THE TRANSITION FROM SOCIALISM:
STATE AND CIVIL SOCIETY
IN THE USSR

Chandran Kukathas   David W. Lovell   William Maley

Editors

The Transition
from Socialism

State and Civil Society
in the USSR

Longman Cheshire

Longman Cheshire Pty Limited
Longman House
Kings Gardens
95 Coventry Street
Melbourne 3205 Australia

Offices in Sydney, Brisbane, Adelaide and
Perth. Associated companies, branches, and
representatives throughout the world.

Edited by Trischa Baker
Typeset by David W. Lovell and William Maley in 11pt Goudy.
Printed in Hong Kong

National Library of Australia
Cataloguing-in-Publication data:

The Transition from socialism: state and civil society in
the USSR.

Includes index.
ISBN 0 582 87046 1.

1. Communism – Soviet Union – History – 20th century. 2.
Soviet Union – Politics and government – 1917–   . I.
Kukathas, Chandran. II. Lovell, David W., 1956–   .
III. Maley, William, 1957–   .

947.084

CONTENTS

PREFACE

This book is the second product of the collective efforts of its three editors; it cements, if cement were needed, a happy and fruitful collaboration. It would not have been possible without the willing assistance of the colleagues represented in its pages, many of them from different parts of Australia who joined us for seminars where early versions of their essays were presented and discussed.

We owe a special debt to the Politics Department at the Australian Defence Force Academy, for meeting the costs associated with bringing many of the contributors to our seminar series in Canberra. We thank the dedicated audience at those seminars for providing useful commentary.

Finally, we should like to express our gratitude to Ron Harper of Longman Cheshire, for continuing to deal good-naturedly with three frustrated publishers; and to our Longman Cheshire editor Trischa Baker, who eliminated many of the typographical errors and inconsistencies we ourselves had overlooked.

Chandran Kukathas   *December 1990*
David W. Lovell
William Maley

1

Civil society
and Soviet studies: an
introductory essay

DAVID W. LOVELL

I

In November 1917 the Bolshevik party led by Vladimir Lenin took power in Russia, and consolidated its grip on power over the next four years. Dogmatic as socialist theorists, the Bolsheviks proved flexible as policy-makers because their policies were usually subordinated to the maintenance of their rule. From the earliest times in the Russian Social Democratic Labour Party (forerunner of the Soviet Communist Party), the focus had been on leadership—of the working class in general, and of the party in particular. Indeed, it is difficult to conceive of Bolshevism apart from Lenin: an exceptional, though scarcely endearing, leader and strategist. Those in the Party who followed him and fought for his mantle, even if not exceptional, were made to appear so. At one level, then, the history of the USSR can be written in terms of its leaders.[1] The leader with whom the present changes in the Soviet Union will irretrievably be linked is Mikhail Sergeevich Gorbachev. This is not to deny the importance of the party and the institutions for governing which it created or moulded to its purposes; it is rather to stress that the relations between state and party, and between party and leader— both areas subject to what Trotsky once called 'substitutionism'[2]— have made it possible from time to time for one man to have enormous influence, and for his idiosyncrasies to fashion policy almost without restraint. The focus of this book, by contrast, is only incidentally upon leadership, because the formation of civil society which the volume charts may provide a bulwark against unaccountable and unresponsive leaders.

Lenin, Stalin, Khrushchev, Brezhnev, Andropov, Chernenko: this is the line of Gorbachev's predecessors. Their official titles may not have been the same, but each emerged unmistakably as leader. Except for Andropov and Chernenko, whose tenure of the highest position was brief, each impressed his stamp upon the character of the Soviet system. Though Gorbachev has been leader for only six years he, too, has already made his mark. And what an extraordinary and unprecedented mark it has proven to be! The future of the Soviet system itself is at stake. With Lenin we readily associate the Revolution and the consolidation of the Bolshevik predominance within the framework of 'Soviet power'. With Stalin, ruthless campaigns against oppositions—real and supposed—within party and state, industrialisation, the collectivisation of agriculture and a disastrous foreign policy: all resulting in tens of millions of Soviet deaths.[3] With Khrushchev, an attempt to remove the fear of arbitrariness, and with Brezhnev, a dull routinisation of every aspect of life, together with nepotism and corruption: the grey years of a system in decline. Underlying all those periods beyond the first were similar and chronic economic and political problems, to the handling of which each leader brought his own particular style. Yet to the problems of food and housing shortages, shortages of consumer goods, poor quality of producer and consumer goods, environmental destruction, endemic political corruption and the difficulties of non-Party members in having any significant political voice,[4] each of these leaders had no answer which did not involve some combination of further exertions, greater sacrifices and more hardship. By the time of the Brezhnev period, and perhaps long before, these appeals had lost their effectiveness. The consumption of alcohol at this time[5] (albeit a tidy revenue-raiser for the Soviet government) pointed not just to a further diminution in the standard of living of ordinary Soviet people, but to their alienation from a political and economic system founded on the claim that it was designed to benefit them.

These are the endemic problems, compounded by the weariness of the Soviet people, to which Gorbachev has forcefully addressed himself in part because, as Lenin once observed of other pre-revolutionary situations, the old system is no longer perceived as being able to go on in the same way.[6] The Soviet system is, in part, a grand exercise in subordinating social relations to the human will. It is also testament to the futility of such an attempt. The exertions of the Soviet people themselves, whether encouraged, cajoled or bludgeoned by their rulers, have been enormous. Their results have not, on balance, been worth the costs. But there is a deeper point to be made. The very attempt to control all aspects of one's life, of which modern communism is an example, is doomed to failure. Social life is too complex; the methods we have for analysing it are, at the finest levels, intrinsically distorting; the ways we have of intervening are too clumsy. In addition, individuals initiate and create social relations which then have a life of their own, in which individuals participate, but over which they have only limited control: the market is a prime—and in this case very relevant—example. Such social relations bring benefits as well as risks. To try to bend them to our wills tends to destroy whatever benefits they may have. The point of this classical liberal view, which the editors (though not necessarily all the other contributors to this volume) embrace, is that attempts such as the Soviet to master society and history are inevitably destructive and produce vastly more misery than they are promoted to eradicate. The cogency of this view aside, Gorbachev has begun a series of changes in many of the aspects of the Soviet system, once considered fundamental to it, which are a product of the realisation that public disaffection with Soviet life may ultimately have brought down the system itself. These changes, associated in the economic sphere with the term *perestroika*, or 'restructuring', and in the political sphere with *glasnost'*, or 'candour', are proving to be far less cosmetic than they initially appeared. What sort of change will they add up to? It is this broad question that each of our contributors addresses, with particular reference to the notion of 'civil society', which I shall introduce below.

Gorbachev's rule began in 1985 with little indication of the reforms which would change the face of Soviet and world politics. He may at first have moved cautiously because his support among fellow Politburo members was not certain or secure. But when he published *Perestroika* in 1987,[7] Gorbachev signalled that something fundamental had to be done if the Soviet system was to be saved at all. What prompted Gorbachev to this realisation? We can list at least some of the probable factors. Among the first things to note about Gorbachev are his relative youth (b. 1931); his long official experience with·agriculture (perhaps the consistently weakest sector of the Soviet economy); the vastly different style of his leadership, much more like a Western politician and using the same (electronic) means of communicating with the Soviet people; and his apparent openness to unpleasant truths.[8] Yet while these factors may have helped to shape his perception of the strengths and weaknesses of 'really existing socialism', it would be a mistake to conclude that Gorbachev alone is responsible for the unravelling of the command administrative system. Although opinions are divided, it seems to us rather that Gorbachev began a process which assumed its own momentum.

What will be the result of these reforms? It appears that they may produce a different system altogether, which to many indicates that Gorbachev's proposals amount to a revolution in the Soviet Union. 'Revolution' is a term which we have become accustomed to use to describe a dramatic shift in the social basis of political power:[9] a point which is—thus far—difficult to concede in the Soviet case. Yet the very power of the term at least emphasises the possible extent of the changes, and the possible depth of opposition to them. One can expect opposition to Gorbachev's proporals from those who have profited from the Soviet system, and from those who wish to see further and faster changes. On the whole, Gorbachev has handled these internal challenges skilfully. Not only does he have the public style of a Western politician among his constituents, which makes him appear accessible to them and interested in their concerns and well-being, but he does not lack the abilities of a Soviet politician brought up in an atmosphere of patronage, of conciliating bureaucratic interests, and of removing individuals within leading party organisations who might threaten his power base. As the locus of power itself shifts to electoral institutions and public fora, as it seems to be doing, Gorbachev may be compelled to take a more Western approach and throw the weight of his newly-created (and worryingly powerful) Presidential office behind his proposals. It will be interesting to see whether, or for how long, he can control the processes he has begun. By their very nature, it seems that he will become one of a number of influences—though a very important one—upon their outcome, but that he cannot be their sole determinant. Perhaps he will become their victim. *Perestroika* does not now depend on M.S. Gorbachev. Already, we must conjure with other names: for example that of Boris El'tsin, Chairman of the Supreme Soviet of the Russian Soviet Federative Socialist Republic.

What preceded these changes, and can help to explain them? Among the most important factors we can identify are the low levels of general economic growth[10] and the consistently poor—sometimes disastrous—Soviet grain harvests over the last ten to fifteen years. Rampant environmental destruction was another. Furthermore, on 25 April 1986, the Chernobyl Number 4 Reactor was involved in a serious accident which led to the 'melt-down' of the reactor's core. The accident itself, and the efforts to contain the damage it caused, spoke volumes about the state of Soviet technology, about Soviet management of particular enterprises and management of information, and about Soviet ability to respond effectively to any civil emergency. The Chernobyl accident and its aftermath were an indictment of the Soviet system. *Glasnost'*, Zhores Medvedev has convincingly maintained, is one of the legacies of Chernobyl.[11] Indeed, David Holloway has suggested that, 'By giving a new impetus to the environmental movement, Chernobyl has thus helped to strengthen civil society in its efforts to control the actions of a powerful state ... Chernobyl must be seen, therefore, not only as a technological disaster and a human tragedy, but also as an important event in the political evolution of Soviet society'.[12]

It was in 1989, however, that the changes in the Soviet Union seemed to pass the point of no return. This was the year when communist regimes throughout Eastern Europe—most created after post-Second World War Soviet military interventions, and supported by Soviet military and economic 'aid'—succumbed to the enormous pressures for reform generated among their own populations. Older rulers were replaced; elections in Poland and Hungary displaced the ruling party; in Romania, the leader was overthrown by his people, and killed.[13] The Soviet Union made it clear that it would not intervene, and began to withdraw units of its military forces, sometimes at the behest of their 'hosts'. 1989 was also the year in which, after an ill-advised ten-year military intervention in neighbouring Afghanistan, the Soviet Union withdrew its troops from that devastated country—though not its military aid to the puppet regime of Najibullah.[14] Indeed, the successes of Gorbachev's policies are so far to be seen chiefly in the area of foreign relations, particularly in an easing in world tensions between the USSR and the USA, and between the Warsaw Pact and NATO, for which he has was awarded the 1990 Nobel Peace Prize. The recent reunification of Germany as well as the Soviet response to the Iraqi invasion of Kuwait underline at least a benign influence abroad. By contrast, Gorbachev's successes at home are mixed (witness, for example, the reactions of Soviet citizens to news of Gorbachev's Nobel Prize), and are political rather than economic. But even in politics the record will remain inconclusive until a fundamental feature of the Soviet system—the fusion of the Communist party with the state, substantially through the operation of the *nomenklatura* system[15]—has been obliterated in practice. Until then, criticism within elected bodies (of which there is much) and political pluralism (of which there has been a vast increase) cannot be duly translated into changes in state policy.

II

I have been writing as though the economic and political spheres of Soviet life were separate. Analytically, of course, they are separable, but one of the characteristic features of the Soviet system is the deliberate connection between the two as a means of ending the sorts of invidious and inhuman conflicts which Marx had seen as characteristic of capitalist societies. Yet as an example of humans controlling their creations, and transcending alienation, this connection of the two spheres is a chimera; but there are other aspects to consider. It is at once a potential (if limited) source of strength, given that it can enable the whole national effort to be directed at certain specific goals, and a source of chronic weakness, for what is good for exceptional circumstances, say of national emergency, rebels against becoming the rule. Societies resist being turned into what Michael Oakeshott has called 'enterprise associations'.[16]

It is at this point that the notion of 'civil society', on which this book is focussed, becomes useful as both an analytical tool and, for those who wish to pursue these things, as the basis for a political programme. The term 'civil society' has a long history, but it has become prominent in the recent debates in Eastern Europe and the USSR over the future of socialist regimes.[17] It is a way of connoting the separateness of certain social relations, especially those involving exchange, from those which characterise politics. Its users accept that social life is divided into separate spheres; its advocates accept that social life *ought* to be divided into separate spheres. The future of socialist states can thus be seen in terms of whether they are able to create, or re-create a civil society, or perhaps simply re-invigorate elements of an existing civil society which had been suppressed under socialism but not destroyed. The difference in formulation represents a difference of emphasis akin to that which became evident in the 1960s debate over the concept 'totalitarianism'.[18] Indeed, C.M. Hann has recently declared that the notion of 'civil society' is unhelpful precisely because it relies on an unrealistic contrast between the 'pluralist West' and the 'uniform totalitarian East': 'the revival of civil society ... often turns out to be no more than a surrogate for the persistence of totalitarian theories in other guises'.[19] Of course it is probably impossible for every organisation and every aspect of life to be related directly to the state, but this process has gone further in socialist systems than anywhere else. It has done so on the dubiously grounded theory which counsels that the abolition of civil society will remove the divisions and conflicts which bedevil modern societies, a move which has not led to the parallel disappearance of the state but to its extension and aggrandisement. Our view, by contrast, suggests that separating the economy from state direction—perhaps the most important step in the revival of civil society—is a prerequisite to the establishment of genuine political freedoms and economic prosperity among Soviet citizens. Such a separation is slowly being accomplished in the Soviet Union. Its continuation is surrounded by uncertainties, and it may well be accompanied by hardship, but its promise for Soviet citizens is surer than the hollow exhortations by communists to work ever harder within the existing system.

There are many objections to the revival of civil society, some of them coming from Soviet workers and consumers themselves. There are also differences among analysts as well as Soviet leaders over the appropriate pace of such a change. The revival of civil society will undoubtedly give rise to social and economic inequalities as well as unemployment: so does the Soviet system. The difference lies in the fact that under civil society effort will be more directly rewarded. The revival of civil society will see cheating and profiteering: so does the Soviet system. The difference lies in the fact that under a settled civil society, consumer education, a market ethic, and the rule of law will force these phenomena to the periphery rather than accept them as endemic. The revival of civil society will mean that those who own and direct the means of production will have power over those who do not: so it is also in the Soviet system. The difference lies in the fact that under civil society, the dispersion of economic power means that political and legal power cannot be monopolised, and that checks and safeguards against the abuse of power are able to operate. Where civil society differs entirely from the command economy which it will replace is in the more efficient allocation of resources, the greater productivity and material wealth it will provide, and not least in the heightened civility of relations between its people. No longer will the forms of equality, the obligatory 'Tovarishch', belie enormous disparities of status, but people will be in many important respects the equal of each other and demand consideration and respect because of it.

'Civil society' is a complex concept, and the essays in this work explore various aspects of it, and often give those aspects different emphasis. As a framework for discussion, it thus provides a starting point. It is a more useful starting point for understanding the changes underway in the USSR, the editors believe, than that provided by 'democratisation', for example. It is popular to conceive of the current reforms within the Soviet Union as aspects of, or contributions to, democratisation conceived as an extension of the ability of citizens to contest for public office. This is a view which is popular also among Soviet politicians. The latter at least give the lie to Soviet pretensions to democracy for the last fifty years. But the notion of *perestroika* and *glasnost'* as instruments of democracy is not a particularly helpful one because of the very abasement of the term 'democracy' to which the Soviet experiment and its protestations has contributed.[20] 'Democracy', etymologically, denotes 'rule by the people'. What is it to 'rule'; and who are 'the people'? These are not hollow questions: as Andrei Platonov once acidly remarked, 'Without me, the people is incomplete'.[21] Representative democracy, the only modern form of rule which can give democracy any substantial meaning, intensifies these questions. And *liberal* democracy requires, for genuine and enforceable political freedoms, that its political separation of powers be backed up by a social separation of powers.[22]

This is not to say that all of our contributors are convinced that the extent of the utility of 'civil society' is vast. It is, as T.H. Rigby puts it, no 'precision instrument'. For all that, it remains valuable.[23] All of the contributions to this collection, save one, were written with the current reforms in mind. The editors asked the contributors to address, within their fields of expertise, certain topics: we made no attempt to impose any particular methodology or conclusions upon them. Of the exception to this process, something more needs to be said in connection with discussion of 'civil society'. In 1974, Leszek Kolakowski wrote the piece we reprint here: 'The Myth of Human Self-Identity: Unity of Civil and Political Society in Socialist Thought'.[24] It ably summed up, at a time when the importance of the concept of 'civil society' was barely recognised in the West, what we believe is a fundamental flaw in socialist social theorising. That flaw is to believe that a perfect unity of personal and communal life is possible any longer, if it was ever so. Indeed, in the essay by Chandran Kukathas and David W. Lovell, this socialist view is seen as a product of a larger debate about the character and prospects of modern society which exercised a number of major thinkers during the eighteenth and nineteenth centuries.

The Kukathas-Lovell essay is based on the view that politics, as the constant process of conciliating interests, will always be indispensable in modern societies, a view which socialists ignore or deride at their peril. The dispensability of politics, allied with the harmonisation of interests, are notions which rely on a view of human community which has greater affinity with the peculiarities of Periclean Athens than with modern realities and potentialities. They were, nevertheless, popular among those horrified at the dissolution of the old social ties, and at the apparent disintegration of society itself in the period begun by the Industrial and French Revolutions. Though this may explain their use, it does not justify it. Theoretical neatness and monism have conspired in a 'solution' to the social problem which simply translates it to a new level.

Eugene Kamenka and Alice Erh-Soon Tay point to the relative weakness of civil society in pre-Revolutionary Russia—indeed, to the militarisation of society and government. Likewise, they emphasise the importance of the state in the Chinese political tradition. The major promise of the events of 1989–1990 in Eastern Europe and the Soviet Union lies in the development towards *constitutional* governments. But for the rule of law to prevail, they maintain, a strong civil society is only one factor.

Vladimir Shlapentokh takes the historical story a step further by outlining the fate of Russian civil society under Lenin and Stalin. His essay documents the extent of state interference in, and control over, the economy, politics, and everyday life; it enables us to understand better the significance of the Gorbachev era. T.H. Rigby's essay examines the recent development of civil society in the USSR by identifying its various 'vestigial elements' under what he has elsewhere analysed as Soviet 'mono-organisational socialism'.[25] Rigby stresses the importance of privacy in sustaining and strengthening such elements. If it were not for them, current Soviet reforms would not have moved so quickly or gone so far. For Rigby, then, civil society is a factor in the reforms, as well as being one of their chief beneficiaries. Yet while Kukathas and Lovell concentrate on the role of a market economy in civil society, Rigby lays stress on non-market activities.

Leslie Holmes looks at the changing balance between coercion and normative forms of legitimation as bases of communist power in the USSR. He emphasises the role of eudaemonic legitimation under Gorbachev, and its links with power exercised through legal-rationality. The emergence of a market, he argues, is critical to these forms of legitimation, though they undermine the principles of communism. Legal-rationality and civil society (focussing principally on independent political activity), he argues, are incompatible with Leninism. Holmes anticipates a further expansion of civil society as the balance of the mode of legitimation shifts.

Stephen Fortescue presents a case-study of the efforts to encourage an economic civil society by making industrial ministries more accountable to the state or more 'economic'. His evidence indicates that the gains from various proposals are minimal because ministries retain their capacity to react in traditional ways. Fortescue suggests that ministries react in defensive ways to targets imposed on them by the plan, and that the solution to this impasse is ultimately in the hands of the politicians, not the bureaucrats.

William Maley looks at the unleashing of nationalist passions which has been perhaps the most spectacular domestic accompaniment of Gorbachev's reforms. He develops a distinction between two different ideal types of nationalism, both of which may have anti-communist effects, but only one of which may be amenable to the development of civil society. Maley's essay emphasises the importance of the values of the autonomous associations that comprise a civil society: those associations which are tolerant of others' values, he argues, must predominate. Nationalism may be a powerful solvent of the Soviet federation, but only certain of its forms are amenable to the development of civil society.

Carlyle Thayer examines the recent transformation of Soviet alliance relations under the 'new political thinking'. He looks, in particular, at the changing military and economic dimensions of the relations between the USSR and Vietnam. Thayer argues that dramatic changes in traditional Soviet alliance relations are due in part to the development of civil society and the consequent devaluing of ideology in foreign relations. Alliance relations between the two, he concludes, have 'withered on the economic vine'.

III

In looking at Gorbachev's USSR, I am reminded of an incident during the 1968 Tet Offensive of the Vietnam War: US Air Force Major Chester L. Brown is reported to have explained that in order to save the town of Ben Tre it became necessary to destroy it. Gorbachev's reforms seem to have begun as an attempt to save state socialism; in their midst, state socialism has been the greatest loser. Perhaps Gorbachev did not at first realise the extent of the problem, or the radical solutions which would be required to inject innovation and enterprise into the command economy. For it is not just a question of 'abuses', or 'corruption', or the fat of the *nomenklatura* which has created the problems of consumption in the USSR: they are built into the foundations of such an economy. If the USSR is powerful, it is so almost despite itself: enormous resources—officially 70.9 billion roubles for 1990—have been channelled into the military budget.[26] If it feeds its population, it does so by relying, paradoxically, on private plots. If it has created vast productive units and enormous outputs in heavy industry, it has done so by sheer force of will, and at the expense of their quality and, ultimately, of its own people.

This is not to say that centralised or 'planned' economies are impossible: it is to say that *rational* calculation and balanced, sustained production are impossible within them. This is the theme of László Csapó's essay, even though Csapó is unconvinced of the utility of 'civil society'. Indeed, the experience of the command economy works against Gorbachev's reforms, and threatens ultimately to bring them to an end, and Gorbachev to his political end. For the exertions required to build one part of the economy have been at the expense of the other parts, and the immediate imbalance caused has always been justified as a short-term sacrifice to pay for the better life to come. Communism, in other words, has always asked—and when it has not asked, it has forced—its people to take it on trust that things will get better, that consumer goods, housing, health, and so on will get better if only they will work in a certain way now. This trust has evaporated. If Gorbachev relies upon the Soviet people to take him on trust that, in five or ten years of *perestroika*, things will get better, his political future is built on sand. Gorbachev does not have the luxuries of time or trust. Thus the transition from socialism in the USSR may yet turn out to be a bloody, or inconclusive, affair. Politics, as it is practised in the West, and as Gorbachev has adapted to it rather well, is about trust, about the balancing of short- and long-term goals, and about recognising and conciliating different interests. It may be well for an ascetic voluntarily to deprive himself of worldly goods in the quest of worldly satisfaction, or the hope or expectation of an other-worldly reward, but asceticism as a political programme is no vote-winner; and votes have begun to count in the USSR.

The other phenomenon with which Gorbachev's reforms must wrestle is the culture of dependence which has been fostered in the USSR since 1917. It is a common criticism of welfare programmes in the West that they discourage the initiative of the recipients, and alter the behaviour of recipient groups who become welfare-dependent.[27] The Soviets have been 'welfare recipients' for more than seventy years. The initiative and enterprise on which their material improvement depends does not seem to abound among them. Being thrown into the market, rather than eased into it—'cold-shower capitalism'—may cause great hardship, but perhaps ultimately less than the failed experiment in communism. This, too, is Csapó's view; for him, it makes the case for Western economic aid to the Soviet Union and Eastern Europe more palatable.

IV

The impetus for this collection derived from the assumption that the distinction between state and civil society provides a useful perspective on the processes of change in the Soviet Union. The distinction itself is not new, nor is its application to socialist regimes. The Poles have been conducting analyses of this sort since early in the 1970s, stimulated perhaps by Gramsci's contributions to Marxism (which posited the *superstructural* identity of 'civil society', and thus stressed the importance of political *and cultural* leadership—'hegemony'—in any cogent revolutionary strategy),[28] and certainly by the role of Solidarity.[29] What is distinctive about this book, however, is its stress on the state-civil society distinction as a key to understanding the communist project, which may be described as an attempt to translate the theoretical critique of this distinction into a practical programme. For many of us, the point is that the success of political freedoms in the Soviet Union depends on the revival or reinvigoration of civil society—in effect, to create rival or countervailing powers to the power of the state—and that this in turn depends on the implementation of the right to private property and the restoration of the market, including the market in capital goods. There is no certainty about the links between private property and political freedoms: the former provides the necessary but not sufficient basis for the latter. The only certainty is that the attempt to destroy private property and the market is the prelude to the loss of political freedoms and the downgrading of living standards.

Few would deny that there are costs associated with market economies, but their benefits are overwhelming. The command economy has proved a failure, even in the provision of public goods where one might have expected success. The command economy must be considered fundamentally flawed, because of its inability to price its products appropriately, while the market economy is—in this respect—a constantly self-correcting mechanism. The benefits of the market are apparent, but its set-up (and not merely its running) costs are large, in psychological, social and economic terms. They will prove a fearsome barrier to further progress away from socialism. Economic reform in the USSR towards a market economy is hindered by a popular feeling against the motive of economic incentive. Wealth is wanted, but wealth requires enterprise, incentive, and risk-taking. It is not clear that the Soviet people are willing to pay this cost. Therefore, politically, if the move toward a market economy is proposed, this becomes a large problem: perhaps the central problem of the present time. The political reforms having progressed about as far as they can; the time is ready for movement on the economic front. But will there be a market in capital goods? Who will become the shareholders (capitalists)? What will become of the unemployed? Will contracts be honoured? How will the market and the consumers be protected from the unscrupulous? Civil society is not simply the market: it requires certain habits and attitudes and expectations. They are not created overnight. They deem that differentials in wealth give rise to emulation and enterprise rather than resentment and envy. The prospects for successful economic reform and recovery in the USSR seem, on this scale, and from our evidence of consumer discontent, to be very bleak. 'Profiteering' needs to receive a public absolution, and 'interest' must once again be liberated as an acceptable motivation in economic and political spheres.[30] Above all, the Soviet Union needs the standards of legality which are basic to a market economy.

Political science is not mere prophecy, though good political science can illuminate the ways ahead. The contributors to this book are conscious that the processes they describe, so closely associated with Mikhail Gorbachev, may not continue in their present form. They are aware that the pace of reform in Eastern Europe and the Soviet Union may slow or halt, and that 'reform' may produce chaos or despotism. All these essays point to a process that is difficult, full of obstacles and problems, and with an outcome which is uncertain. If events in the USSR overtake us, so be it. But the analyses in this book will continue to contribute to an understanding of the failure of communism in general and Soviet communism in particular. The advent of Gorbachev and the progress of his reforms has overtaken much of the traditional Soviet analyses: but they are not thereby rendered worthless. None of these essays is especially sanguine about the future of the USSR: if the authors are united on anything, it is perhaps on a scepticism about the prospects for a successful, liberal end to the current Soviet reforms.

Whatever their immediate fate, the changes occurring in the Soviet Union today are profound. For the editors' part, we believe that they constitute the transition from socialism. Like the transition *to* socialism, it is not easy to anticipate the pace, or even the ultimate destination of this process. Likewise—to repeat at the risk of monotony—the costs may be great. But if such a transition is to succeed, it requires the revival of civil life and a diminution of the state's pretensions. It requires, in other words, a healthy civil society.

Notes

1   For a detailed discussion of the place of the 'personal ruler paradigm' in the analysis of Soviet politics, see T.H. Rigby, 'The Soviet Political Executive, 1917–1986', in Archie Brown (ed.), *Political Leadership in the Soviet Union* (London: Macmillan, 1989) pp. 4–53.

2   See Baruch Knei-Paz, *The Social and Political Thought of Leon Trotsky* (Oxford: Oxford University Press, 1978) pp. 192–199. Trotsky's position was developed in his anti-Leninist *Our Political Tasks*, first published in 1904.

3   See Дмитрий Волкогонов, *Триумф и трагедия: Политический портрет И.В. Сталина* (Moscow: Izdatel'stvo Agentstva pechati Novosti, 1989).

4   For some details of these problems, see Mervyn Matthews, *Poverty in the Soviet Union* (Cambridge: Cambridge University Press, 1986); Nick Eberstadt, *The Poverty of Communism* (New Brunswick: Transaction Books, 1988); Igor Birman, *Personal Consumption in the USSR and the USA* (London: Macmillan, 1989); and Mervyn Matthews, *Patterns of Deprivation in the Soviet Union Under Brezhnev and Gorbachev* (Stanford: Hoover Institution Press, 1989).

5   See Vladimir G. Treml, *Alcohol in the USSR: A Statistical Study* (Durham: Duke University Press, 1982).

6   'It is only when the *"lower classes" do not want* to live in the old way and the *"upper classes" cannot carry on in the old way* that the revolution can triumph': V.I. Lenin,'"Left-Wing" Communism—An Infantile Disorder', in V.I. Lenin, *Collected Works* (Moscow: Progress Publishers, 1977) Vol.XXXI, pp. 21–118 at p. 85. For an account of Lenin's 'sociology of revolution' see Norman Wintrop, 'Marx, Lenin and Modern Revolutions' in David Close and Carl Bridge (eds), *Revolution: A History of the Idea* (London: Croom Helm, 1985) pp. 89–119 at pp. 107–117.

7   M.S. Gorbachev, *Perestroika: New Thinking for Our Country and the World* (London: Collins, 1987)

8   See Zhores Medvedev, *Gorbachev* (Oxford: Basil Blackwell, 1988).

9   See Theda Skocpol, *States and Social Revolutions: A Comparative Analysis of France, Russia, and China* (Cambridge: Cambridge University Press, 1979)

10 See, for example, Alec Nove, *Stalinism and After: The Road to Gorbachev* (Boston: Unwin Hyman, 1989) especially pp. 177–186.

11 Zhores Medvedev, *The Legacy of Chernobyl* (Oxford: Blackwell, 1990).

12   David Holloway, 'The Catastrophe and After', *New York Review of Books*, vol.37, no.12, 19 July 1990, pp. 4–6, at p. 6.

13   For a discussion, see Jan Pakulski, 'Eastern Europe and "Legitimacy Crisis"', *Australian Journal of Political Science*, vol.25, no.2, November 1990, pp. 272-288.

14   See Amin Saikal and William Maley (eds), *The Soviet Withdrawal from Afghanistan* (Cambridge: Cambridge University Press, 1989).

15   For detailed discussions of the *nomenklatura* system, see Bohdan Harasymiw, 'Nomenklatura: The Soviet Communist Party's Leadership Recruitment System', *Canadian Journal of Political Science*, vol.2, no.4, December 1969, pp. 493–512; Bohdan Harasymiw, *Political Elite Recruitment in the Soviet Union* (London: Macmillan, 1984) pp. 153–186; John Miller, 'Nomenklatura: Check on Localism?', in T.H. Rigby and Bohdan Harasymiw (eds), *Leadership Selection and Patron-Client Relations in the USSR and Yugoslavia* (London: George Allen & Unwin, 1983) pp. 62–97; and T.H. Rigby, *Political Elites in the USSR: Central leaders and local cadres from Lenin to Gorbachev* (Aldershot: Edward Elgar, 1990) pp. 73–126.

16   See Michael Oakeshott, *On Human Conduct* (Oxford: Oxford University Press, 1975) pp. 114–118.

17   See, for example, John Gray, 'Glasnostications', *Times Literary Supplement*, July 21–27, 1989, pp. 798, 809. Other recent discussions of civil society and socialism include S. Frederick Starr, 'Soviet Union: A Civil Society', *Foreign Policy*, no.70, Spring 1988, pp. 26–41; James P. Scanlan, 'Reforms and Civil Society in the USSR', *Problems of Communism*, vol.37, no.2, March-April 1988, pp. 41–46; William Green Miller (ed.), *Toward a More Civil Society?: The USSR under Mikhail Sergeevich Gorbachev* (New York: Harper & Row, 1989); John Gray, 'Totalitarianism, Reform, and Civil Society', in Ellen Frankel Paul (ed.) *Totalitarianism at the Crossroads* (New Brunswick: Transaction Books, 1990) pp. 97–142; David Lane, *Soviet Society under Perestroika* (London: Unwin Hyman, 1990) pp. 89–107; Vladimir Tismaneanu, 'Nascent Civil Society in the German Democratic Republic', *Problems of Communism*, vol.38, nos.2–3, March-June 1989, pp. 90–111; David Strand, 'Protest in Beijing: Civil Society and Public Sphere in China', *Problems of Communism*, vol.39, no.3, May-June 1990, pp. 1–19; and Janina Frentzel-Zagorska, 'Civil Society in Poland and Hungary', *Soviet Studies*, vol.42, no.4, October 1990, pp. 759-777.

18   See Leonard Schapiro, *Totalitarianism* (London: Pall Mall, 1972). The concept of totalitarianism was developed in the 1950s in Hannah Arendt, *The Origins of Totalitarianism* (London: George Allen & Unwin, 1967), and in Carl Joachim Friedrich and Zbigniew Brzezinski, *Totalitarian Dictatorship and Autocracy* (Cambridge: Harvard University Press, 1965). On the rediscovery and widespread use of the concept of totalitarianism by Eastern and Central European thinkers, see Jacques Rupnik, 'Totalitarianism Revisited' in John Keane (ed.), *Civil Society and the State: New European Perspectives* (London: Verso, 1988) pp. 263–289. More recently, the concept has been put to use by Soviet scholars: see А.А. Кара-Мурза, and А.К. Воскресенский (eds), *Тоталитаризм*

как исторический феномен (Moscow: Philosophical Association of the USSR, 1990).

19 C.M. Hann, 'Second Economy and Civil Society', *Journal of Communist Studies*, vol.6, no.2, June 1990, pp. 21–44 at p. 31.

20 An abasement reflected in C.B. Macpherson, *The Real World of Democracy* (Oxford: Oxford University Press, 1966).

21 Quoted in Евгений Евтушенко, 'По моему мнению', *Советская культура*, 15 April 1986, p. 3.

22 A point made with some force by Robert A. Dahl, *A Preface to Democratic Theory* (Chicago: University of Chicago Press, 1956). Richard Sakwa, by contrast, has argued that the appropriate way to conceptualise the present changes in the Soviet Union is in terms of 'commune democracy', a strand of participatory democratic thinking within the Marxist tradition. See Richard Sakwa, 'Commune Democracy and Gorbachev's Reforms', *Political Studies*, vol.37, no.2, June 1989, pp. 224–243. Such an approach seems to accept the transcendence of state and civil society which, as this and other essays in this collection argue, is at the root of the problem. On the more general challenge of constructing an appropriate theoretical framework for understanding the current developments in the authoritarian regimes of the Soviet Union and Eastern Europe, among others, see Lucian W. Pye, 'Political Science and the Crisis of Authoritarianism', *American Political Science Review*, vol.84, no.1, March 1990, pp. 3–19.

23 In this most of them differ, for example, from the view of Zbigniew Rau, 'Some thoughts on Civil Society in Eastern Europe and the Lockean Contractarian Approach', *Political Studies*, vol.35, no.4, December 1987, pp. 573–592, who suggests an analysis of the new Eastern European situation in terms of a Lockean contract.

24 First published in Leszek Kolakowski and Stuart Hampshire (eds), *The Socialist Idea: A Reappraisal* (London: Weidenfeld and Nicolson, 1974) pp. 18–35.

25 T.H. Rigby, *The Changing Soviet System: Mono-organisational Socialism from its Origins to Gorbachev's Restructuring* (Aldershot: Edward Elgar, 1990).

26 See Д.Т. Язов, 'Новая модель безопасности и вооруженные силы', *Коммунист*, no.18, December 1989, pp. 62–72. For differing views on the proportion of the USSR's Gross Domestic Product absorbed by military expenditure, see Paul Dibb, *The Soviet Union: The Incomplete Superpower* (London: Macmillan, 1986) pp. 80–89; Franklyn D. Holzman, 'Politics and Guesswork: CIA and DIA Estimates of Soviet Military Spending', *International Security*, vol.14, no.2, Fall 1989, pp. 101–131; James E. Steiner and Franklyn D. Holzman, 'Correspondence: CIA Estimates of Soviet Military Spending', *International Security*, vol.14, no.4, Spring 1990, pp. 185–198; and Steven Rosefielde, 'Soviet Defence Spending: The Contribution of the New Accountancy', *Soviet Studies*, vol.42, no.1, January 1990, pp. 59–80.

27 See, for example, Charles Murray, *Losing Ground: American Social Policy 1950–1980* (New York: Basic Books, 1984).

28 See Noberto Bobbio, 'Gramsci and the Concept of Civil Society' in John Keane (ed.), *Civil Society and the State: New European Perspectives*

(London: Verso, 1988) pp. 73–99. Gramsci's notes on 'civil society' are collected in Quintin Hoare and Geoffrey Nowell Smith (editors and translators), *Selections from the Prison Notebooks of Antonio Gramsci* (London: Lawrence and Wishart, 1971) pp. 206–276.

29   See Z.A. Pelczynski, 'Solidarity and "The Rebirth of Civil Society" in Poland, 1976–81' in John Keane (ed.), *Civil Society and the State: New European Perspectives* (London: Verso, 1988) pp. 361–380.

30   See Albert O. Hirschman, *The Passions and the Interests: Political Arguments for Capitalism before its Triumph* (Princeton: Princeton University Press, 1977) for an account of an earlier acceptance of the legitimate role of 'interest'.

2

The Significance of Civil Society

CHANDRAN KUKATHAS
& DAVID W. LOVELL

> The limitations of political emancipation are immediately evident
> in the fact that a state can liberate itself from a limitation without
> man himself being truly free of it and the state can be a free state
> without man himself being a free man.—Karl Marx, 'On the Jewish
> Question'

I

We are currently witnessing changes in the Soviet Union and its
Eastern European satellites which may herald the most significant
social and political transformation since the Second World War, and
which have already begun to alter the face of world politics. The
political crisis of communism has finally caught up with its chronic
economic disorder, as leaderships crumble under the weight of
popular protest. The first signal for the new-found power of
popularity in communist systems was given by Soviet President
Mikhail Gorbachev's refusal to use Soviet troops to prop up
discredited Eastern European communist parties. The second can be
found in his allowing more public debate, freer soviet elections, and
non-communist deputies inside the Soviet Union itself. For the first
time in communist history, liberalisation is being initiated and
endorsed by the central power of the socialist bloc.

With this liberalisation come profound hopes as well as justifiable
fears: hopes for political and economic freedoms, and for a removal
of the burdens of a doomed attempt to pre-empt history; but fears of a
resurgence of insular and destructive chauvinism, and of the weight

of a culture of dependence resistant to the new challenges and opportunities. One of the greatest problems which faces the Soviet President (one which may cut short his political career and the *perestroika* and *glasnost'* by which it has lately been characterised) is the long-simmering nationalities question and the related issue of secession from the federation of Soviet Republics. The whole process admits few certainties.

There are thus good reasons why, although we celebrate the changes, we should remain cautious when assessing their depth, extent and possible longevity: freedoms given are freedoms which can be taken away. Furthermore, the concept 'democracy', around which much of the popular anti-government sentiment in socialist states has crystallised, is slippery. Certain versions of it are amenable to rulers of all stripes. 'People power' may help to remove tyrants, but others often ride to power on its back. While demands for democracy provide some indication of what citizens of socialist states aspire to— governments which can be made and replaced regularly and peacefully, are accountable for their actions to the governed and are responsive to the freely-expressed wants of their citizens—it is far from obvious that democracy is the key to the emancipation of the Communist world. Indeed, it is our contention that to understand what is happening and what is needed there we must focus on a somewhat different notion: the notion of *civil society*.

Communism, in many ways, was a challenge not to democracy but to civil society. Its greatest theorist, Karl Marx, in conceiving communism as a flourishing of human freedom, saw the threat to that freedom coming not from democracy but from the sharp separation in the modern world between the civil and political aspects of men's existence. For Marx, freedom was absent because men's fully human, 'universal' aspects were diverted into an abstract sphere while their 'real' lives, in *civil society*, were dominated by considerations of narrow self-interest, or 'particularity'. It was not that Marx objected to political emancipation as such; rather that he saw it as only a part of the story of human emancipation. In the Hegelian terminology which permeated his early work, Marx spoke of the political state as 'man's *species-life*, as *opposed* to his material life'.[1] As long as civil society existed, and its mores prevailed, human emancipation would be incomplete, if not wholly illusory. The communist revolution would bring freedom not simply by instituting new political forms, but by transforming— *transcending*—civil society, and bringing into being a social order in which the distinction between the realm of the social and the realm of the political had vanished. Indeed, Marx at first described this vision of integral man as 'true democracy'.

The communist regimes of the real world, harsh and authoritarian as they have been, may be distinguished from other similarly repressive regimes not by their evident disdain for liberal democracy, but by their assault on society itself. To varying degrees, all have tried to transform society and its human 'material': to break down and destroy the traditional structures of civil life, and to reconstitute the social order in accordance with a more-or-less settled plan.

It is in this context that we need to come to terms with the significance of civil society. Our concern in this essay is to explain why an analysis of the transformation of the Soviet Union and Eastern Europe should take special cognisance of civil society, and should be conducted in terms which give this notion a central place. What is currently happening there, we suggest, is the re-birth of civil society, or the re-constitution or re-invigoration of its vestigial elements. To this end, we begin by offering a brief account of what we understand by civil society, and of how the separation between state and society was welcomed by Montesquieu; we then turn to look at the subsequent criticisms of civil society advanced by its most important detractors, notably Rousseau and Marx; and from there we develop some broader conclusions about the nature and significance of civil society.

II

What, then, is *civil society*? According to the essay by Leszek Kolakowski reprinted in this collection, 'civil society is a whole mass of conflicting individual and group aspirations, empirical daily life with all its conflicts and struggles, the realm of private desires and private endeavours'. Thus understood, civil society amounts to a complex association of individuals joined with one another in relations shaped by personal interest, economic interdependence, and legal and customary rules. Within civil society one would thus expect to find persons who associate with one another for friendship, or to pursue common goals, or in order to trade goods, services, and ideas. One would expect to find a variety of civil associations, including churches, clubs, universities, and business enterprises, along with the various bodies and practices which go to make up the institution of law. Excluded from the realm of civil society are political relations and the institutions of the state. But civil society is not just a location; it has a content denoted by the characteristic relationships it engenders. Its critics, as we shall see below, present the units of civil society as individuals, and their relations as essentially *egoistic*; we are persuaded that its significance lies in the *independence* of *civil associations*.

It is the distinction to be drawn between civil society and the state that, in fact, gives the notion of *civil* society its point. We have noted that civil society is a complex of institutions and practices which make up 'the market', as well as associations of individuals who join together to pursue all sorts of goals beyond narrowly economic ones. These productive and social activities share a large measure of independence from government—though the precise extent of that independence is subject to dispute, since civil associations are in constant relationship with governments through laws, regulations, subsidies and commerce. Arguably, the *existence* of a civil society may be ascertained by the extent of those social activities which are independent of government initiative, regulation or subsidisation; its *health* by the extent to which its constituents and activities depend upon, or look to, government for support. What is less contentious, however, is that there is a conceptual distinction to be drawn between the civil and the governmental aspects of society.

That said, however, it should be noted that the distinction between civil society and the state is a relatively recent one. The term 'civil society' itself has a long history, forming part of a European tradition traceable, as John Keane has suggested, 'from modern natural law back through Cicero's idea of *societas civilis* to classical political philosophy—above all to Aristotle, for whom civil society [*koinonia politiké*] is that society, the *polis*, which contains and dominates all others'.[2] But in this tradition, civil society is coterminous with the state. As recently as the seventeenth and eighteenth centuries, when Locke, Hume and Rousseau referred to civil society, it was political society that they had in mind. It was in this period, however, that the distinction between the social and the political began to emerge.

The conceptual differentiation of state and civil society paralleled their historical differentiation, as a new sort of society—in which human relations were mediated increasingly through the market—emerged from the sixteenth and seventeenth centuries. The process has been variously described as the transition from status to contract,[3] or the transition from *Gemeinschaft* to *Gesellschaft* associations.[4] In Marx's summary—and there is some truth in it—

civil society arose out of the destruction of medieval society, in which individuals lived as members of associations (such as guilds or estates) which were themselves political societies. As these forms of association broke down, and such communal bonds became less important, individuals were increasingly linked by commercial and legal relationships. At the same time, political relations became less and less an aspect of social and economic interaction. The political role of individuals as citizens came to be sharply distinguished from their social roles as members of civil society.[5]

The development of the distinction between the social and the political also ran parallel to important developments in social theory. Increasingly, social and political thinkers began to take *society* and its structure as the subject of their investigations. The most important contribution to this development was undoubtedly that of Montesquieu who, in *The Spirit of the Laws*, distinguished between the 'political and civil laws' of each nation, and argued that 'Laws should be so appropriate to the people for whom they are made that it is very unlikely that the laws of one nation can suit another'.[6] With this he established 'society' as a separate subject of study— particularly for the would-be legislator.

The general question Montesquieu raised was about the nature of order given the diversity of customs and morals. More particularly, what course should a wise legislator take in order to promote liberty? He concluded that government and laws should conform to the 'humour' or 'disposition' of the people, which were in turn affected by such physical circumstances as climate and geography and by 'moral' factors such as religion and custom. The wise legislator would understand that he could not go against or cut through this variety or particularity, in order to shape or re-model society. Ultimately, the concern of the legislator, or the institutions of government, was to provide the security Montesquieu saw as essential to liberty. In accounting for liberty in this way he was suggesting that rulers needed to concern themselves not directly with the welfare of their subjects, but rather with securing the conditions under which individuals were free to pursue their various ends in safety.

In Montesquieu's social theory there is a strong suggestion first, that under the rule of laws ensuring individual safety society would flourish; and secondly, that such a society would have a civilising effect on human development. This view emerges sharply in his account of eighteenth century England, which he saw as a polity in which individual liberty was secured by constitutional government and a commercial society. Here indeed the civilising nature of commercial society was instantiated:[7]

> Commerce cures destructive prejudices, and it is an almost general rule that everywhere there are gentle mores, there is commerce and that everywhere there is commerce, there are gentle mores.

Commerce, he maintained, while corrupting the purest morals, refined barbarous ones. The spirit of commerce brought with it frugality, economy, moderation, work, prudence, tranquillity, and order. It enlightened and softened men: the natural effect of trade, in the end, was peace. Montesquieu's underlying proposition was that a concern with commerce encouraged people to think of themselves and their material affairs, and this made them tolerant and hardworking.

Notwithstanding Montesquieu's misunderstandings of the institutions of eighteenth century England, and his ingenuous account of the workings of commerce, he established a vigorous counterpoint to the advocates of ancient republicanism and its emphasis on the glory and virtue of the republic. In emphasising the value of commerce in encouraging people in their private material pursuits, he was concerned to point out how good a thing it was that people were distracted from concern for, or devotion to, the fatherland or the king. In an attack on political moralism, Montesquieu tried to persuade the French monarchs that grandeur was more likely to be realised through economic expansion than military conquest.[8] More generally, he insisted that the very nature of society meant that it was not open to the legislator to control at will or whim; society had an independent life of its own.

Montesquieu's work exerted a considerable influence on later French thinkers such as Benjamin Constant, Alexis de Tocqueville and Emile Durkheim.[9] And his impact on his Enlightenment contemporaries was no less significant. Later in the eighteenth century, in the social thought of David Hume and Adam Smith, we find some of the earliest and most impressive attempts to account for the nature of society as a self-sustaining or spontaneous economic and legal order.[10] And while they did not make explicit any distinction between state and civil society, these thinkers attempted to offer an account of the role or place of political institutions given the same assumptions about the nature of society. Both were familiar with Montesquieu's writings. And like Montesquieu, they tried to show that the proper purpose of political institutions was not to shape or reconstruct society but to preserve the constitutional order within within which the self-regulating processes of the social order might be allowed to function.[11]

In many ways Hume and, especially, Smith were more sober in their assessments of the workings of society. Although convinced of the benefits of commerce, and of the system of private property generally, they also saw its imperfections. Smith, anticipating many of the concerns of Hegel and Marx, recognised the problems faced by the emerging industrial society. The boredom and the dulling of the senses induced by repetitive factory labour Smith feared would produce a society of dullards, easily manipulated by political leaders. Moreover, the unplanned drift to the cities he thought would lead to the breakdown of moral structures as individuals 'escaped' from local mechanisms which monitored social behaviour and kept destructive inclinations in check. Yet the solutions to these problems, he maintained, lay not in social transformation but in piecemeal reform within society, through such measures as education.[12]

While thinkers such as Montesquieu, Hume and Smith did not operate with a formal distinction between state and civil society, they nonetheless made clear a view that civil life had a considerable measure of independence from governmental institutions. Moreover, they went to some length to argue that the development of this private realm was generally benign. This view was strongly contested by theorists who were sceptical, if not openly hostile, to this tradition of thinking; the most important of them was Jean-Jacques Rousseau.

III

If Montesquieu was the champion of modern civil society, Rousseau was its greatest challenger. While the former saw it as the realm within which men were civilised, the latter found it corrupting and destructive of human freedom. Contrasting society with an imaginary natural state, Rousseau described how man had been corrupted by his acquisitiveness, which had transformed his very nature for the worse. Burdened by the artificial wants and needs created by society, men came to compare themselves with one another, and learned to deceive one another in order that they might assert their pre-eminence. At the root of the problem for Rousseau, lay the division of labour and private property, by which people were at once locked in relations of (inter)dependence, and yet set against one another by their conflicting material interests. Bernard Yack is right to argue that Rousseau 'is the first to suggest that the spirit of modern social interaction is the obstacle to human satisfaction and completeness'.[13]

Rousseau saw the key to the disorders of modern society in institutions separating the individual from his fellows. The right of property, enshrined in the law, served simply to reinforce competition and inequality, setting rich against poor, owners against workers. While Adam Smith hailed the benefits of the division of labour, Rousseau stressed its divisive impact. Under its institutions, the prevailing human relations were exchange relations; and these were unsatisfactory because they were primarily relations of interest. Human association was thus founded not on fellow-feeling but on ties of self-interest. Having 'lost' his natural liberty, the individual was now chained to his fellows; in modern society there was neither freedom nor community.

The problem with civilisation, according to Rousseau, is that egoism and sectional interests have so much scope. Egoism did not exist in the state of nature: '*Amour-propre* is a purely relative and factitious feeling, which arises in the state of society, leads each individual to make more of himself than of any other, causes all the mutual damage men inflict one on another'.[14] The contracting of man out of the state of nature brought with it great advantages, but also deep problems related to the development of civil society, with its possessiveness, and the distinction between *mine* and *thine*. As Rousseau famously declared: 'The first man who, having enclosed a piece of ground, bethought himself of saying "This is mine", and found people simple enough to believe him, was the real founder of civil society'.[15] The problems of civilisation, in particular inequality and the subjection of some men to others, had thus begun:[16]

> Man must now, therefore, have been perpetually employed in getting others to interest themselves in his lot, and in making them, apparently at least, if not really, find their advantage in promoting his own. Thus he must have been sly and artful in his behaviour to some, and imperious and cruel to others; being under a kind of necessity to ill-use all the persons of whom he stood in need.

For Rousseau, property was the basis of much evil—rivalry and competition, and conflicting interests—and since the right to property was so poorly established, the rich man conceived a profound plan: to turn his potential adversaries into allies. This he did by setting up political institutions based on ideas of justice, but which in fact legitimised property holding and the existing distribution of inequality.[17] Law converted usurpation into a right. Property, above all, gave rise to the pursuit of individual interest at the expense of the social interest, and was thus a threat to freedom. 'What can be thought', he asked rhetorically, 'of a relation, in which the interest of every individual dictates rules directly opposite to those the public reason dictates to the community in general—in which every man finds his profit in the misfortunes of his neighbour?'[18]

Given that there was no prospect of return to a state of nature, the problem was to show how freedom could be had in the modern world. Although Rousseau changed his mind about the suitability of various kinds of political institution, he made clear that the solution to the problem of modern society lay in eroding the distinction between the public and the private affairs of individuals. Society, he argued in *The Social Contract*, had to be conceived of as embodying a 'General Will'. This General Will, he wrote elsewhere, 'which tends always to the preservation and welfare of the whole and of every party, and is the source of the laws, constitutes for all the members of the State, in their relations to one another and to it, the rule of what is just or unjust.'[19] Such a 'will' was a genuinely communal interest in the well-being of society as a whole, which could be truly 'willed' by each and every individual not distracted by private, selfish concerns. Society had a common interest which amounted to more than merely the sum of private interests.

Only a mode of political association in which each individual gave up his natural liberty to the whole community, subordinating his individual will to the collective will, could overcome the inequality and social disunity which disfigured modern society. Rousseau's models for political society were the ancient Greek poleis, especially Sparta, with their strongly developed civic virtue and public-spiritedness. Modern, or 'civilised' man was, by contrast, selfish and obsessed with money. Modern institutions produce 'divided souls', since love of community conflicts with natural self-love.[20]

The freedom Rousseau conceived of consisted in the harmonisation of particular wills with the General Will, or the suppression of the former by the latter, as when individuals are 'forced to be free'[21] or when partial associations are outlawed. Rousseau's practical advice was, in some respects, rather tame. He suggested, first, that governments ought to 'prevent extreme inequality of fortune',[22] and secondly 'that there should be no partial society in the State, and that each citizen should express only his own opinion ... But if there are partial societies, it is best to have as many as possible and to prevent them from being unequal'.[23] In other respects, Rousseau's views are quite radical. It is arguable whether he intended that there should be no private existence at all. Yet he did assert that: 'Each man alienates, I admit, by the social compact, only such part of his power, goods, and liberty as it is important for the community to control; *but it must also be granted that the Sovereign is sole judge of what is important*'.[24] In Rousseau's conception, freedom advanced in proportion as the distinction between the individual and society was eroded: 'The better the constitution of a State is, the more do public affairs encroach on private in the minds of the citizens'.[25]

IV

Rousseau perhaps did more than any other philosopher to give currency to the idea that the key to the achievement of human freedom was the overcoming of the conflict of interest inherent in the realm of social interaction among private individuals: the realm of civil society. Yet while he offered a thorough critique of 'civil society', he did not take the trouble to explore the contrast between civil society and the state. The thinker who did most to expound the conceptual distinction, by making it central to his political philosophy, was G.W.F. Hegel. Hegel's reflections largely coincided with the French Revolution of 1789,[26] in which the political sphere was formally separated from the civil. The factors which once directly decided where all power lay (birth, wealth, education) now had less significance, for the political sphere had become—in principle, if not in actuality—a sphere of formal equality. In his *Philosophy of Right* Hegel offered an account of the nature of civil society as a stage in historical development which culminated in the emergence of the modern state. But he also supplied an analytic account of civil society as the realm of human interaction which mediated between the family and the state. It is this account of civil society as a sphere of legal and economic activity which has been most influential in modern political analysis, not least because it provided the target for the criticisms put by Marx against modern civil life.

Hegel was influenced by a vision of ancient Greek virtue,[27] and he is an important link between Rousseau and Marx. He, too, attempted to defend a conception of freedom and describe its political and social preconditions. But Hegel's mature project did not advocate the abolition or transcendence of civil society.[28] In this he disappointed the hopes raised by his early philosophy, which suggested that freedom as self-determination could be attained not just in consciousness but also in the world, and provided his Young Hegelian epigones with material for diverse interpretations and projects.[29] Man, Hegel finally concluded, is fully at home in the realm of Absolute Spirit, in the community of shared knowledge, not in the social community. Hegel was nevertheless influenced by Rousseau's understanding of the dichotomies of the modern world. Central to his analysis was the contrast between the individual and society, and like Rousseau he longed for a reunification. At first, Hegel saw these dichotomies as historical rather than human limitations; later, he saw them as a product of the *maturity* of society.[30] The break in Hegel's attitude to the polis, and the related vision of a unified civil-political existence, came around 1805–06, when he began to argue that public freedom can be realised without destroying individual self-preference. Individualism, he argued, was an achievement of the modern world.[31]

Hegel came to believe that civil society, the sphere of individualism (or 'subjectivity'), was important in a fully developed community, because it was characterised by the rule of impersonal law, and by relations that included—but were not solely—relations of the market economy. But he was not a classical liberal, for whom the state was a necessary evil, a shield for civil society. The state, for him, was an ethical institution, and membership of it was necessary for the moral well-being of men. Men formed genuine communities only when they shared some basic moral ideals. In Hegel's account of ethical life, civil society is one of the three major spheres: family, civil society, and state. The family is held together by ties of sentiment, the state by the impartiality of civil service and a kind of altruism. In civil society, individuals are free to pursue their own interests and differences; they are united by mutual need. Civil association was brought about by the free play of self-interest: unconsciously and automatically. And civil society was composed of three 'moments': the system of needs (the economy); the administration of justice; and the police and corporation.[32] Of Hegel's views it would be more correct to say that civil society and the political state were two aspects of the state, two kinds of public authorities. Civil authorities served primarily individual or group purposes; political authorities served primarily the purposes of the whole people.

Hegel argued that the state is too large and impersonal to serve as an object for the immediate affections of its citizens. It must, of course, provide a framework of laws within which the market can operate, but its laws are chiefly procedural rules, in the interests of all, and are not designed for the moral edification of citizens. Such opportunities as there are for civic virtue come from the institutions of civil society, especially those Hegel called 'corporations', which included a whole range of professional associations and voluntary organisations, as well as those we normally associate with the market: 'As the family was the first, so the Corporation is the second ethical root of the state, the one planted in civil society'.[33] These corporations are the source of socialisation and education for their members; they, rather than the state, have welfare functions (because of the danger 'the rabble' presented to social stability); and they have functions of political representation (in the Assemblies of Estates). The corporation thus mediates between the individual and the state, but it also prepares the individual for politics, chiefly through his contributions to its internal workings:[34]

> Under modern political conditions, the citizens have only a restricted share in the public business of the state, yet it is essential to provide men—ethical entities—with work of a public character over and above their private business.

This theory of liberal corporatism is a system of self-regulation by quasi-autonomous social groups.[35] Relations between the state and civil society were mediated by Hegel's 'universal class', the bureaucracy. If, for Hegel, there can be no return to the Greek polis, how can we be at home in the world? His answer was that the role of the state is to create the conditions in which this could be achieved within family and civil society.

V

Under the influence of Rousseau, and reacting against Hegel's *Philosophy of Right*, the young Marx was a fierce critic of civil society. For Hegel, the units of civil society were complex foci of value; for Marx, civil society was chiefly *bourgeois* society—the market economy—and its relations simply those of self-interest and calculation. Both Hegel and Marx used the term '*bürgerliche Gesellschaft*' to describe this phenomenon, but with different intent. As Marx claimed in the *Communist Manifesto*, the bourgeoisie 'has left no other nexus between man and man than naked self-interest, than callous "cash payment"'.[36] It had even, he argued, 'reduced the family relation to a mere money relation'.[37] This is why he soon turned to the study of political economy to investigate the 'anatomy' of civil society. Marx's conception of freedom as autonomy differed from Hegel's in demanding that heteronomy be eliminated in the world, and in identifying the sources of that heteronomy in capitalism. Marx advocated a socialist revolution, not a revolution in consciousness. And in his developed conception, he nominated certain social classes as bearers of public virtue and private greed.

Marx first came to grips with the conceptual problems raised by the existence of civil society in his paragraph-by-paragraph confrontation with parts of Hegel's political philosophy. Hegel had argued that the spheres of particular interest (family and civil society) could be reconciled with the sphere of the general interest (the state). Marx was hostile to this view, believing that universality consisted in the *abolition* of particularity, not in reconciliation with it.[38] Marx advocated 'true democracy', which he called 'the true unity of the general and the particular'.[39] Under this democracy, the political state—a product of the modern separation of public and private life—is annihilated. 'The abstraction of the *state as such* belongs only to modern times, because the abstraction of private life belongs only to modern times. The abstraction of the *political state* is a modern product'.[40]

Marx was impressed by the ancient Greek poleis where, he asserted, 'the *res publica* is the real private affair of the citizens'.[41] He criticised Hegel for positing the separation of state and civil society, and for constructing an identity between them: not for misdescribing the empirical reality, but for acquiescing in it.[42] For Marx, the separation of civil and political society was a straightforward contradiction because, in its political act, 'civil society must completely give itself up as civil society, as civil estate, and assert an aspect of its existence which not only has nothing in common with the real civil existence of its essence but stands in opposition to it'.[43]

Marx was concerned not just that the principles of the two spheres were in conflict, but that they placed individuals in an invidious position.[44]

> Civil society and the state are separated. Hence the citizen of the state is also separated from the citizen as a member of civil society. He must therefore effect a *fundamental division* within himself ... Hence, in order to behave as an *actual citizen of the state*, and to attain political significance and effectiveness, he must step out of his civil reality, disregard it, and withdraw from this whole organisation into his individuality ... His existence as a citizen of the state is an existence outside his *communal* existences and is therefore purely *individual* ... The separation of civil society and political state necessarily appears as a separation of the *political* citizen, the citizen of the state, from civil society, from his own, actual, empirical reality'.

Differences within civil society therefore have no political significance: there are no longer political estates, only social estates. This transformation from the Middle Ages was accomplished by the French Revolution. At present, Marx argued, civil society has elections as its chief political interest, and though individuals may be 'commissioned as representative of *general* concerns, ... they actually represent *particular* concerns'.[45] Here is the key to transcending the distinction: '*elections unlimited* both in respect of the franchise and the right to be elected. But the completion of this abstraction is at the same time the transcendence of the abstraction. In actually positing its *political existence* as its *true* existence, civil society has simultaneously posited its civil existence ... as *inessential*'.[46]

Marx's ideas about the separation of civil from political society were employed in a distinction between political and human emancipation. 'Merely' political emancipation—the making of one's political attributes independent of the features of one's civil life (wealth, birth, religion)—was an illusory emancipation: 'the *state* can free itself from a restriction without man being *really* free from this restriction'.[47] The distinctions of birth, rank, education and occupation remain restrictions upon his autonomy. Not only was political emancipation illusory, but it gave rise to a fundamental division within the life of man:[48]

> Where the political state has attained its free development, man—not only in thought, in consciousness, but in *reality*, in *life*—leads a twofold life, a heavenly and an earthly life: life in the *political community*, in which he considers himself a *communal being*, and life in *civil society*, in which he acts as a *private individual*, regards other men as a means, degrades himself into a means, and becomes the plaything of alien powers.

Civil society is an expression of man's separation from his community and from his real self: an expression of his alienation. The sole bond which holds men together in civil society, according to Marx, 'is natural necessity, need and private interest, the preservation of their property and their egoistic selves'.[49] And the political sphere is subordinated to private interest.[50]

Civil society is dissolved into independent individuals, whose relations with one another are regulated by formalised laws. All 'species-ties' between men are ended, and 'egoism and selfish need' are put in their place, giving rise to a situation where 'atomistic individuals ... are inimically opposed to one another'.[51] Human emancipation occurs when man in civil society really becomes political man, when he becomes a 'species-being' in his everyday life, and consequently when he does not see 'politics' as a separate activity. By claiming that 'The state is based on the contradiction between *public* and *private life*, on the contradiction between *general interests* and *private interests*',[52] Marx could argue that politics cannot solve the social problem because it is itself expressive of that problem. He maintained that the social revolution would ultimately usher in a period when the division between state and civil society would disappear, and politics would become unnecessary.

VI

The inspiration of the critics of civil society is thus laid bare. What stands out in the work of the critics is an attachment to the view that the true nature of man is reflected in the *general* aspects of his existence—selfless, other-regarding—which so far find their expression in politics. Furthermore, they believe that once the political sphere has become institutionally separate, and is subject to its own rules and logic, then man suffers a crisis in trying to reconcile the different aspects of his existence: chiefly the civil and political. The nature of civil society is such as to bring into constant, and sometimes quite personal, conflict the particular and the general; considerations of personal well-being collide with those of communal well-being. We are inclined at this point to object to the reality, or historical veracity, of the image of 'civic virtue' to which these notions appeal. That man was an essentially political being was an ideal shared by a few ancient Greeks for a limited period of time, and its exclusivity was palpable. It can be argued not that man was losing something he once had, but that as a consequence of positing the boundaries of the political sphere, the *location* and extent of those boundaries could become the subject of rational discussion and argument, and that every man had at last attained the potential to have a political existence (*if* the boundaries permitted it—and that was something which he could contest—and *if* he chose to exercise his right). Politics had at last become attainable. But what sort of politics? Liberalism emerged at about this time because it was an argument for politics as a 'second order' activity: once politics had been demystified, it could be put in its place.

Of course, the proper place of politics continues to be disputed: here is the importance of considering the work of our three critics— Hegel, who accepted the separation of state and civil society, but who argued the need for a 'universal class' (the bureaucracy) to mediate the two, and for an ethic in which society could unite; and Rousseau and Marx, who argued that this separation was a division *within* man (translating directly, in Marx's analysis, into a *social* division),[53] and who refused to countenance its psychic and social consequences. Marx's 'universal class' (the proletariat) was devised not to straddle the division or make it workable, but to *transcend* it.[54]

It was in the political sphere, Marx believed, that man's universality—his true social and species nature—could genuinely be expressed. But it would have to be a political sphere quite different from the one which confronted man after 1789: separate, and abstracted from his real, everyday concerns (the sphere, as Marx put it, of 'abstract universality'). This is the point at which Marx employs Rousseau's analysis of the division that man undergoes when faced with the sphere of abstract universality. In civil society, in his everyday economic and social life, man is expected to act in a certain way: protective of his own and his family's interests, as a calculating individual, ready at every point to maximise his gains and to seize the opportunities presented by others' misfortunes. In the political sphere, by contrast, he was expected to follow another code entirely: to consider the general good rather than his own, and to show compassion to the less fortunate. Marx's point, and Rousseau's, was that this division created tensions within man and society which could only be overcome if the ethic for man was the same in both spheres—that is, if the spheres themselves disappeared. The sphere of abstract universality would be replaced by a life of genuine universality. Politics as we understand it would be unnecessary. Hegel, by contrast, believed that the associations of civil society could inculcate a sort of civic virtue, a compassion for the plight of *some* others, and a consideration for the interests of *some* others. His point was that the state should remedy what it could in civil society: that it had to be alive to genuine and widespread social ills.

We are inclined also to object to the image of 'the general' which the critics of civil society appear to share. That conflicts and tensions arise between the individual and society is an obvious feature of social life. Yet they are inescapable if we are to avoid the sort of 'barracks-room communism' which Marx disdained, for the complexity and changeableness of human interests bespeak not *a solution*, but *resolutions*. In recognising and accepting this, Hegel was the more astute. Like the early political economists, he perceived that individual industry, acquisitiveness and motivation could have desirable social effects. Individual self-interest has its ugly aspects, but if they were its sole or predominant aspects (as the critics sometimes believed), civil society itself could not survive.

VII

By understanding the weaknesses of the critique of civil society—
especially those of its most forceful advocate, Marx—we should
become clearer about the significance of a discussion of civil society
in the present Soviet context.

Amongst the difficulties which beset Marx's social philosophy,
three stand out as of special importance here. The first has to do with
his insistence that man's nature was most truly expressed in the
general aspects of his existence. The second lies in his claim that man
possesses a fundamental, *universal* human nature whose expression
is frustrated by the existence of civil society. The third is his view
that the separation of the civil and the political was a barrier to
man's freedom. We shall discuss these difficulties in turn.

That Marx thought man's nature was most truly expressed in the
political sphere of his life is evident in his statement that, in pre-
communist society, man leads a twofold life: 'life in the *political
community*, in which he considers himself a *communal being*, and
life in *civil society*, in which he acts as a *private individual*, treats
other men as a means, degrades himself into a means, and becomes
the plaything of alien powers'.[55] It is in man's nature as a communal
being that Marx finds what is finest about the human species. The
private realm, for him, is the realm of egoism and exploitation. It
was also the realm of illusion, in which man mistook his rights—of
property, of trade, of religion—for real freedom, when he was not
really free from property, or trade, or religion. This 'right of man to
liberty is based not on the association of man with man, but on the
separation of man from man'.[56]

But is all separation 'alienation'? Is all alienation of a piece? And
what conceivable sort of unity can overcome alienation? The desire
for association with others is clearly one which is often extremely
strong: few people wish to spend their lives wholly isolated from the
company of others. Equally, it is an exaggeration to suggest that this
is, or ought to be, the most important of our desires. In fact the desire
for a measure of independence and privacy seems to have been as, if
not more, important. Some would go further to suggest that it is the
peaceful private life, undisturbed by the unwelcome intrusions of
others, which is to be most highly prized. There may be times when
communal attachments come to the fore—in times of war or
natural disaster, for example—but the sooner we are able to return
to the privacy of our own pursuits the better. As Oakeshott puts it:
'When the springs dry up, the fish are all together on dry land. They

will moisten each other with their dampness and keep each other wet with their slime. But this is not to be compared with their forgetting each other in a river or a lake'.[57] If civil society ends traditional social ties (some renewed form of which its critics seem to hanker after), it does not spell the end of all satisfying social attachments. The latter are more specialised, diverse, flexible and freer,[58] and civil society has its discontents, but 'alienation' seems unable to encompass or appreciate this new complexity.

To this Marx might, of course, have objected that such arguments merely reveal the critics' own alienation. The valuing of privacy and separateness may reflect the extent to which we are dominated by the forces of 'particularity' that prevail in civil society. This leads us to the second difficulty with Marx's views: why think we have a universal nature in any strong sense? It is not necessary to deny that human beings share some important similarities, beginning with their biological characteristics, and extending to their capacity for rational calculation, their passion and interestedness, and their desire for a measure of social acceptance. But this is not to say, as Marx suggested, that the diversity of cultures, religions and national loyalties which shape actual individual identities are therefore aberrations which distort rather than disclose man's essence. There is no universal human identity beyond what is given to individuals by the accidents of birth in that realm of particularity called civil society.

If this is the case, then Marx's concerns about the separation of civil society from the political realm are quite unfounded. If this separation reflects the 'double life' man leads, as a communal being at one moment, and a private individual at another, it simply embodies a central aspect of the various competing roles within human experience. And it points to the notion that there is no single part of that experience—no particular way of life—that has any overriding claim to pre-eminence. Civil society confirms for us the variety of ends people pursue; political society is a reflection of the need to find ways to deal with the conflicts which arise in, but cannot be resolved by, civil society. It is no more difficult for man to step from civil society into the role of citizen in political society and then back again, than it is for him to hunt in the morning, fish in the afternoon, and criticise after dinner.

What are the implications of these criticisms of Marx for our understanding of the significance of civil society? If our criticisms are sound, civil society is important because of its contributions to the constitution of human identity and the fulfilment of individual aspirations. It is certainly, as Marx thought, the realm of self-interest and 'particularity', as well as the arena in which cultures, traditions, and localities compete for individual allegiance and vie for pre-eminence. But it would be, and has been, disastrous to assume that there is some unique human essence—a quintessential humanity—to be liberated by the suppression or destruction of the particularities of civil society.

As an ideology, communism has been distinctive in rejecting the worth of the realm of particularity; in practice it has, to varying degrees, launched an attack on that realm in attempts to suppress religious, cultural and ethnic traditions. It has succeeded simply in suppressing or distorting their expressions. The ideological and political collapse of communism suggests that we should redirect our attention to the target of its attack: to reassert the functions of the traditions and institutions of civil society, and to ask what is necessary if its development or regeneration is to be made possible. In inquiring into the possibility of the reassertion of civil society we would be asking some very fundamental questions, not simply about some abstract notion, but about the very prospects for civil life after communism. It is also to reassert a different view of politics, defended by Bernard Crick, as an activity concerned not with social planning or design, but with maintaining order in complex societies by conciliating different interests by giving them a share in power.[59]

In this regard it is necessary to address some important problems which arise from the nature of civil society. While it is easy to exaggerate the harms caused by competition and conflict among rivals in the economic arena, there is no doubt that civil society is the realm of potentially disruptive conflicts among competing interests and traditions of behaviour. Modern society has long been characterised by a pluralism not only of ethnic groupings, but also of religious, linguistic and cultural traditions. Thus, civil life is generally shaped not only by particular traditions of behaviour, and their respective norms of right conduct, but also by the interaction between the different traditions. Two problems consequently emerge. First, differences between the communities which live by different traditions may lead to disagreement (and conflict) over the terms of the broader civil association—consider, for example, the call from some British Muslims for the extension of the blasphemy laws to deal with the publication of Salman Rushdie's *Satanic Verses*. Secondly, the very fact of propinquity, and the interaction among different communities—through trade, for example—can weaken communal bonds, producing individuals who are more cosmopolitan but less committed to the values and practices of particular communities. This creates a problem of conflict within communities in which those wishing to preserve the integrity of their own traditions of conduct find it increasingly difficult to do so in the face of numerous opportunities for individual members to break away as members of a wider society. Once again, the result can be an increase in sectional demands for the rules of the wider society to conform more closely to the requirements of their particular interests.

The issue that needs to be addressed is properly a political one: how to specify the terms under which the broader civil association—civil society—has to be governed, given the fact of a pluralism of communities and traditions. More specifically, with respect to the re-developing societies of Eastern Europe, it is necessary to tackle the problem of how civil society is to be re-established, since the overthrow of old regimes and the abolition of totalitarian political structures appears to have awakened long-suppressed national and ethnic conflicts. Political emancipation itself can do little more than create the need for more fundamental social and political settlements.

Here then, we think, lies the significance of civil society as a subject for investigation, or as a focus for those inquiring into the transformation of Eastern Europe. Mere political emancipation is not what is most important; as Marx himself noted, albeit with quite a different point in mind, 'the limitations of political emancipation are immediately evident in the fact that a state can liberate itself from a limitation without man himself being truly free of it'. Soviet civil society, in particular, after emancipating itself from political society, needs to demand that politics serves *its* requirements, rather than vice versa.

Notes

1   Karl Marx, 'On the Jewish Question', in Karl Marx and Frederick Engels, *Collected Works* (London: Lawrence and Wishart, 1975) Vol.III, pp. 146-174 at p. 153.

2   John Keane, 'Despotism and Democracy: The Origins and Development of the Distinction Between Civil Society and the State 1750-1850', in John Keane (ed.), *Civil Society and the State* (London: Verso, 1988) pp. 35–71, at p. 35.

3   Sir Henry Maine, *Ancient Law* (London: J.M. Dent, 1917) especially pp. 67–100.

4   Ferdinand Tönnies, *Community and Society* (East Lansing: Michigan State University Press, 1957).

5   For an illuminating discussion of the development of civil society from
     mediaeval times see Antony Black, *Guilds and Civil Society in European
     Political Thought from the Twelfth Century to the Present* (Ithaca:
     Cornell University Press, 1984).

6   Baron de Montesquieu, *The Spirit of the Laws* (Cambridge: Cambridge
     University Press, 1989) p. 8.

7   Ibid., p. 338.

8   For a discussion of Montesquieu's defence of commerce see Judith Shklar,
     Montesquieu (Oxford: Oxford University Press, 1987) pp. 107–108.

9   For discussion of Montesquieu's influence see Shklar, *Montesquieu*,
     Chapter 6; and Raymond Aron, *Main Currents in Sociological Thought*
     (Harmondsworth: Penguin, 1965) Vol.I, Chapter 1. On Montesquieu's
     influence on Constant see Stephen Holmes, *Benjamin Constant and the
     Making of Modern Liberalism* (New Haven: Yale University Press,
     1984).

10   Some have argued that the earliest important contribution to the theory
     of spontaneous order was that of Bernard Mandeville in his 1714 work
     The Fable of the Bees, or Private Vices, Public Benefits (Indianapolis:
     Liberty Press, 1988). The most distinguished modern theorist is F.A.
     Hayek. See F.A. Hayek, *Law, Legislation and Liberty* (London: Routledge
     and Kegan Paul, 1982) Vol.I, Chapter 2.

11   On Hume see F.A. Hayek, 'The Legal and Political Philosophy of David
     Hume', in V.C. Chappell (ed.), *Hume* (London: Macmillan, 1970) pp.
     335–360.

12   On this point see in particular Andrew Skinner's introduction to Adam
     Smith's *The Wealth of Nations Books I–III* (Harmondsworth: Penguin,
     1986) especially pp. 79–82.

13   Bernard Yack, *The Longing for Total Revolution: Philosophic Sources of
     Social Discontent from Rousseau to Marx and Nietzsche* (Princeton:
     Princeton University Press, 1986) p. 35.

14   Jean-Jacques Rousseau, 'A Discourse on the Origin of Inequality', in
     Jean-Jacques Rousseau, *The Social Contract and Discourses* (London:
     J.M. Dent, 1973) pp. 27-113 at p. 66, n2.

15   Ibid., p. 76.

16   Ibid., p. 86.

17   Ibid., pp. 88–89.

18   Ibid., pp. 106–107.

19   Jean-Jacques Rousseau, 'A Discourse on Political Economy', in Jean-
     Jacques Rousseau, *The Social Contract and Discourses* (London: J.M.
     Dent, 1973) pp. 115-153 at pp. 120–121.

20   According to Shklar, 'It mattered far less to Rousseau whether the heroes
     of Sparta and Rome had ever really existed, than that such men could *not*
     be found at all in modern times': Judith N. Shklar, *Men and Citizens: A
     Study of Rousseau's Social Theory* (Cambridge: University Press, 1969),
     p. 13.

21   This paradoxical expression has given rise to numerous, divergent
     interpretations of Rousseau's politics, some of them usefully collected in
     Guy H. Dodge (ed.), *Jean-Jacques Rousseau: Authoritarian Libertarian?*
     (Massachusetts: D.C. Heath, 1971).

22 Rousseau, 'A Discourse on Political Economy', p. 134.
23 Jean-Jacques Rousseau, 'The Social Contract', in Jean-Jacques Rousseau, *The Social Contract and Discourses* (London: J.M. Dent, 1973) pp. 163-278 at p. 185. For a discussion of this view—and a defence of Rousseau—see Alfred Cobban, *Rousseau and the Modern State* (London: George Allen & Unwin, 1964), pp. 45–48.
24 Rousseau, 'The Social Contract', p. 186: emphasis added.
25 Ibid., p. 239.
26 See Joachim Ritter, *Hegel and the French Revolution: Essays on The Philosophy of Right* (Cambridge: The MIT Press, 1982) especially pp. 35–89.
27 See Raymond Plant, *Hegel* (London: George Allen & Unwin, 1973) pp. 17–40.
28 Charles Taylor, *Hegel and Modern Society* (Cambridge: Cambridge University Press, 1979) pp. 100–111, argues that Hegel differs significantly from Rousseau in accepting an 'articulated differentiation' of society as both unavoidable and compatible with freedom.
29 Yack, *The Longing for Total Revolution*, pp. 209ff. points to the differences between Hegel's earlier and mature conceptions of freedom. On the developments within Hegel's works, and the reactions by Young Hegelians to them, see William J. Brazill, *The Young Hegelians* (New Haven: Yale University Press, 1970) especially pp. 29–70.
30 Yack, *The Longing for Total Revolution*, p. 196.
31 G.W.F. Hegel, *Hegel's Philosophy of Right* (Oxford: Oxford University Press, 1952) §182, Addition: pp. 266–267.
32 Ibid., §188: p. 126.
33 Ibid., §255: p. 154.
34 Ibid., §255, Addition: p. 278.
35 See the discussion in Steven B. Smith, *Hegel's Critique of Liberalism: Rights in Context* (Chicago: University of Chicago Press, 1989) pp. 140–145.
36 Karl Marx, 'Manifesto of the Communist Party', in Karl Marx and Frederick Engels, *Collected Works* (London: Lawrence and Wishart, 1975) Vol.VI, pp. 477-519 at p. 487.
37 Ibid., p. 487.
38 For a discussion of the logic behind this view, see Eugene Kamenka, *The Ethical Foundations of Marxism* (London: Routledge & Kegan Paul, 1972) pp. 37–47.
39 Karl Marx, 'Contribution to the Critique of Hegel's Philosophy of Law', in Karl Marx and Frederick Engels, *Collected Works* (London: Lawrence and Wishart, 1975) Vol.III, pp. 1-129 at p. 30. This work, and Marx's subsequent *On the Jewish Question*, are discussed in Leszek Kolakowski, *Main Currents of Marxism: Its Origins, Growth and Dissolution* (Oxford: Oxford University Press, 1978) Vol.I, pp. 122–131.
40 Marx, 'Contribution to the Critique of Hegel's Philosophy of Law', p. 32.
41 Ibid., p. 32.
42 Ibid., pp. 50–51. Hegel, however, was not uncritical of civil society, and of the poverty and alienation which accompanied it. But, as Avineri

explained, 'For Marx ... this split of man into *bourgeois* and *citoyen* is the measure of his alienation, whereas for Hegel it is the basis of his integration into it': Shlomo Avineri, *Hegel's Theory of the Modern State* (Cambridge: University Press, 1972) p. 104n. Jean Cohen also stresses the richness of Hegel's understanding of civil society, contrasting it with Marx's 'impoverished' analysis (which he argues is fundamental to the inability of Marx's class theory properly to encompass modernity): Jean L. Cohen, *Class and Civil Society: The Limits of Marxian Critical Theory*(Oxford: Martin Robertson, 1983) pp. 24–25.

43   Marx, 'Contribution to the Critique of Hegel's Philosophy of Law', p. 77.

44   Ibid., pp. 77–78.

45   Ibid., p. 123.

46   Ibid., p. 121.

47   Marx, 'On the Jewish Question', p. 152.

48   Ibid., p. 154.

49   Ibid., p. 164.

50   Ibid., p. 164.

51   Ibid., p. 173.

52   Marx, 'Critical Marginal Notes on the Article by a Prussian', in Karl Marx and Frederick Engels, *Collected Works* (London: Lawrence and Wishart, 1975) Vol.III, pp. 189-206 at p. 198.

53   'The estrangement of man, and in fact every relationship in which man [stands] to himself, is realised and expressed only in the relationship in which a man stands to other men': Karl Marx, 'Economic and Philosophic Manuscripts of 1844', in Karl Marx and Frederick Engels, *Collected Works* (London: Lawrence and Wishart, 1975) Vol.III, pp. 229-346 at p. 277. This is a proposition which Robert Tucker, for one, finds 'theoretically untenable': Robert C. Tucker, *Philosophy and Myth in Karl Marx* (Cambridge: Cambridge University Press, 1972) p. 148.

54   See David W. Lovell, *Marx's Proletariat: The Making of a Myth* (London: Routledge, 1988) pp. 17–56.

55   Marx, 'On the Jewish Question', p. 154.

56   Ibid., p. 162.

57   Michael Oakeshott, 'Introduction' in Thomas Hobbes, *Leviathan* (London: Blackwell, n.d.) p. lxvi.

58   See Karl Popper, *The Open Society and Its Enemies* (London: Routledge and Kegan Paul, 1966) Vol.I, pp. 174–175.

59   Bernard Crick, *In Defence of Politics* (Harmondsworth: Penguin, 1964) p. 15.

3

The Myth of
Human Self-Identity:
Unity of Civil and Political Society
in Socialist Thought

LESZEK KOLAKOWSKI

These remarks are not historical. Their aim is to point out a
soteriological myth hidden in the traditional Marxist anticipation of
socialism as based on the identity of civil and political society. I will
try to reveal a continuity (though not identity) between this
soteriology and contemporary totalitarian variants of socialism and
to say why the Marxian ideal of unity is in my opinion
impracticable. A short historical remark may be useful, nevertheless,
to bring into relief the background against which Marxian thought
seems to have developed.

Marx's ideas on the relationship of civil society to the state took
shape in his criticism of four doctrines which differed widely in the
negative influence they exerted on his thought. They are: (1) Hegel's
and then Lassalle's theory of the state; (2) the classical liberal
concept; (3) anarchist (mostly Bakuninist) criticism of the state; (4)
totalitarian communism.

The first two may be called liberal in the sense that they both
involved a separation of the political from the civil society as a
permanent feature of human life and both rejected the idea that the
state could ever replace the civil society or, at the other extreme,
become superfluous; in other words, they were neither totalitarian
nor anarchist. Both Hegel and Lassalle, however, differed from
classical liberal tenets in that they went beyond a purely utilitarian
concept of the state and attributed an autonomous value to it as the
highest form of human community. The classical liberal doctrine
envisaged the state in strictly utilitarian terms as a necessary device

which societies had to apply in order to keep inevitable conflicts of particular interests within well-defined legal limits and thus prevent society from turning into an unrestricted war of all against all; that is, from eventually falling prey to the tyranny of the strongest.

When we confront the Marxian strictures on Bakunin we may sometimes feel it difficult to square them with his criticism of Lassalle; the former is attacked for blaming the state as the main source of all social evil, the latter for worshipping it as the most splendid achievement of the human spirit. We may state, however, that Marx's basic conception of the relationship between political and civil society, as expounded in 1843 in the unfinished *Critique of the Hegelian Philosophy of Right* and in the *Jewish Question*, h a d persisted intact throughout his intellectual development, and there is no reason to maintain that it was ever denied in later writings.

To be sure, Marx started in Feuerbachian fashion by blaming Hegel for his 'inversion' of the relation of 'subject' to 'predicate' in dealing with the question. For Hegel, he says, the real human subjects become predicates of the universal substance embodied in the state. Real priorities are thus reversed since 'the universal' may be only a property of an individual being and the genuine subject is always finite. It is not the state that creates 'real individuals'; the state, on the contrary, is an 'objectified man'. The stated aim of democracy is to restore the state to its real human creators. When stating that 'the universal' needs human subjectivity to reach its own perfection, Hegel not only makes the separation of the state from human beings eternal but sanctions the illusion of the state as the embodiment of the universal interest. Hegel believed indeed that the spirit of the state, its superiority over all particular interests, is incorporated in the consciousness of functionaries, since only they can identify their particular interest with the universal one and make possible the synthesis of general good with the aspirations of particular layers of society. Consequently, Hegelian philosophy supports the ideological illusion of the Prussian bureaucracy that considers itself the incarnation of the universal interest. Marx stresses, however, that when bureaucracy becomes an autonomous principle and when the interest of the state gains independence as the interest of the bureaucracy—and is thus a 'real' interest— bureaucracy must fight against the aspirations of other particular orders which gave it birth.

Marx thus took over the Hegelian distinction of civil society and the state, while denying their permanence and the necessity of their separation. The civil society is a whole mass of conflicting individual

THE MYTH OF HUMAN SELF-IDENTITY   43

and group aspirations, empirical daily life with all its conflicts and struggles, the realm of private desires and private endeavours. To Hegel, its conflicts are rationally moderated, kept in check and synthesised in the superior will of the state, this will being independent of any particular interest. To Marx the state, at least in its present form, far from being a neutral mediator, is the tool of some particular interests disguised as the illusory universal will. Man as citizen and as private person is two different and separated beings, but only the latter, the member of the civil society, is the 'real' concrete being; as a citizen he participates in the abstract community owing its reality to ideological mystification. This mystification was unknown in mediaeval society where class division was directly expressed in the political order, that is, the segmentation of the civil society was reflected in the political organism. Modern societies, having abrogated the direct political validity of class stratification, split social life into two realms, and this division is carried over into each individual existence; it became a contradiction within every human being, torn between his status as a private person and his role as a citizen. Consequently political emancipation—in defiance of Bruno Bauer's philosophy—must not be confused with human emancipation. The former may politically cancel the differences between people in ownership or in religion, that is, make the differences politically insignificant and thus liberate the state from religious or class distinctions (by, for example, the abolition of ownership qualifications in political activities or of legal privileges for certain denominations). This change, important though it may be, does not abrogate either religious or class division in society and allows them to keep working. It leaves untouched the separation of civil from political society; the former is still a realm of real life, egoistic and isolated for every individual, the latter provides life with collective character but only in an abstract illusory form. The aim of human—as opposed to political—emancipation is to restore to collective life its real character, or to restore the collective character to civil society. At the end of the *Jewish Question* we find the important sentence which expresses—still in philosophical and embryonic form and not yet in class terms—the great Marxian hope for universal human emancipation; a hope that was to continue determining all his further efforts to outline his vision of a society abolishing for ever the dichotomy between man's personal and his collective existence:

> Only when the real individual man will absorb back the abstract citizen of the state and—as individual man, in his empirical life, in his individual work, in his individual relationships—will become

> the species being, only when man will recognise and will organise
> his 'forces propres' as *social* forces and, consequently, will not
> separate from himself the social force in form of *political* force any
> more, only then the emancipation of man will be accomplished.

Nobody can pretend to find in this sentence everything that Marx
would say later about the meaning of the future kingdom of
freedom. But everything he said grew out of this primordial hope. In
the quoted sentence the concept of 'human emancipation' lacks any
mention of class struggle and the mission of the proletariat. And yet,
the same vision of man returning to perfect unity, experiencing
directly his personal life as a social force, makes up the philosophical
background of Marxian socialism. In all later writings which were
to define his position in contrast to liberal, anarchist and communist
totalitarian doctrines, the same eschatological concept of the unified
man remains.

What is wrong with this hope? Is there any historical connection
between the Marxian vision of the unified man and the fact that real
communism appears only in totalitarian form, that is as the
tendency to *replace* all crystallisations of the civil society by coercive
organs of the state? How can this connection be grasped?

While we cannot examine in detail the intricacies of the problems
in the chronicles of Marxist doctrine here, I must summarise,
however crudely, the paramount points of Marxian criticism of the
four approaches just mentioned.

Anarchism—Stirner and Bakunin. Bakunin's concept was based
on three premises. First, that state institutions are the main sources
of all social evil. Second, that people left to themselves and free from
the burden of political machinery will develop their natural ability
for friendly co-operation within loosely organised small
communities. Third, that any attempt to rebuild the state, once the
existing one has been crushed, will end with another and still worse
version of the same tyranny; a new apparatus made up of the former
workers cannot but refurbish or reinforce eternal slavery and the
upstarts who run it will be instantly converted into turncoats from
their class and will guard their freshly acquired privileges against
that class. To Marx the first two arguments were obviously wrong
and based on ignorance of well-proved historical facts. Since the
origin of the state is to be looked for in civil society, and not
conversely, Bakunin's demand for the demolition of the state
amounts to putting the carriage before the horse. The existing
political bodies do not produce inequality and exploitation, but
express them; briefly, the alienation of labour precedes political

alienation. To dissolve the political framework of the capitalist order, while retaining the relations of production unaltered, would be to preserve conditions which would be bound soon to create the same framework again. As to the third point, Marx never dealt with it. It remained open for his followers. His comment on the Paris Commune, in particular his saying that the working class cannot take over the ready made state machinery but has to smash it, was welcomed, to be sure, by Bakunin's acolyte Guillaume as a shift towards the anarchist standpoint. Wrongly so, as later writings (especially the *Critique of the Gotha Programme*) would reveal.

The classical liberal concept corresponded to the idealised model of capitalist society as analysed in *Capital*. Marx was aware, of course, that the real patterns of capitalist economy do not coincide perfectly with this model, which presupposes that the state is utterly inactive in economic life and allows the laws of free competition to work unbridled. Still, this was the model he was dealing with in his major work. The liberal concept—the state limited to the role of watchman and forbearing to interfere in the 'free contract' relations between entrepreneurs and wage earners (not to speak of other aspects of industrial activity)—was not, strictly speaking, 'wrong' in Marx's eyes, as far as it matched the genuine tendency of capital. What was wrong was the ideological delusion that this kind of separation met the inalterable requirements of human nature or that, once laid down, it would last indefinitely. According to this concept the maximum productive efficiency and consequently the optimum general good is secured within a political framework based on the minimum interference in economic relations. The state has to care about security; welfare and wealth will look after themselves. Marx's anticipated organisation of society was exactly the opposite: political government would become superfluous while economic management, 'the administration of things', would exhaust the functions of the public organs. The expression 'withering away of the state' comes from Engels but it fits into Marxian predictions. The question arises: what premises do we have to admit in order to believe that a social organisation free from any mediating and coercive power and from any political bodies is practicable? What conditions would make conceivable a society which can 'administer things' without 'governing people'?

Hegel's and Lassalle's cult of the state was attacked by Marx from another point of view. Lassalle did not share, of course, the ideal of the economic neutrality of the state. On the contrary, he believed that the workers, through the parliamentary system, could influence the state and compel it to help in organising independent productive co-operatives which would eventually dominate economic life. For Marx, Lassalle utterly neglected the class character of the existing state and cherished a utopian fancy that the state, which is in fact a self-defensive device of the privileged classes, may be employed as an organ of socialist transformation. By considering the state as a value in itself and overlooking its class function Lassalle reveals his historical ignorance.

Marx did not deny that the state apparatus may play an independent role in the class struggle; this happens, he thought, in exceptional circumstances which he analysed in the case of 'Bonapartism'. Moments of temporary autonomy of the state occur as a result of stalemate in a sharp class war. Marx did not try to synthesise his general view on the state as an organ of class domination and his remarks on these exceptional conditions. Nor did he lay down any theoretical view about how the socially indispensable functions of the state can coexist with its role as the oppressive instrument of the propertied classes. No wonder that what the Marxist movement took over from its founder was the crude idea that the state is 'nothing more' than an organ of class rule, the fist of the owners held over the head of the exploited, and that, since the basic class antagonisms are irreconcilable, the 'capitalist state' can never be at the service of workers' welfare.

Marx's criticism of totalitarian utopias takes up much less space in his writings. It does appear in the '44 Manuscripts' as criticism of primitive egalitarian communism, willing to destroy anything that cannot become the private property of all, that is, everything that distinguishes individuals from each other, and to abolish talents and all personal qualities which make cultural creativity possible. Far from promising the assimilation of the alienated world, this communism pushes alienation to the extreme when it tries to debase the whole society into the present position of workers. To this Marx opposes what he calls 'the positive abolition of private property', an expression he did not explain and which, it seems, he did not use subsequently. Its meaning may be guessed from the context, dealing with religious alienation and the anticipated abolition of atheism. The latter loses any meaning once human self-affirmation no longer depends on negation of God to become positive self-affirmation. One may guess that his analogy suggests a meaning for the 'positive' abolition of private property: a society which no longer depends on the negation of private property is probably a society in which the very question of private property has moved out of people's consciousness and stopped troubling their minds. Nor does this explanation give us any plain clue to the meaning of communism, except that Marxian criticism bears out what we can easily gather from elsewhere: that the 'man of communism' was modelled in Marx's imagination (in contrast to many utopias of the Enlightenment) on pictures of universal giants of the Hellenic and Renaissance worlds, rather than on the patterns of barracks and monasteries. This last point cannot be disputed. What remains obscure is the relation of this buoyant perspective to the structure of the imaginary communist world and to the gloomy reality of the real one.

A pattern of Marxian thought on the question may be expressed as follows:

1. The alienation of labour can be accounted for by the division of labour resulting from technical development.

2. The alienation of labour induced class division and gave birth to special apparatus intended chiefly to protect by coercive measures the vested interests of the privileged strata.

3. In mediaeval European societies the fabric of this apparatus reflected directly the class structure and its function was obvious.

4. In industrial societies the political superstructure and civil society became separated; not in the sense that the former stopped serving the latter, but in the sense that the true nature of political society has been concealed behind legal equality and personal freedom. Consequently, the image of the relations between the two was bound to become mystified in the minds of those involved.

5. At the same time, traditional social ties and loyalties have been utterly shattered in a society where the profit motive rules economic activity unchallenged. As a result, the political society—distorted though its picture may be in the social perception—makes up the only form of (apparent) community, the only place where individuals recognise (in the abstract) the social character of their existence.

6. This results in the almost perfect split of every individual into his real but self-centred life in civil society, on the one hand, and his communal but abstract existence as state member on the other. Social functions (especially work) are perceived as private matters and particular interests (in political functions) wear the mask of social service.

7. The state may emerge as an autonomous social force only in the exceptional circumstances of a temporary equilibrium in the fierce class combat. Nor is the state likely to take over important economic

functions within the capitalist order.

8. The task of communism is to reunite the two aspects of human life which have fallen apart, the personal and the collective, not by destroying the former (as primitive communism would) nor by simply removing the latter while leaving civil society to itself (as anarchist dreams would have it), but by organising a society organically incapable of producing separate political organisms.

9. This restoration of human unity will be brought about by the violent smashing of the protective shell of the existing state, expropriating the exploiting classes and handing over the means of production to the producers. Once the latter are in a position to command all the accumulated forces of production, they will abolish naturally the profit motive in their economic activity and subordinate it to social needs only.

10. Given these conditions, class antagonisms will no longer emerge and, consequently, no organs of political rule will be needed. The public organs will be entirely devoted to the 'administration of things,' education and the welfare of the people.

11. As a result, not only will the split between the social and personal functions of individuals be healed, but so will the division between subject and object of the historical process (transparence of social relations, control of associated individuals over their life-processes, and so on), between man and his natural setting, between desires and duties, and between essence and existence.

What became of this scheme and, in particular, of its forward perspectives? Among socialists hardly anybody before the October Revolution seriously doubted its validity. Lenin's *State and Revolution*, written a couple of months before October, may appear like a daydream today, but it must have looked the same on the very day after the seizure of power. The totalitarian development of post-revolutionary Russian society is often accounted for not only by the exceptional conditions (non-exceptional ones, alas, are not found) at the moment of revolution (overwhelmingly agrarian society, isolation and the collapse of hopes of revolution in the West, economic devastation, political exhaustion), but also by the peculiar tradition of this country in the relation between civil society and the state. According to some Russian historians of the nineteenth century, the predominance of the state over civil society went so far that, far from being a product of class division, the state itself produced social classes by a series of measures imposed from above; the very size of the underpopulated territory and the need for constant military protection from invasions compelled the state to build up a larger and larger apparatus of administration and war and to harness the whole economic activity of the country in the service of the state. All important economic changes were due to the initiative of the state. As a result, the main features of what we today call a totalitarian system were virtually existent in the pre-revolutionary tradition: the predominance of the principle that all citizens' activities (including economic) have to have aims which coincide with those of the state; that no spontaneous crystallisations of social life may be allowed to grow unless they conform to the aims of the state; that each citizen is the property of the state. The unusual autonomy of the Russian state in relation to civil society was not denied by Russian Marxists (Plekhanov, Trotsky), even if they did not go as far as those who devolved on the former the entire responsibility for the construction of the latter, including the very formation of social classes.

But this is not the question we are dealing with. The question is whether, apart from peculiar circumstances and the peculiar tradition of the country where the first attempt was made to found a social organisation on Marxian premises, any suspicion may be justified as to the connection between these very premises and the real results of this attempt. To ask this does not amount to putting the frivolous and unanswerable question: 'What would Marx say if he saw the work of his followers?', since it is obvious that he could not see it without surviving for many decades longer than he did, that is, without changing himself in a way that we cannot possibly guess. Nor do we ask if the patterns of contemporary communism have been, as it were, fully preordained by, or prefigured in, the Marxian scheme. It is plain, if not notorious, that an ideology is always weaker than the social forces which happen to be its vehicle and try to carry its values. Consequently, since no real interests involved in social struggles are reducible to the simplicity of an ideological value system, we may be certain in advance that no political organism will be the perfect embodiment of its ideology. To state this of Marxism, as of any other ideology, we can dispense with historical knowledge. To those who think about the prospects of socialist development the real question is: does inquiry into the Marxian idea of the unity of civil and political society lead us to presume that any attempt to set up such a unity will be likely to produce an order with strongly pronounced totalitarian traits?

It should be stressed that we are not the first to broach this topic. Otherwise we could be suspected of looking for a *harmonie préétablie* between an idea and its subsequent embodiment just to resolve intellectual anomalies and to put the contingency of history into apparent order. Actually the same question had been repeatedly raised—mostly by anarchists and syndicalists, but by some Marxists as well—long before the answer could be found in the empirical realities of the socialist state.

The main reason advanced for putting it was that Marx was deluding himself in predicting a socialist organisation with centralised economic management but without political power and social oppression. Such a system—according to Bakunin's criticism— is bound to engender a new class of rulers either from working-class renegades or from the intelligentsia. Waclaw Machajski even maintained that Marxian socialism is an ideological device of the intelligentsia trying to replace the then privileged classes and to seize power in order to profit from their socially inherited cultural and intellectual superiority. Sorel insisted that all leaders who expected the socialist revolution to be carried through by political parties were just the new would-be revolutionary despots and that, no matter how democratic the phraseology they used, people like Jaurès or Turati announced only another form of oppression over the working class. Similar utterances can be quoted from French syndicalists and Proudhonists. Sorel expected a new oppressive society to emerge from any programme of political (that is, party sponsored) revolution, as opposed to the movement of real workers. The latter could win only if they managed to get rid of the supremacy of intellectuals and to become masters of production directly and not through political functionaries or managers.

Socialists did not, of course, accept this line of reasoning. Some of them, however, pointed out the dangers of a new despotism which could emerge if either the revolution occurred in 'immature' conditions or the leaders failed to interpret the meaning of Marxian socialism properly. Jaurès wrote that if socialism resulted in a group of rulers controlling the right to all economic decisions in addition to their political power, this would mean delivering up to a handful of people an omnipotence before which the might of Asiatic despots would turn pale. Plekhanov, in his polemics against revolutionary populism, noted that if by chance a conspiratory movement succeeded in seizing power in economically backward conditions, it would only establish a kind of oriental satrapy or renew Tsarist despotism on a communist basis. He repeated similar warnings against Bolsheviks who were, in his opinion heirs of narodnik conspiracy, rather than Marxists.

There were others who emphasised the moral rather than the economic preconditions of socialist society, if this society were not to degenerate into a new oppressive class system. I quote Edward Abramowski, a theorist of anarcho-cooperatism, who is less known in the West, being a Pole. He wrote in 1897:[1]

> May we venture an opinion that the rise of the socialist system could omit its previous stage of moral revolution? That one could organise communist institutions without finding in human souls the corresponding needs, without having the foundation in the consciousness of people? ... Let us suppose for a moment that a revolutionary Providence, a conspiratorial group professing socialist ideals, happily succeeds in mastering the state machinery and establishes communist institutions with the help of the police disguised in new colours. Let us suppose that the consciousness of the people takes no part in this process and that everything is carried out by the force of sheer bureaucratism. What happens? ... The new institutions have removed the fact of legal ownership, but ownership as a moral need of people has remained; they have banned official exploitation from production, but have preserved all the external factors out of which injustice arises and which would always have a field large enough to operate in—if not in the economic sphere, then in all other fields of human relations. To stifle aspirations to ownership the organisation of communism would have to apply extensive state power; the police would replace those natural needs out of which social institutions grew and by virtue of which they freely develop. Moreover the defence of new institutions would only be possible for a state founded on principles of absolutism, since any effective democracy in a society beset by violence under the new system would threaten that system with rapid decay and would bring back all the social laws which would have survived in human souls untouched by revolution. Thus, communism would not only be extremely superficial and impotent, but would turn into a state power oppressing individual freedom; instead of the former classes two new classes would emerge—citizens and functionaries—and their antagonism would necessarily appear in all domains of social life. Consequently, if communism in such artificial form, without moral transformation of people, could even survive, it would contradict itself and it would be a social monster such as no oppressed class ever dreamt about, least of all the proletariat that is fighting for human rights and is called upon by History itself to achieve the liberation of man.

Thus the concept of the rise of a socialist 'new class' had not waited for Burnham. It had been anticipated long before people were able to find it in experience (after the October Revolution Kautsky seemed to have been the first to apply this concept to the new society, in 1919). We must, however, make the distinction between critics who warned against the new communist class society, which would result if the revolution failed to find appropriate economic or moral conditions, and those who claimed to have found the germ of a totalitarian order in the very concept of socialism as elaborated by Marx. The two kinds of arguments are logically independent.

Let us turn to the latter way of arguing, as we know it from anarchist writers. I think that there is considerable justification for this criticism. To say so I do not need to share anarchist ideals or to consider them either feasible or consistent. I will try to repeat in modified form those critiques which are noteworthy, and to adduce some other remarks on the subject, not necessarily taken from the same sources.

1. The crucial point in the Marxian ideal of unity is his distinction inherited from the 'utopian' socialists—between the administration of things and governing the people. This distinction is vague, since we cannot imagine how things can be administered without people being used, controlled and organised for this purpose. Management of the economy involves control over people and it is not prima facie clear what is meant by saying that this would be not a 'political' but a purely 'economic' control. It is self-evident that economic planning involves the planning of the labour force and labour organisation. In effective planning and management three kinds of instruments can be employed: material incentives, moral motivations and physical coercion. The first presupposes a free labour market (economic activity depending on private motives, striving after personal profit, competition between working individuals) and is hardly compatible with the Marxian image of the unity of social and personal life. The second presupposes a formidable moral revolution in men's minds; what reason is there to believe that such a revolution is likely or possible? The experience of socialist countries speaks clearly against any hope of using moral incentives as a lasting and efficient basis for production; most phraseology intended to arouse 'enthusiasm for work' was used rather to cover various means of pressure and violence. It seems hardly necessary to stress the incompatibility of the third kind of instrument with the Marxian programme. If, however, we read the notorious attacks of Trotsky on Kautsky from 1920, we notice that to him the system of compulsory labour was not a transitory necessity of the civil war period but a permanent feature of socialist society.[2]

> The principle itself of *compulsory labour* service has just as radically and *permanently replaced* the principle of free hiring as the socialisation of the means of production has replaced capitalist property... The only solution of economic difficulties that is correct from the point of view *both of principle and of practice is to treat the population of the whole country as the reservoir of the necessary labour power* ... The foundation of the militarisation of labour are

those forms of state compulsion without which the replacement of
capitalist economy by the socialist will for ever remain an empty
sound ... No social organisation except the army has ever considered
itself justified in subordinating citizens to itself in such a measure,
and controlling them by its will on all sides to such a degree, as the
state of the proletarian dictatorship considers itself justified in
doing, and does ... For we have no way to socialism except by the
authoritative regulation of the economic forces and resources of the
country, and the centralised distribution of labour-power in
harmony with the general state plan. The labour state considers
itself empowered to send every worker to the place where his work is
necessary [emphasis added].

Trotsky mentions, to be sure, the 'enthusiasm for work' residing in
the working class, but he is aware that the planned economy cannot
rely upon this factor. His idea, roughly speaking, is: 'Let the workers
work for almost nothing—and go where we want them to go, out of
revolutionary enthusiasm. If they fail to do so, they will do the same
anyway under the persuasion of the policeman's gun.' In other
words, Trotsky promised us socialism conceived of as a permanent
concentration camp. He did not seem to be worried about the possible
incompatibility of this programme with Marxian doctrine. Two
circumstances may none the less be adduced in his favour. First, a
free market for the labour force seems indeed to run against the
Marxian concept of socialism. Second, he offered a practicable
solution to a question which Marx left unanswered. Indeed, if we set
aside the free market, then coercion and moral motivations are left
as the only possible stimuli for work; and the second proved to be
utterly unreliable. In fact, all three factors have been applied, in
differing proportions, in the history of socialist states. Material
incentives seem now to be on the way towards prevailing in
economic organisation.

2. Following on the question of stimuli for work the question
arises of the stimuli for production itself. Marx recognised that civil
society is ruled by private interest and that, left to themselves, people
will produce and trade anyway; however, they are unable to master
the global results of their joint productive activity and the latter turn
against them in the form of quasi-natural catastrophic laws.
However, if the motives of private profit in production are
eradicated, the organisational body of production—that is, the
state—becomes the only possible subject of economic activity and the
only remaining source of economic initiative. This must, not by
bureaucratic ambition but by necessity, lead to a tremendous growth
in the tasks of the state and its bureaucracy. This is what really
happened. The civil society—as opposed to the state apparatus—has

to be left economically passive and deprived of any reasons for, or possibilities of, taking the economic initiative. Without impulses from the state apparatus no economic activity arises in the society, except on the insignificant fringe of small private producers considered as relics of the past. What is not planned by state organs is simply not produced, whatever the social needs may be. Some changes, slowly and reluctantly initiated in socialist countries to restore the influence of the market on production prove economically efficient to a certain degree, but in the same degree run counter to the Marxian version of unity.

These two circumstances may justify the suspicion that, far from promising the fusion of civil with political society, the Marxian perspective of unified man is more likely to engender, if put into practice, a cancerous growth of quasi-omnipotent bureaucracy, trying to shatter and paralyse civil society and leading the (rightly blamed) anonymity of public life to its extreme consequences.

3. This trend becomes still more likely if we consider the third point: the question of the autonomy of political bodies as distinct from social classes. It is in fact difficult to imagine what reasons could be advanced in favour of the belief that, once social classes (in Marx's sense—based on the criteria of the ownership of the means of production and the appropriation of surplus value) have been abolished, the conflict of private interests will stop. The class struggle in capitalist society is a historical form of the struggle for the distribution of surplus product. Why should we presume that the same struggle for surplus product will not go on within an economy based on public ownership (whether that means an authoritarian or a democratic system)? And since public ownership must inevitably beget social layers endowed with privileges in controlling the means of production, the labour force and the instruments of coercion, what reasons could we possibly have to deny that all devices will be employed to safeguard the position of these layers and increase their privileges? (Unless, of course, we predict a sudden restoration of the angelic nature in the human race.)

It is arguable that, in dealing with these questions and in predicting the return of man to the lost unity of his social and personal existence, Marx admitted, among others, two very common false premises: that all human evil is rooted in social (as distinct from biological) circumstances and that all important human conflicts are ultimately reducible to class antagonisms. Thus he entirely overlooked the possibility that some sources of conflict and aggression may be inherent in the permanent characteristics of the species and are unlikely to be eradicated by institutional changes. In this sense he really remained a Rousseauist. He also overlooked the formidable force of human aspirations for power for its own sake and the extreme antagonisms arising from the relations of power as such, irrespective of the social origin of given ruling bodies. Of all the famous sentences which have had a dizzy career in history, this is one of the most striking in its falsity: that the history of all hitherto existing societies is the history of class struggles. That political bodies are nothing more than instruments of classes; that their interests may always be identified with the interests of the classes they are supposed to represent; that they do not produce interests of their own of any noteworthy importance; that people delude themselves if they imagine they struggle for other values (for freedom or for power, for equality or for national goals) as values in themselves, since these values are only vehicles for class interests—all these beliefs are consequences of this one sentence. They gave to Marxism its stupendous efficiency and its catechismal simplicity. Needless to say, Marx's work shows convincingly that in all detailed analyses his thought was much subtler and more differentiated than this sentence would suggest. And yet without basically taking this belief he would not be able to nourish his hope for a unified man.

Let us conclude:

1. There is no reason to believe that the restoration of the perfect unity of the personal and communal life of every individual (that is, the perfect, internalised identity of each person with the social totality, lack of tension between his personal aspirations and his various social loyalties) is possible, and, least of all, that it could be secured by institutional means. Marx believed such an identity had been achieved in stagnant primitive communities. However, even if this romantic image is well founded, nothing substantiates the hope that it can be resuscitated in the predictable future: it would presuppose an unprecedented moral revolution running against the whole course of the past history of culture. To believe that a basis for such a unity may be laid down first in coercive form (the violent destruction of civil society and its replacement by the omnipotence of an oppressive state) and will grow subsequently into an internalised voluntary unity, amounts to believing that people who have been compelled to do something by fear are likely later to do the same thing willingly and cheerfully. From everything we know about human behaviour the opposite is more probable.

2. The social equivalent of this unity of person was thought of as the unity of civil and political society. This in its turn was conceived

of as a community in which political power had become unnecessary. Such a community is inconceivable unless one of two conditions is fulfilled. The first: that no conflicts of interest arise between groups or individuals, so that economic management does not need to be associated with political power and public instruments of mediation or moderation are not necessary. Only if all conflicts of human interests were rooted in class division (in the Marxian sense of the word)—which is obviously not the case—could we expect this condition to be satisfied in the future. The second condition: that all decisions in public matters, however insignificant, are taken directly by the community as a whole in a democratic manner. Such a system, if practicable, would not abolish conflicts of interest (and thus would not comply with the requirements of perfect unity) but would be capable of moderating them without creating separate political bodies for this purpose. This ideal was patterned in anarchist thought upon mediaeval Swiss villages and, of course, cannot be attributed to Marx. If not for historical, then for technical reasons it is obviously impracticable in any community larger than a mediaeval Swiss village. Societies based on a universal—and still spreading—interdependence of all elements of the technological and economic structures are bound to produce separate bodies both for economic management and for mediating the conflicting aspirations of different sections, and these bodies will in turn always produce their own particular interests and loyalties.

3. The growth of the economic responsibilities of central powers is an undeniable tendency which may be noticed in different political systems. Not only is the trend towards nationalising larger and larger segments of production, transport, trade and exchange system inevitably accompanied by the rise of bureaucracy. The same may be said about all tasks which, it is widely acknowledged should rest on the shoulders of central powers: the welfare, health and education systems, the control of wages, prices, investment and banking, the protection of the natural environment and the exploitation of natural resources and land. It is not impossible, but it is difficult to be consistent when one fulminates at the same time against both the growth of bureaucracy and the uncontrolled wastefulness of the operation of private industry; more often than not, increasing control over private business means increasing bureaucracy. The urgent question is how society can tame its expanding bureaucracy and not how it can dispense with it. Representative democracy presupposes separate bodies with special privileges in deciding on public matters, and thus it cannot secure the ideal of the perfect unity

of civil and political society. It may be said in general that representative democracy carries a great number of vices and only one virtue. All its blemishes and dangers are easily found in the Marxist literature. And its only virtue is that nobody as yet has invented anything better.

*　*　*

I believe that socialist thinking which is centred on its traditional topics (how to ensure for the working society more equality, more security, more welfare, more justice, more freedom, more participation in economic decision) cannot at the same time be infatuated with prospects of the perfect unity of social life. The two kinds of preoccupation run against each other. The dream of perfect unity may come true only in the form of a caricature which denies its original intention: as an artificial unity imposed by coercion from above, in that the political body prevents real conflicts and real segmentation of the civil society from expressing themselves. This body is almost mechanically compelled to crush all spontaneous forms of economic, political and cultural life and thus deepens the rift between civil and political society instead of bringing them closer to each other.

If it is asked whether this result was somehow inscribed in the original Marxian thought, the answer is certainly 'no' if 'inscribed' means 'intended'. All evidences are there to show that the primordial intention was the opposite of what grew out of it. But this primordial intention is not, as it were, innocent. It could scarcely be brought to life in a basically different form, not because of contingent historical circumstances but because of its very content.

The dream of a perfectly unified human community is probably as old as human thought about society; romantic nostalgia was only a later incarnation. This dream has been philosophically reinforced by that element in European culture which arose from neoplatonic sources. There is no reason to expect that this dream will ever be eradicated in our culture, since it has strong roots in the awareness of a split which humanity has suffered apparently from the very beginning of its existence after leaving animal innocence. And there is no reason to expect that this dream can ever become true except in the cruel form of despotism; and despotism is a desperate simulation of paradise.

Notes

1   Edward Abramowski, 'Etyka a rewolucja' in *Filozofia spoleczna* (wybór pism) (Warsaw, 1965), pp. 179–180.
2   L.D. Trotsky, *The Defence of Terrorism: A Reply to Karl Kautsky* (London: Labour Publishing Co., 1921) pp. 126, 125, 130, 131.

4

Communism, Civil Society and Freedom

EUGENE KAMENKA & ALICE ERH-SOON TAY

I

In 1967 the faithful throughout the Communist world and many of their sympathisers outside it celebrated the centenary of *Das Kapital*. It was, they then agreed or pretended to agree, part of an epoch-making vision that charted the 'correct' future for humankind. By 1983, commemorating the centenary of Marx's death, even the faithful within an increasingly divided Communist world were far less certain. Marx was a great thinker and his heart—mostly but not always—was in the right place. But Marx was also dated. He was a nineteenth-century genius, not a twentieth-century one. He produced no eternal verities, drew no simple and reliable map for the path to Utopia. For some who then still called themselves Communists, he undervalued the importance of ethics and human relationships—of truth, kindness and sincerity—or of the need for stable rules of social conduct. Perhaps, some suspected, he should have paid more attention to political culture and democratic traditions. Certainly he knew nothing about Asia. He was no Stalin—but had he helped to make Stalin possible? The answer was no longer a confident decisive no. For others, Marx had exaggerated the centrality and irresistibility of the economic, or of the needs of material production, in the centuries before his time and in the century after. His view that socialist production for use meant the abolition of market relations and of a market for commodities was mistaken. His faith, or that of his successors, in a command economy was exaggerated.

And so it goes on. For the past thirty years, 'Marxists' in and outside Communist countries have been telling us, with an air of discovery, what the rest of us knew all along—that Marx's thought, though often interesting, was both complex and 'contradictory', providing neither a clear and coherent science of society nor irrefutable evidence that socialism must triumph or that it would be a good thing—an era of unprecedented and complete human liberation. If there were, in our time, Marxist rebels and Marxist thinkers, there were also Marxist dictators, torturers and secret policemen, cynics and liars. Were they Marxists because that ideology made their job easier, gave them more power? Whatever the answer, they have ended by totally discrediting, in those countries they have ruled or still rule, both Marxism and the Communist Party.

Even before that, the great debate about the meaning and truth of Marxism had long ceased to be a debate that involved in any sustained or serious way the industrial working class in advancing Western economies. In the West, it fled back, first, from the great meeting halls of the labour movement to radical sects increasingly based on the university and then to the intellectual 'worker' nourished by the public sector, to the drop-out, to the deprived and oppressed who were kept out of industrial society rather than exploited by it. Then there came those—some lesbians and homosexuals for instance—who found in Marxism a pattern for, rather than a solution to, their attempt to reshape and redescribe the world. Thus, instead of transforming either industry or capitalist civilisation, Marxism itself became an industry, and an increasingly scholastic one at that. 'They, they may have won all the battles but we, we had all the best books'. In fact, even that was never true. Much of the best social commentary of the twentieth century has been done by ex-Marxists.

Now, the great debate is simply over. Communism has disintegrated as an ideology, as a system of government, as a revolutionary force. Most of us will soon have trouble in remembering that Marxists long claimed and felt an unconditional superiority in the understanding of history and the elaboration of a science of society. For Marxism was not merely the desire to overthrow regimes based on exploitation and inequality or to build a cooperative commonwealth, a free association of producers. Its alleged superiority lay not in its deeper moral sensitivity and conviction, but in its systematic, scientific character. It deduced the future from the present; it steered by a superior chart. Whether (to use the dichotomies of the time) that 'science' was in fact primarily inductive-empirical or logico-deductive and analytic (a philosophy rather than science) is a separate matter. What did become clear was that it could be saved only by expressing its central tenets so generally or with so many qualifications that it became unfalsifiable.

The collapses and revolutions predicted by Marx took place, but in the wrong societies and settings, at the wrong times and with excessive participation by Marx's favourite non-class, the peasantry (or peasant conscripts) and Marx's most despised colleagues, intellectuals and ideologues. Those brought to power by these *soi-disant* Marxist revolutions have strutted the historical stage in a manner that brought them and Marx's theories and predictions little credit. They have fallen or are falling victims to another revolution—one that Marx did not envisage.

The difference between a Marxist and an anarchist, it was said in the grand old days of confidence, is this: an anarchist wants to know when the revolution will occur; the Marxist asks, what will happen on the day after the revolution? Today, that latter question is being asked by ex-Marxists and by non-Marxists about the remarkable revolutions that have taken place in much of Eastern Europe, to a more limited extent in the USSR and that are still being fought in Bulgaria, Romania, the People's Republic of China and, perhaps, Cuba, North Korea, Mongolia and Vietnam.

To what extent were these remarkable revolutions uprisings from below or collapses of confidence from the top? Did they constitute a rejection of political dictatorship, of one-party rule, or a vote of no-confidence in a state-run economy and pervasive indicative planning, or both of these? Even more radically, were they a total rejection of socialism as an ideology, a re-elevation of liberal democracy, nationalism, religion or any other authority that is not Communist? Some of those participating in these upheavals, indeed, insist that the events of 1989 and 1990 constitute Eastern Europe's, and perhaps China's, belated revolution of 1848—a revolution on behalf of civil and political rights, political pluralism, national and individual self-determination and constitutionalism—the binding of government and administration by law. Nothing lends more plausibility to this view than two striking features that stand at the centre of recent upheavals. The first feature is the extent to which the Communist period is not seen as a viable cultural or political basis for further development. That is why even the Communist Parties themselves are changing their names. The past is discredited. Even its industrial achievements and sociological transformation are no longer valued. They seem to pale into insignificance beside those of the West except in those areas from sputniks to Olympic medals where massive concentration of state resources can produce showy but socially insignificant results. To the dissidents and revolutionaries in what was once the Communist world, Leninist Marxism now presents itself as a blind alley demanding that one retrace one's steps. The call is for a return to the period before the Marxist revolutionaries took power—to its culture, its political discussions and proposals, its faith and hopes. Russian Orthodoxy, Menshevik Georgia, even the *Zemstvo* and the *Kadets*, the May Four Movement in Peking and the long-censored doubts of Lu Xun and Liang Qi-Qiao seem more relevant, more *aktuell*, to those engaged in making the new revolutions than the *Communist Manifesto* or Lenin's *What is to be done?* Of course, this is even more so in those countries where Communist rule can be presented as a period of external, foreign domination: in the Baltic States, in Hungary, East Germany, Poland and Czechoslovakia.

The second feature, closely linked with the first, is the remarkable re-emergence in Eastern Europe, in the Soviet Union and in China of so many of the problems and conflicts that characterised the situation on the eve of so-called liberation 45 or 75 years earlier. East Germany in its internal composition of forces and conflict of ideas appeared, in its final days as a state, to be reliving much of the period 1919–1931, though in a different international setting. So, in many ways, do Poland, Hungary, Romania. Over the Marxist ascription of primacy to productive forces and relations of production, the recent revolutions in the Communist world have reasserted and exemplified the continuing strength and importance of national and cultural traditions and situations, of religion, geo-politics, language, law and custom, and even what Communists call 'the cultural level of life and work'. Even more, they have elevated what Marxists so long denied: the central and lasting importance of political morality, of respect for people as individuals, for the pluralism of values, institutions and groups.

This is not the place to discuss whether the collapse of Leninism is unequivocally and in every respect the collapse of Marxism, let alone of socialism. There are many Marxes and many Marxisms, as there are many Jesuses and forms and understandings of Christianity. Neither the founder nor the disciples speak to us with one voice— coherently, consistently and unambiguously. No great ideology sinks from history totally without trace. There has been no shortage of

Marxists who thought Lenin a bad or irresponsible Marxist or no Marxist at all, a voluntarist driven by lust for political power or excessive faith in it, putting his trust in will and force, not in history and working class organisation. There have been many who foresaw, as Rosa Luxemburg and Karl Kautsky did, the consequences with considerable accuracy: the dictatorship of the proletariat would become a dictatorship over the proletariat; the socialist revolution would impoverish instead of enriching the masses and its representatives would be forced to suspend elections and organisational freedoms in order to stay in power.

The experiment, then, has failed. If Marxism was the science of liberation, it has shown itself, at least in Lenin's hands, to be bad science and at least some of Lenin's mistakes and illusions must be sheeted home to Marx. For those who have lived under Communism, the dismissal of the independent force and value of moral and legal traditions and arrangements, of political pluralism and human rights independent of the state seems the most serious and unpardonable of Marx's omissions. In the 1960s, there were humanist Marxists who believed that such errors could be rectified theoretically within the Marxist system and practically within a more intelligent but still basically monocratic socialism. There are no such believers now accepted as sincere or honest. As we had to tell the then but by now former First President of the Polish Supreme Court, people in Eastern Europe have not rebelled against a socialist interpretation of human rights that puts 'perhaps excessive' weight on social, economic and cultural rights instead of civil and political rights. They have rebelled against the rule of liars and cynics who believed in no rights at all and behaved accordingly.

II

The term 'civil society', as several contributors to this volume stress, emerged in the 17th and 18th centuries. It began as an affirmation or recognition of human capacity to create political organisation distinct from a state of nature; in the hands of Adam Ferguson, especially, it came to be used to emphasise the social or at least the economic rather than the political, the pursuit of economic goals or even private interest as distinct from the elevation of public order or control. For Hegel, as Chandran Kukathas and David Lovell say in chapter 2, the less than truly universal interests of family and civil society had their own value, though they required ordering and completion by a state that represented the universal demands of reason or in an allied version of Rousseau's general will. For Marx modern civil society was Hobbes's war of all against all, the unchecked pursuit of private interest in separation from any conception of the public good, of a universal, that is, universalisable, human interest. It was the world of economic greed, of industry and trade. It was also the consummation of that historical process of alienation which drove universality and the pursuit of the common good out of the life of citizens and gave it a separate and illusory existence in religion, in the sovereign, in the state, in the bureaucracy. All of the latter could only be pretended carriers of the rational and the universal. All of them were unable to heal the split between public and private, universal and particular, created by private property in the means of production and the consequent differentiation of society into classes, without destroying the foundation of their own existence. In individualistic society, the human community had been banished into the blue mist of heaven. Civil society, the world of economic greed and competition, subjugated everything to its interest and way of working. Yet, it was unable to achieve coherence or stability; it carried within it the seeds of its own destruction. The philosophical underpinnings of these views and their theoretical and practical implications have been explored very thoroughly in the last 45 years. Even in quasi-Marxist circles, they are no longer accorded the respect they were once given. For the simple dichotomies of universal and particular, rational and self-contradictory, do not survive serious discussion or analysis. They are not a foundation for social theory. To speak of conflict and co-operation *is* to do serious social theory. But then we are no longer in the world of exclusive logical categories that know no problems of balance and no distinctions of degree.

The late 20th century has come to view civil society in a more complex and also more favourable way. The free market is praised both economically and politically. Private vices, if not totally unchecked, are again held to produce public benefits. Even among socialists, as Robert Miller has rightly recognised,[1] the difference between Marx's concept of civil society and Antonio Gramsci's has been influential. For Gramsci, civil society was not atomistic or shaped only by greed. It was, as David Forgacs (cited by Miller) has put it, 'an ensemble of organisms', of social activities and institutions. It includes trade unions and other voluntary associations, church organisations and political parties not directly controlled by the state. Civil society, in short, is everything social that is not directly part of the government and its organs of repression, though the latter for

Gramsci included the courts and not only the police. Gramsci, of course, was Marxist enough to believe that civil society is shaped by a dominant social group, a ruling class, but he saw it as a sphere of both hegemony and consent, much of it unforced consent, and as a sphere in which opposition to a ruling class could similarly be organised. The strength of civil society in Western Europe, he thought, made the Leninist strategy of capturing power through conquest of the state machinery quite impossible—one would have to capture a whole network of fortifications that lay around the bastion of the state and that were not simply dependent upon it for their existence and strength. Socialism, the Italian Communist Party later came to conclude, therefore required much more than the abolition of private ownership and a socialist state's control of the economy; it required a democratic culture built up in centuries of bourgeois development. It required a society not dominated by the state or shaped exclusively by its will.

Throughout the world, but especially in the formerly Communist world, there is today a collapse of confidence in the state as the organiser and controller of society, though there is in the West still no lack of demand for its help and protection provided it is given without obligation. Those with a Marxist or quasi-Marxist education readily fall back on the term 'civil society' as a way of indicating that there is worth and dignity, energy and political capacity, outside the state and its organs. The term 'civil society', popular in the USSR, Eastern Europe and among Chinese dissidents, is not there used as a term of art with specific reference to Hegel's or Marx's use of it. It is used to refer simply to all that in a society which is not created or controlled by the state as part of its operations. Political democracy, constitutionalism and the rule of law, it is now widely believed in the formerly Communist world, flows out of a vigorous and independent civil society: free trade unions, charitable and cultural institutions that are independent of the state, lawyers and colleges of lawyers, churches, autonomous universities, courts and parliaments, and so on.

Surprisingly—or perhaps not surprisingly—many in the formerly Communist countries echo consciously or unconsciously the views on bureaucracy and the state which John Stuart Mill expressed in his *Principles of Political Economy*, in his *Representative Government* and in *On Liberty*. Mill opposed 'concentrating in a dominant bureaucracy all the skill and experience in the management of large interests, and all the power of organised action existing in a community'. He believed that 'the disease which afflicts bureaucratic governments, and which they usually die of, is routine. They perish by the immutability of their maxims; and, still more, by the universal law that whatever becomes a routine loses its vital principle'.[2] Expanding functions of government and its greater efficiency would end in monopolising the talent of the nation. The bureaucracy would do everything and nothing could be done outside it or against its wishes. What Mill had not dreamt of and what the citizens of Communist countries know all too well, is the degree of corruption, cynicism and inefficiency that could take hold of such a pervasive and all-powerful bureaucracy, still at the mercy of its political masters, but highly privileged in relation to a non-affluent population.

Those still clinging to their earlier more Marxist education recall Antonio Gramsci's remark that Leninism as a programme for seizing state power through a coup based on the capital was possible only in societies such as Russia, where civil society was too weakly developed to form that intricate web of fortifications around the ruling class ideology and its state power. Since Leninism, for Russian, Chinese and East European radicals, is bad, civil society is therefore good, a guarantee against usurpation of power before or after a revolution. The weakness of its development is seen by many as the root cause of Leninist Communism in the Soviet Union and China and, hence, in the world.

The more and less academic elaborations of this view—that Communism finds a natural home in traditionally state-centred and bureaucratic societies where nothing outside the state is capable of acting as the carrier of economic transformation and progress—are well known. Gramsci gives us one version; Karl Wittfogel[3]—whose work began within Marxism—another; a host of Western non-Marxist writers and of East European ex-Marxist dissidents have added more. In both Russia and China, the story runs, for various historical reasons, the state has been a pervasive force, a managerial state, taking responsibility for all social development, controlling or seeking to control everything that is politically relevant. In such states, classes were weakly developed—forms of stratification and not of independent power and organisation. Property, and with it law, had no true independence or autonomy. Power, position and wealth were all fundamentally dependent on the state and its favour. As it was before Communism, so it continued and in conquered societies became after, perhaps even more so. To throw off Communism in Russia and China, but not in Poland, Hungary or Czeckoslovakia, therefore, is to throw off one (or two) thousand years of history, to join a new world community largely based on Western history, structures and development.

III

Analysing the history of Russia and China is a complex and inexhaustible project, in which one has to steer between the Scylla of gross oversimplification and the Charybdis of missing the wood for the trees. There is no claim associated with the concept of an Asiatic mode of production or with that of a Russian or Chinese state always stronger than the rest of society that has not been challenged, in many cases seriously and responsibly. Yet the difference between the Tsar as Autocrat of all the Russias and the Emperor of China as Son of Heaven on the one hand and any European monarch remains. Chinese Communists themselves, recognising that the unification of China under the Qin and Han introduced a new and in many respects unique social form, have to call it bureaucratic feudalism as a way of accepting that direct social power lay primarily in the hands of a state-appointed and state-controlled bureaucracy. At least some of the continuing weakness of civil society in China, furthered by ideologies that have inculcated contempt for the merchant and made his position insecure, rest in the fact that almost all educated Chinese have seen their loyalty and their career opportunities as intimately bound up with state service, with the capital as the political and cultural centre of China. For almost half of China's history, the capital's writ did not run throughout the provinces, or at least through all of them. There were times of trouble, of competing dynasties, of foreign invasion. But the ideal of a China unified under the Emperor and a bureaucracy that served him remained stronger, far stronger than any competing ideal. In many ways, it still is.

In Europe, the emergence of Russia as a world power was as remarkable as that of Prussia.[4] It, too, was based on the militarisation of society and government—on the building of a powerful state and army and the attempted pervasive regulation of social and political life for largely military purposes. That has a long history, a history that Russians themselves have seen as sombre and tragic, as great and terrifying, and as essentially different from that of Europe. The debate is not over that fact but over its causes and explanation. The late Tibor Szamuely, in his *The Russian Tradition*,[5] took up the theme of geopolitical military necessity.

Russia, Szamuely argued, was for almost all of its history a great frontier—a frontier whose armed struggle against invaders had a length, intensity, and ferocity unparalleled in the annals of any other nation. Secure existence on that frontier involved a continuous process of opening up and colonising the vast spaces of eastern Europe and northern Asia through unflagging migration and resettlement. (Between 1300 and 1600, the Muscovite state expanded from 20,000 square kilometres to 5,400,000 square kilometres and it continued to grow at the rate of 35,000 square kilometres a year.) Military service and migration, the colonisation of the country, became the central features of Russian history. They called for effort on a scale undreamt of by Europe, but had to be carried out under the most difficult circumstances—meagreness of resources, shortage of manpower, lack of technological development and the harshest of climatic and physical conditions.

So, as Russian historians agree, Russia was conquered—not once, but in a crucial sense twice: first by the Mongol army, the terrible Golden Horde, and then by Mongol politics and statecraft, by the Mongol State Idea, according to which all men were equal in the totality of their duty to the state—a state seen as exercising an irresistible, pervasive *Imperium mundi in statu nascendi*, an *imperium* before which all opposition or disobedience was an act of treason, to be punished as such.

The Mongol Horde that conquered Russia in 1237 was then the most fearsome instrument of war yet devised. It smashed princedoms that had grown from the first Russian state established, with its capital in Kiev, by Norse invaders toward the end of the ninth century. Those princedoms bore a close resemblance to the state formations then being set up in western Europe. They comprised large and wealthy cities and important waterways, conducted a flourishing foreign trade and, according to Szamuely, were based on land held in unconditional, allodial possession, on free fighting men entering and leaving the princes' service at will and on a peasantry which was mostly free.

In the life and political systems of those grand duchies there was the basis for a western European political development, leading to pluralism, to a feudalism based on contractual obligations and ultimately, perhaps, to capitalism—a view that has now been revived by many a Ukrainian nationalist and westernising Russian. There was, however, Szamuely argued, one feature pointing in another direction—Kiev, though not on the scale of Greece and Rome, was a slaveholding society to an extent not known in northern and western Europe. But even before the Mongol Conquest, Kiev had been engaged in a losing struggle with one wave of invaders after another: Khazars, Pechenegs, Polovtsy. The centre of gravity, by the end of the twelfth century, was shifting north-east and there, for the rest of Russian history, it was to remain. Kievan Rus might have some bearing on the subsequent history and development of Lithuania and Poland and of Ukranian national aspirations, but to the growth of the new Muscovite state it becomes irrelevant.

The two hundred and fifty years of the Tatar yoke have remained in the collective memory of the Russian people as a period of tragedy and humiliation. For the intellectuals this was the period that sent Russia off, for better or for worse, on its unique and fateful path. The rule of the Great Khan, as the Russian historian Kliuchevskii put it, 'was the hard Tatar knife that cut through the knots into which the princes had entangled the country's affairs.' The Yoke laid the foundations for national unity and for the growing power of the grand dukes of Moscow. From Ivan I (1325–1341), nicknamed 'Kalita' or 'Moneybags' (for he was Farmer-General of the tribute collected by the Tatars from Russian lands) to Ivan III, the Great, who in 1480 proclaimed Russia's independence from the Tatars, these grand dukes threw themselves with Mongol cunning and intrigue into the process of enriching their states, of keeping the Mongols' trust while robbing them as much as they dared and, above all, of 'collecting the Russian lands', bringing all that they could under the rule of their state in preparation for a rebellion based on the prior destruction of their rivals.

Once independence had been wrested from the Tatars, once national unity had been established, three centuries of relentless military struggles followed—against the Swedes, the Poles and Lithuanians, the Crimean Tatars, the Turkish Empire. For three hundred years after the Yoke had been thrown off Russia continued to be dominated by the military frontier. For this frontier, in the sixteenth century already, she provided every spring and summer 65,000 fighting men at a time when the mightiest European armies were composed of 10,000 or 12,000 men, drawn from a much larger and much richer population. Only the most brutal autocracy, only utter insistence on the duty of every Russian to serve the state year after year, could have ensured national survival between the fifteenth century and the end of the eighteenth. Certainly, with Ivan IV's smashing of the independence of the old *boyar* nobility, with the institution of state serfdom and service lands, with the dissolution of the last vestiges of Russian representative bodies, with the institutionalisation of the autocracy under the first Romanov Tsars in the seventeenth century, this was what Russia got. Even the Church or its Holy Synod became a department of state and the Old Believers who resisted this subordination to temporal power were persecuted without mercy.

The political system of Muscovy, Szamuely argued, was thus a system founded on the utter centrality and pervasiveness of the state. The land, the property and the persons of Russia's citizens belonged, in principle, to the state. The social categories or classes were determined by the state and determined in terms of their varying, but always severe, obligations to the state.

When the nearly disastrous war against the Swedes forced Peter the Great, at the beginning of the eighteenth century, to recognise that Russia must be modernised technologically, that a window through to Europe must be hacked out of the frozen ice, the autocracy and its system were in principle only strengthened: the state became the centre and carrier of the reorganisation of Russia, as it had been the centre and carrier of its struggle against the Tatars. His successors, in the eighteenth century, did remit the nobles' obligation of service, thus making the nobles seem, superficially, to be members of a social class rather than men in a form of employment, as they had been hitherto. But when the half-mad Tsar and Emperor Paul I confided to the Swedish Ambassador that in Russia 'only he is great to whom I speak, and only while I am speaking to him', he was telling no more than the truth.

Szamuely's eminently readable book was also a journalistic one; it paints history with broad strokes and without scholarly caution or precision. But it captured vividly and accurately what thinking Russians for more than a century and a half have felt about their own history before and after the Communist seizure of power and how the people saw (and see) the state as grasping, unprincipled and irresistible. It is not a climate in which public morality and public responsibility flourish.

Russia, says the folk proverb, cannot be measured with a yardstick. Neither, added the poet Tiutchev, can she be fathomed with the mind. One can only have faith in her. For centuries most Russians have displayed such faith: an incredible attachment to a country, a history and a form of government that has brought them little but outrageous suffering. Those who lost that faith and gained another, like Petr Chaadaev, were confined to a lunatic asylum or ruthlessly repressed in other ways. Most took and to some extent still take pride in that suffering; the constant deprivation and insecurity that put them above material interest and gave them 'soul'. Behind that Russian pride and Russian soul, there has lain a raging, agonising uncertainty, a split personality, a tortured desire to emulate the West and to avoid becoming like it. It is the stuff of which great literature is made—and a great literature was indeed created.

The scholarly versions of Russian history do not differ from this more popular and impressionistic version all that much. There is argument about the extent to which the Varangian Norse Kingdoms and princedoms in Russia were like or different from their north and west European counterparts, though there is general agreement that the rulers had far less attachment, if any at all, to the territory or the people they literally acquired. There is argument about the role and importance of slavery, of burghers, of popular assemblies and of free landholding. But about the centrality and overwhelming power and pretension of the ruler and his state in the Muscovite order, there is no argument. Some ascribe the overwhelming powers and ambition of the Russian state as an instrument of autocracy to the Mongol-Tatar yoke and the influence of Mongol and Chinese statecraft. Others stress the Byzantine model of Caesaro-Papism in which church and state combine to rule, or in which the church is totally subordinated to the state. The difference between neo-Platonist eastern Christianity and the Aristotelianism of the western Church had also been thought significant. Others again, like Szamuely, have emphasised Russia's lack of natural boundaries and defences, the constant threat from Livonian Knights, Lithuanians, Poles and Swedes in the west, Tatars and a succession of central Asian kingdoms and tribes in the east and south. Richard Pipes[6] argues that Russia's economic conditions and external situation required her to organise militarily and therefore politically in a highly efficient manner, while her climate, her poor roads and great distances, and her economy generally inhibited such organisation. The state, he says, did not grow out of society nor was it imposed upon society externally. It developed rather out of princely power over their private domains. The prince's authority spread—not without meeting massive resistance—to the free population outside these domains. Russia became a 'patrimonial state' in which the lines separating ownership from sovereignty were weak or non-existent, in which private property was not seen as a realm over which public authority normally exercised no jurisdiction. Property was rather a true patrimonium—of the prince. The prince and the Tsar *owned* his kingdom. In Russia, Pipes argues, the separation between sovereignty and authority exercised as ownership occurred very late and very imperfectly: the ruler was both the sovereign of the realm and its proprietor. No social class—the peasantry, *dvorianstvo* (the serving nobility that replaced the *boyars)* or the 'missing bourgeoisie'—was strong enough to challenge the state. True, in the 19th century, the Tsarist government, in the central provinces at least, became captive to the landowning classes it had created, but those classes, threatened by the peasantry, were simply not strong enough to wrest formal power from the Tsar. Deprived of a base in the power of property, Russian opposition to the autocracy became almost entirely intellectual, elevating ideas and thus encouraging the further extension of attempted ideological control by the state, but also the growth of an intelligentsia that defined itself by the belief that ideas could produce social change.

The Mongol-Tatar Yoke resulted not only in the importation of a Mongol and thus to some extent Chinese model of statecraft and administration but also in a brutalisation and further de-democratisation of Russian political life. As Pipes puts it:[7]

> there can be scarcely any doubt ... that domination by a foreign power, which in its worst form lasted for a century and a half, had a very debilitating effect on the political climate of Russia. It tended to isolate the princes from the population further than they were already inclined to be by the workings of the appanage system, to make them less conscious of political responsibilities, and yet more eager to use power to accumulate private properties. It also accustomed them to regard authority as by its very nature arbitrary. A prince confronted with popular dissatisfaction had merely to threaten with calling in the Mongols to secure obedience—a practice that easily grew into habit. Russian life became terribly brutalized, as witnessed by the Mongol or Turco-Tatar derivation of so many Russian words having to do with repression, such as *kandaly* and *kaidaly* (chains), *nagaika* (a kind of whip) and *kabala* (a form of slavery). The death penalty, unknown to the law codes of Kievan Rus, came in with the Mongols. During these years, the population at large first learned what the state was; that it was arbitrary and violent, that it took what it could lay its hands on and gave nothing in return, and that one had to obey it because it was strong. All of which set the stage for the peculiar type of political authority, blending native and Mongol elements, which arose in Moscow once the Golden Horde began to loosen its grip on Russia.

That brutalisation, and suppression of initiative from below was to be maintained by serfdom and the slow development of a genuinely urban culture.

IV

If the concept of Communism as resting on an earlier Caesaro-Papism or Oriental Despotism in Russia and China is academically complex, it is—in Russia and China, but not for Eastern Europeans—also politically and psychologically difficult. Latvians and Lithuanians, Poles and Hungarians, let alone Czechs, have little difficulty, and indeed take much joy, in ascribing the unchecked excesses of Communism to the servility and lack of freedom bred by Russian and Chinese political traditions. Some Russians and Chinese agree; many more would like to find and stress alternative traditions within their own society that do not doom them to servility and powerlessness *vis-à-vis* the state. But Russians have no political traditions from below that they can fall back on in any serious way. The revival of the old parliamentary assembly, the Duma, early in the 20th century lasted less than ten years. The peasant commune, the *Mir*, was probably state-instituted for taxation purposes and was certainly not a vehicle of progress whatever the Narodniks may have thought. Russians historically had been defined by three things, even in their own eyes: their capacity for suffering, their share in great power dominance that produced fantastic geographical expansion of their political rule, and their Russian orthodoxy. But only Protestants and Old Believers have any record of asserting religion *against* the state, of building independent religious communities and institutions.

Still, the Communist period, as we now see, after Stalin's death did witness important developments toward urbanisation, Westernisation and even a 'middle class' culture having more than only literary foundations. But all of these, in Russia, are still weak and in the rest of the former Communist world poor. This is why an important element in the current amazing enthusiasm for building or restoring the institutions of civil society in the former Communist world is the more prosaic desire to attract foreign capital as charity, investment or loan. It is widely believed in Communist societies that foreign governments and foreign institutions will favour non-governmental organisations and institutions over governmental ones for these purposes; that civil society, in short, can be built with foreign help. In the Soviet Union, a charitable trust is being established, officially under the control of citizens and not government officers, to collect funds at home and abroad to aid what is now admitted to be the enormous number of people living under the poverty line whom the state has not the money to help. A specifically Russian Cultural Foundation has been set up in the RSFSR[8] to receive donations and artefacts at home and abroad as part of a campaign to foster and invigorate the love and appreciation of the specifically Russian cultural heritage in art, architecture and religion. Dissidents and ex- or crypto-Communists vie with each other in arranging readings from Solov'ev or Shestov, in making available Orthodox Easter food (*paskha* and *kulich*), in honouring non- and anti-Communists reviled until very recently. Civil society, coupled with religion and nationalism (for Russians, the two are virtually one), now plays the role that *Volk* played in Germany: it separates culture and politics from the existing state authorities.

Has all this a future? Can it develop or even survive, without falling into all the conflicts that Marxists call contradictions, into conflicts that fatally undermine the prospects for a pluralist and democratic society ruled by and in the spirit of Western conceptions of law?

The break-up of the Soviet Empire internally and externally, like the break-up of other empires, has seen a remarkable revival of old-fashioned nationalism in every territory that had come under Soviet domination or continuing Soviet influence—from Mongolia to Czechoslovakia, from Cuxhaven to Vladivostok. This is the most serious and in some ways the most promising step toward transforming the Russian tradition of statecraft with its all-powerful ruler and its provincial governors (even if they were later called party secretaries) who ruled it through their personal connection with the centre and their ability, in the last resort, to summon troops. Much of the new nationalism is a liberating reaffirmation of national independence, both culturally and politically, of popular participation and home rule, of some earlier democratic institutions and traditions, which the Communists had sought to destroy. Much of it is less pretty than this—insular, chauvinist, driven by hatred of near and often similar neighbours. Neither Catholicism in the east nor Russian Orthodoxy has succeeded, in this context, in becoming a force for universalism or reconciliation, or, at least, tolerance. Many cannot conceive of a true Pole or a true Poland that is not Catholic—but they do not see a Catholic Lithuanian or a Uniate Ukrainian as brothers and sisters in Christ or even as constituting no threat to the integrity of the Polish people and the Polish state. Neither does the Orthodox Ukraine feel one with an Orthodox Russia. It is all too easy to repudiate Communism by saying that the Communists were actual (though often concealed) or 'spiritual' Jews who hated the country they brought to disaster. Religion in much of Eastern Europe is an ingredient in nationalism and can and does give it a nasty intolerant edge. It has not there acted as a solvent. Communism was the last religion that sought to unify humanity in the name of an ideology propounded from the centre: we are still only beginning to realise how great its failure was. It transformed Azeris and Tatars, Armenians and Kalmyks, Russians, Ukrainians and Kazakhs far less than we had ever dreamt—at least in their perception of themselves and their role in the world. It drew off elites, as the British did in India, Russianising them and also turning them ultimately into critics and rebels. But it maintained its rule and the semblance of harmony by leaving the prejudices of the many largely intact. Not Communism, but world travel, and communication, and common material problems and demands, have provided such broadening of the horizons as we can find. A democratic humanism more strongly developed in such countries as Czechoslovakia than in Poland, let alone Russia, will be badly needed.

Against this broadening of the horizons among an educated elite, and, in states bordering upon the West, among a wider public, we have to set the remarkable extent to which the Communist world, until recently, insulated itself against some of the main UN- and American-inspired changes in social attitudes taking their departure from the revulsion against Nazism and later from the Civil Rights movement. The Communist world cheapened and deadened the moral impact of Nazism by absolving the German people and their collaborators of any historic national responsibility. It treated Nazism as third-stage imperialism, a product of world capitalism. It minimised the independent force and horror of anti-semitism and other national chauvinism; it avoided moral as against political judgment. A whole host of moral sensibilities that have grown stronger and stronger in the West are consequently weakly developed in the East. There will be and there already is a price to pay for that in the expulsion or welcomed departure of gipsys, Jews, and guest workers, in anti-semitism, in intolerance of minorities, in the danger of lack of principled universal moral convictions in and moral demands upon government after the dust settles. It must also be said, however, that there are in the former Communist countries many voices, especially in the leadership of the democratic and anti-chauvinist forces, that emphasise precisely the past lack of moral sensibility and judgment and seek to emphasise the need for it now—most strongly perhaps in what was once East Germany.

Democracy is not the solution to problems. It is a *sine qua non* for the sustained exposure of lies and illusions, of cynicism, dishonesty and incompetence in government. For those who have just come out of the darkness, especially for the intellectuals among them, the first priority was to see the triumph of truth, the exposure of lies, and the end of the power to enforce compliance with evil. For that, they needed what they called civil society—men and women, institutions and activities, not incorporated in the state apparatus, not subject to pervasive dictation from above. In some countries such as Poland, East Germany and Hungary, there was more in the way of tradition and living actuality to draw on than in other countries, such as Bulgaria and Romania. In some—such as Serbia or Azerbaijan—the non-state popular tradition was as suspect in its militant chauvinism as the state tradition. In all countries, a total surrender of state power to civil society could easily lead to exacerbated conflict, tension and disunity, while facing the problem that the experienced were inevitably tainted by their participation in Communist administration and politics. It is at this point that generalities cease to serve and national specificities and the presence or absence of stable institutions, stable mass movements and of statesmanship come to the fore.

In the meantime, it is important to note that democracy as the direct unmediated rule of the people is not the ideal or the reality being born in the revolutions of 1989–90 any more than they were born in 1766, 1789, or 1848. At the political level, the principal achievement or aim of 1989–90 is the actual or demanded imposition of parliamentary democracy and constitutionality, of the rule of law not only on citizens but on government, and its servants, coupled with the breaking of an economic impasse through the liberation of enterprise and the restoration of honesty into work relations. But what sort of constitution and what sort of law? And can their future be guaranteed except through the strengthening of civil society *vis-à-vis* the state? Can that be done without a successful overhaul and restructuring of the economy—a process that will inevitably produce and intensify problems before solving them? Certainly, in the Communist world as in other worlds, economic breakdown, civil disorder, national and religious tensions and the continuing gulf between the intelligentsia and the people can lead to demands for and the reality of an authoritarian populist or even military leadership.

Here it becomes clear that civil society as a concept of practical and theoretical analysis has very limited value except as initial slogan for rallying those not tainted by involvement with a discredited state. At the political level, the countries formerly ruled by Communists need to create or recreate a *Rechtsstaat*, to impose the rule of law and respect for law on their citizens, their economic entrepreneurs and managers, their political parties and their political leaders and government officers. They are aided in this, above all, by an international political and legal climate; they will be hindered, in some countries very seriously, by the lack of past traditions, by economic shortages and chaos, by chauvinism and national tensions, by the weak development of a legal profession, judicial independence and 'legal culture'. The battle for law will be both necessary and difficult, for much of the population and the leadership still misunderstand law by seeing it as consisting merely of a set of decrees.

T.H. Rigby, in chapter 6, emphasises that the Kingdom of Lies created by Communist rulers was successfully resisted only by three social phenomena the state did not succeed in controlling: the family, memory and cultural endeavour and tradition. These were the strongest elements of successful resistance on which much else, including the conquest of trade unions, depended. For citizens coming out of monocratic socialism, they represent the kernel of civil society. Both national consciousness and religious tradition can become and in many places have become intimately linked with them, expanding into the vacuum left by discredited state ideology— though doing so in varying degrees in different sections of the population. Trade union consciousness is more limited in appeal and troublesome for governments bent on attracting investments and building up markets but trade unions are and will be a significant element in the dispersion of power and the articulation of recognised interest groups that speak out freely. For even a people's revolution is always conducted and supported only by a section of the people and conflicts of views and interests among the supporters themselves emerge as the excitement dies down. It is at that time that two perennial but ever-important questions acquire renewed urgency. One is the relationship between freedom and authority. Another is the possibility of creating structures that derive legitimacy from the character of civil society, of the community at large and not from the traditions of the command structure, the state and bureaucracy, against which people have rebelled. This is the central question in Eastern Europe today. Its solution requires a combination of principled understanding, tactical flexibility and responsiveness and a capacity to latch onto, reinterpret and create national and popular traditions. It requires statesmanship, including a commitment to democracy and the willingness to defend it by exercising authority when necessary without making it into a way of life.

When we turn to these questions, we are no longer much helped by simply counterposing a concept of civil society to that of the state. We have to turn, rather, to three related historical enquiries that may produce different results in different regions and cultures. First, how did the state and the monocratic political structure acquire and maintain the power they held? Second, what is and what will happen to the relationship between politics and state power—can politics be turned from a tool into a check? And third, can the same be done with law? These three questions may well be linked, and the answer we give may rest on the strength and character of the traditions associated with state, politics and law as much as on any abstract attempt to devise constitutions. But no country today is an island—the traditions are becoming international. That is one of the strongest factors on the side of pluralist and democratic development in the former Communist world. So, as everyone knows, are the rising levels of knowledge, sophistication and expectation among citizens, the increasing complexity of production, distribution and exchange, and the increasing need at all levels for a workforce that can exercise judgment, make flexible responses and work willingly as well as cooperatively. The revolutions in Eastern Europe were partly made possible by the growing recognition of these needs and realities and fumbling attempts to accommodate them; that historic process is not reversible.

Pluralism and democracy, then, are working a transformation in the Communist world and exposing it to all the manifest conflicts and tensions of a free society in a politically and economically difficult period. Both pluralism and democracy will have to be affirmed vigorously and yet tempered by political realism—a task in which the Weimar Republic was singularly unsuccessful. But many nations have managed and there is no reason to think that no others will.

The dismantling of centralised state ownership and control of means of production, distribution and exchange will be of great importance, though there will be an initial danger that the same groups of state and party officials will take over important sectors of the economy by 'privatising' themselves while continuing in their corrupt and self-seeking ways, using existing political and administrative networks rather than developing entrepreneurial skills and moralities. Here, as everyone knows, foreign investment, support and partnership coupled with genuine foreign participation and supervision (always a touchy matter, but in this context essential) could be of great benefit.

On the political side, nothing is more important than the internal and external collapse of the Soviet Empire and its giving way to a pluralist, fragmented system of states with high degrees of autonomy in their political and economic life. The real check on the centralising and authoritarian power of a Soviet President—for which there will continue to be some need—is not so much civil society as the perfectly possible vigorous development of Republican Soviets into independent and critical parliaments, formulating their own policies, making demands on the centre, establishing liaisons among themselves and with independent nations, both outside the Soviet Union and with those parts of the Soviet Union that may indeed opt to secede altogether.

There is, in short, no longer any reason to believe that the Soviet state will be stronger than the rest of society once the rest of society has formed itself once again into distinct national groups and in which even Russian democratic forces can find many new causes for comfort. The development will be uneven, central power will not be and in some cases must not be abandoned overnight. Some regions and even nationalities may produce highly authoritarian and illiberal governments and even majorities. But pluralism will triumph. Or to put it more modestly, Soviet hegemony will crumble.

In China the situation at present is much less hopeful for democracy. Civil society is an equally problematic and in some ways unhelpful concept in analysing Chinese past and present. The rich complexity of clan and guild organisation, the comparative independence of Buddhist and Taoist streams of thought, the vigorous commercialism of the Chinese south and east, have long been successfully confined to a sub-political role. Civil society in that sense has been much more vigorous and colourful in China than in Russia; but its political importance and the social respect accorded to it have been far less.[9] Whatever the actual weaknesses of the Chinese managerial civilisation at various periods of its history, the ideologisation of a great state and bureaucracy as fundamental to China's past, present and future was far more successful than anywhere else in the world. The concept of monocratic socialism has not suffered the same death blow in the People's Republic of China as it has in the former Soviet Empire and bloc. The intelligentsia, or significant portions of it, are perhaps as disaffected as they have ever been. Successfully crushed within the country, they are in danger of retreating to total cynicism. Those who still hope can only wait for a mistake, or a change of heart, at the top. When that happens, and it cannot be ruled out, symbolic revolution could break out again. It is difficult, however, to see 'civil society' doing more than protesting in order to cast down a bad Emperor and promote the leadership ambitions of a good one, who will allow more discussion and adopt better policies, who will bring the work of the government and the good of the people into greater harmony.

To go further, China—like the Soviet Union and the Soviet bloc—needs the break-up of an Empire that provided much of the foundation for monocratic rule. But China is an empire in a much more complex sense than the Soviet Union or the Tsarist Empire ever was. Its nationalities—outside Tibet—are predominantly minorities, surrounded by larger Chinese populations. Chinese or Han nationality is a matter of custom, lifestyle and political allegiance, not of spoken language. But the culture, including the political culture, has been so strong that rebel provinces and rebel warlords have not sought political independence, but simply backed their own candidates for Emperor at the centre. The division of China into independently governed south, east, west and north might well be the only way of erecting serious structural and ultimately cultural barriers against overwhelming central and centralising power. Yet that course is not only fraught with practical difficulties, it would be quite unacceptable to the majority of Chinese and especially of Chinese intellectuals. China's status in the world as a great and unified civilisation matters to them, at the ideological level, more than anything else. Otherwise one might as well emigrate. Yet Taiwan and Hong Kong do prove how great the potential of the Chinese people is, once they are liberated from the weight of that great tentacular Moloch of a state.

This is not to say that China has not been witnessing some of the tensions, expectations and hopes that have produced the momentous changes in Eastern Europe and the Soviet Union. It is to say that they have not gone as far, that they have less conscious unideologised popular support and that the government has not given way, at home or abroad, to an extent that can undermine its capacity to control the situation. Of course, when monocratic power collapses, it does so suddenly, to the astonishment of the world around it and the events in Tienanmen Square in April, May and June, 1989, did have repercussion in and offer inspiration to those who sought freedom in the Soviet bloc. If and when monocratic power gives way, in China as in Eastern Europe and the Soviet Union, there will be a remarkable going back to the ideals and arguments of the years just after 1919. Of that there are many signs already. Communism still holds power in China. But as an ideology and a faith, it has lost the support of all sections of the community except the cynical and the opportunist. It is not now directly challenged by any major sections of the population that counts in this connection except students and research workers because of fear, because they cannot see outside the Party any force or group that can take over and hold China together and because the Party leadership is still willing to close ranks against any attempt to challenge its ultimate authority. For the moment, civil society in China remains as weak a political force as it ever was.

Notes

1   See Robert F. Miller's contribution to Robert F. Miller (ed.), *The Development of Civil Society in Communist Systems* (Sydney: Allen & Unwin, forthcoming).

2   We draw here on Eugene Kamenka, *Bureaucracy* (Oxford: Basil Blackwell, 1989) p. 132, where the references from Mill and other authors worth consulting are set out more fully.

3   See Karl A. Wittfogel, *Oriental Despotism* (New Haven: Yale University Press, 1957).

4   Compare Kamenka, *Bureaucracy*, pp. 101–115.

5   See Tibor Szamuely, *The Russian Tradition* (New York: McGraw-Hill, 1974).

6   Richard Pipes, *Russia Under the Old Regime* (Harmondsworth: Penguin, 1974) *passim*; compare Kamenka, *Bureaucracy*, pp. 107–109.

7   Pipes, *Russia Under the Old Regime*, p. 57

8   Russian Soviet Federative Socialist Republic, the largest of the union republics within the USSR.

9   For a fuller consideration of Chinese history in relation to this question, see Alice Erh-Soon Tay *Law in China—Imperial, Republican, Communist* (Sydney: Annual Lecture on Asian Studies, no. 3, Centre for Asian Studies, University of Sydney, 1986) and Alice Erh-Soon Tay, 'Communist Visions, Communist Realities and the Role of Law', *Journal of Law and Society*, vol.17, 1990, pp. 155-169.

5

The Destruction of Civil Society in Russia (1917–1953)

VLADIMIR SHLAPENTOKH

The definition of 'civil society' used in this essay is similar to that used by authors who describe civil society in negative terms relative to state society (see, for example, the chapters in this book by Kukathas and Lovell, and especially Rigby). That is, civil society refers to any part of society that is not under the direct control of the state. At least two implications follow from this conceptualisation of civil society: first, that the development of civil society can also be described as the process of destatisation, and second, that all sorts of human activity not controlled by the state—including political, economic, and cultural activity—constitute the essence of civil society.

When the Bolsheviks took power in October 1917, they faced a relatively well-developed civil society, complete with political, economic, and cultural activities independent of state control. This society had begun to take shape even before the February revolution and expanded tremendously in the months prior to October. Between February and October 1917, Russians preparing to elect the Constitutional Assembly enjoyed a political order with numerous political parties (before the February revolution there were about fifteen parties in the Russian parliament) and innumerable clubs and associations, absolute freedom of speech and press, and freely elected local governing bodies. At the time, it was said that 'in 1917, Russia was the most free country in the world.' Between the two revolutions, Russia had a well-developed private economy, despite lingering remnants of serfdom and communal bonds in the countryside. Before the October revolution, the trademarks of civil society were especially visible in the area of free speech. By any standard (but especially when compared to Stalin's Russia), freedom of speech and association were almost absolute between February and October 1917. With civil society existing at such a grass-roots level, it took the Bolsheviks almost ten years to destroy Russian civil society (although, for the most part, the job was completed within the first two years after the revolution).

I

When the Bolsheviks took power in October 1917 under the direction of Vladimir Lenin, they came with deeply rooted views on the role of the state and the nature of civil society. These views remained fairly stable immediately following the revolution, but were gradually adjusted and modified to adapt to the demands of mastering and running a country.[1] Lenin rarely used term 'civil society' in his writings. The term is entirely absent from the indexes of all editions of Lenin's *Collected Works*. The term 'bourgeois society,' however, as it was used by Lenin and his colleagues, was the exact equivalent of what we are calling 'civil society'. In fact, the concepts of 'bourgeois' and 'civil' societies were interchangeable in 18th and early 19th century literature, including in the works of the Bolsheviks' teachers—Marx and Engels.[2] In the following remarks, I will briefly discuss Lenin's attitudes toward state and civil society before and after the revolution.

Lenin's hostility toward bourgeois, or civil, society stemmed from his Marxist heritage, with its hatred of anything 'private' or 'individualistic'—terms to which he attached deeply negative meaning. Bourgeois society, for its part, was opposed to Communism because of the latter's emphasis on collectivism and the public cause.[3] Trotsky was opposed to both societies for a yet another reason— bourgeois society was nationalistic and Communist society was internationalist.[4] Lenin appropriated Marx's major ideas about the state, although he assigned the state a far more important role in historical developments than did Marx. Lenin regarded the state as a coercive institution serving the dominant class in class society, and envisioned the disappearance of the state in a classless, Communist society where people could truly be free. Lenin was far more aggressive toward the bourgeois state than were his mentors. He particularly stressed the role of coercion and violence in the activities of the state, and rejected any view of the state as an agent of reconciliation.[5] He focused with equal verve on centralisation as a major feature of the state ('the whole society will be as one factory and one office').[6] He scoured the writings of Marx and Engels looking for quotations confirming his negative attitudes toward any sort of regional autonomy in society. In 1917, when writing 'State and Revolution', Lenin triumphantly declared 'Marx is centralist'.[7]

In the writings of Lenin and his comrades in arms such as L.D. Trotsky or Nikolai Bukharin, it is not the Russian bourgeoisie and its civil society that are the major targets for future revolution, but the tsarist state. Trotsky, for example, characterised the tsarist state as a 'giant centralised feudal-bureaucratic machine'.[8] Lenin's image of the state as a powerful militarised and bureaucratised Leviathan, totally out of the people's control, was strongly enhanced during World War I. During this period, democracy was restrained to a greater or lesser extent in all warring countries. Lenin expected that this restraint would continue after the war.[9] In addition, World War I allowed Lenin and his followers to overcome a contradiction in their pre-war ideology. On one hand, as true Marxists they acknowledged the priority of bourgeois (that is, civil) society toward the state as its instrument. On the other hand, however, they also tried to suggest that the bourgeois state is unaccountable to society and, in fact, serves the interests of the masters of large corporations—a narrow group of tycoons. Although Marx's The 18th Brumaire of Louis-Bonaparte and Engels's The Origin of the Family, Private Property, and the State provided Lenin and his adherents with arguments in favour of an autonomous state, the emergence of a wartime military economy was more influential in their thinking. This economy supported their vision, inspired by the Russian absolutist monarchy, of a nearly autonomous state—a mighty entity far more frightening and powerful than the simple 'executive committee of bourgeoisie' from The Communist Manifesto.

The war allowed Lenin to advance the concept of imperialism as a special stage in capitalism and state-monopolistic capitalism. This concept helped him come to an important conclusion: 'the political superstructure over monopolistic capitalism is the development from democracy toward political reaction'.[10] The theory that democracy has been on the decline in capitalist countries since the end of the 10th century ran blatantly counter to historical data.[11] Yet, the Bolsheviks used this theory as an additional philosophical justification (the Bolshevik leaders, almost all very educated people, enjoyed lofty arguments) for their dictatorial manners and policies both inside and outside the party.[12]

Lenin had an absolute belief in the state as a docile instrument in the hands of the few who control it, whom he thought to be above criticism from any 'civil society.' As a result of this belief, Lenin was especially receptive and devoted to the idea of a dictatorship of the proletariat. This idea suggested the merciless use of the state machine against all who might resist it—in this case, the enemies of the revolution. Lenin espoused the idea of a dictatorship much more vigorously than did either Marx or Engels. Although his contemporaries—including Marxists in Western Europe such as Bernstein and Kautsky and the entire German Social-Democrat Party—abandoned this concept in the late 19th century, Lenin boldly praised a future revolution that would permit the creation of a state machine controlled by the revolutionaries and their party. Lenin's strong faith in the state as a key agent in the society that he sought to create stemmed from his belief in the decisive role of a revolutionary minority and its leaders, in this case the party and its leading bodies. For Lenin, the state machine could produce either the maximum evil or the maximum good, and should therefore be in the hands of the ruling minority. Lenin's position was seconded by Trotsky, who, decades before Keynes and other adulators of the state during the 1930s, described the state as 'the greatest means of organisation, disorganisation, and reorganisation of social relations'.[13] Lenin's admiration for science and, especially, for Marxism contributed heavily toward his belief in the might of the state. Lenin was confident that science could discover the laws of history and that, in fact, Marx had done so. Lenin was further convinced that, equipped with knowledge of historical laws, a minority, a party, could conquer the state machine and use it for the benefit of the people.[14] Lenin's scientism later played an important role as a powerful ideological tool against civil society, depriving civil society of both its rationality and its ability to operate for the benefit of the masses.

As mentioned earlier, Lenin's simultaneously contemptuous and respectful attitudes toward the state were combined with a true Marxist belief in the ultimate withering of the state in Communist society. In such a society, it was argued, self-regulation would make coercion and, by extension, the state, unnecessary. Unlike his teachers, however, Lenin delayed the bestowing of freedoms from the period immediately following the revolution to some more remote time when, with the establishment of a new communist order, the state would simply disappear. Still, prior to the revolution, Lenin did envision the partial withering of the state, as well as the installation of a dictatorship of the proletariat, soon after the revolution.[15] Although the proletarian dictatorship would be directed primarily against the former dominant class, the role of state institutions for the masses would also decline, as would the people's direct participation in managing social affairs.

Lenin's hatred of bourgeois society extended to a future time, when he envisioned no separation between public and private life—a view that influenced the Bolsheviks in the first years after the revolution. Lenin, with his adulation of Marx and the 'public,' used the term 'private' only in disparaging ways. For example, he declared that the religious feelings of the people could not be considered 'private business'.[16] Even with this network of beliefs, Lenin's vision of a new political order that would eventually give way to a Communist society included a strong role for the masses. Unlike Stalin, Lenin had no contempt for the masses. Whereas Stalin did not even bother to gauge the popular mood (sociology was nonexistent in the Stalin era), Lenin was eager to learn the public's attitudes toward major social and political issues. As a result, surveys were conducted even during the civil war. Even before the revolution, Lenin saw the masses as a positive political actor, but only if they followed the lead of the party, which was, of course, more knowledgeable about the course of history. Lenin eagerly accepted Kautsky's thesis that the proletariat was incapable of generating the idea of socialism by itself, needing instead to have the idea presented to it from above. Criticisms of the trade unions and of the workers' movement in general for their 'economism' (that is, being preoccupied with economic concerns at the expense of political concerns) and for 'khvostism' (dragging behind the vanguard) were important elements of Lenin's prerevolutionary political struggle.

As a Westerniser and a committed opponent of populists and others who insisted on the social historical road for Russia, Lenin acknowledged the importance of democratic principles as proclaimed by the Great French Revolution, but not as brought about later by bourgeois society. Lenin's prerevolutionary writings contain several statements in favour of freedom and of the masses' meaningful role in governing society. This was particularly true with respect to those works written in 1905–1907 under the influence of the First Russian Revolution.[17] Still, themes of freedom and real democracy were never dominant in Lenin's prerevolutionary writings, and they yielded to Lenin's obsession with the dictatorship of the proletariat and the necessity of using violence—a favourite word of Lenin's—against the enemies of the revolution. Although Lenin totally rejected contemporary parliamentarianism and universal elections as bourgeois hoaxes ('the universal election law is a tool for the dominance of bourgeoisie'),[18] he never discussed, even superficially, how the masses would participate in decision-making. While praising Soviets as superior to 'bourgeois parlementarianism' (especially after the revolution), Lenin never seriously elaborated the idea of Soviets. Instead, he delivered the traditional invectives against the corrupt bourgeois democracy—tirades which would later be seconded, in almost the same words, by Hitler—and offered only general statements regarding the 'direct participation of the masses in government'.

Even after the revolution and four years of experience, Lenin almost never discussed the working mechanisms of the Soviets, such as the decision-making process and influence of external forces on this process. Given Lenin's preoccupation with keeping total control in the hands of the party apparatus, his failure to discuss these issues is understandable. Lenin wholeheartedly championed coercion as the core of the proletarian dictatorship, and even declared that a successful revolution would have no place 'for freedom and democracy,' because both are 'incompatible with violence'.[19] When praising the experience of the Commune of Paris in 1871, Lenin discussed only the removal of the professional bureaucracy and the army, avoiding any mention of who would guide the ordinary people now in control of the government. Similarly, he was silent regarding protecting the people's freedoms in the new society.[20]

Moreover, in trying to assess Lenin's sincerity regarding the participation of the masses in government, that is, whether he was sincere or merely paying lip service to the dominant ideas of the contemporary socialist movement, it is reasonable to examine his activity as a party leader. Both before and after the revolution (especially after) Lenin was anything but a promoter of democratic principles in his party. In fact, Stalin later labelled the party 'the order of sword-bearers,' which was characterised by iron discipline for all of its members.

II

Given his intellectual and emotional preparedness, Lenin was unshaken by his sudden emergence at the helm of the gigantic country. With the state machine finally in their hands, the Bolsheviks increased their invective against real democracy, asserting that 'Now there are no democratic states. What exist now in Europe, America, and Japan are dictatorships of financial capital'.[21] The practice of government increasingly forced Lenin to focus on those elements of his *Weltanschauung* that were prominent before the revolution. Lenin was convinced that he could perform miracles with the state machine he now controlled. These miracles included building a socialist society in a country as backward as Russia, which would disprove the Marxist doctrine declaring world revolution to be a prerequisite to building a new society. In March 1922, Lenin wrote that 'the proletarian state in Russia ... has absolutely enough ... political power ... and economic strength ... to guarantee the transition to Communism'.[22] Lenin revealed similar convictions in another article written during the same period.[23]

The violence that was so prominent in Lenin's prerevolutionary works increased during the period of the civil war and foreign intervention. The bloody events of 1918–1920 confirmed Lenin's belief that only violence could save the revolution from its enemies. His esteem for the French Jacobins, which had always been high, also increased during this period. In 1920, Bukharin ecstatically cited Marx's famous dictum that 'violence is a midwife of any old society that is pregnant with a new one,' and praised 'revolutionary violence' as the major tool in the creation of a 'new production structure'.[24] Having received a lukewarm, and occasionally even hostile, reception from the workers, Lenin and his comrades spoke increasingly often of the necessity for 'the militarisation of the "population" as a method of self-organisation for the working class and the peasants'.[25] Lenin did not even bother to refer to the Civil War as a temporary justification for such militarisation. During 1918–1922 Lenin proclaimed himself the bitter enemy of all freedoms and all types of democratic procedures for the election of officials, both for society and for the party. In 1921 he forced the 10th Party Congress to pass a rule prohibiting factions inside the party, thus eliminating any free debate among party members.[26]

Presenting Soviets as the newest, most advanced forms of government, Lenin and the Bolsheviks proclaimed with special fervour that the new political order rejected the division of power, the essential element of bourgeois (that is, civil) society. Of course, Lenin continued to pay lip service to democratic principles, although less so than before the revolution. He usually simply equated the dictatorship of the proletariat to democracy or said that 'each female cook has to learn how to manage the state'.[27] In this way, Lenin laid the groundwork for the creation of the ritualistic democracy that reached its peak in the 1930s. At the same time, however, Lenin attacked democracy more harshly than ever (in part because of caustic criticism of the Bolshevik state by Kautsky and other European socialists).[28] Although after the revolution Lenin remained sensitive to the mood and the opinions of the masses, these were not considered directives for the state but constraints to be taken into account. For example, in 1922, Lenin, mindful of the Kronstadt and Antonov rebellions and fearing the collapse of the Soviet state, gauged public opinion before he introduced the NEP.[29] Up until, and even a few years after, Lenin's death, major party resolutions regularly revealed the party's support for the participation of the masses in both elections inside the party and in various social actions. The constraints also imposed by these resolutions, however, reveal the ritualistic nature of these calls for a 'workers' democracy'.[30] Lenin always held that the dictatorship of the proletariat was supported by the party and that his leadership had the support of the working class. When Lenin received the first hints that workers were directing activities against his policies, he swiftly crushed the representative of the proletariat, just as he had done with the labour opposition in 1921.

Lenin was one of the first to understand the importance of the workers' councils (Soviets) that spontaneously emerged during the first Russian revolution of 1905–1907 and then reemerged after the Revolution of February 1917. In these Soviets, as well as in various other bodies, such as the 'Committees of Poor Peasants' (*Kombedy*), Lenin discovered an effective means of controlling and using the masses for the construction of a new society. The Soviets also provided a structural-legal basis for his dictatorship of the proletariat, since, by the early 1900s, it was already unacceptable to rule by force without some form of democratic coverage.

Lenin's views on socialism seem to have changed in the last two years before his death.[31] By all accounts, Lenin reassessed his views on the importance of market and state regulations and moved somewhat in the direction of the position held by Western social democrats; that is, toward the partial recognition of civil society and its economic function. Writing about free cooperation and its importance in the construction of a new society, Lenin, for the first time, used terms such as 'private interest' in a positive way, withholding the venom he usually directed against anything linked to bourgeois society.[32] Still, there is no sign that he changed his views toward the political order. He died an implacable foe of democratic institutions, political pluralism, and even freedom of discussion inside his own party.

III

In the wake of the seizure of the Winter Palace, Lenin and his colleagues revealed themselves to be determined to concentrate power in their hands. They openly intended to turn the state machine into their own instrument and were overtly hostile to any independent activity in society. The following three sections systematically investigate the ways in which the Bolsheviks destroyed civil society in the country. This destruction followed three stages: War Communism, the NEP (New Economic Policy), and the rise of Stalinism.

When the Bolsheviks came to power after the February revolution, the old state machine was, in many respects, almost dead, and a civil society, with numerous autonomous organisations, was rapidly developing. In the months immediately after the October coup, these processes were intensified by the activities of young Bolsheviks. These young believers, inspired by orthodox Marxist views about the withering of the state and what they considered to be old 'bourgeois' institutions, like the family and the school, tried to introduce a new lifestyle founded on autonomy and self-regulation. They based their efforts not on directions from their leaders but on the writings of Marx and Engels, in the Marxist and revolutionary traditions. Thus the Bolsheviks bent on quickly destroying civil society had to deal not only with the old order, but also with their own comrades who sincerely believed in new freedoms.

The first steps toward destroying civil society were directed toward the multi-party system. The disappearance of the so-called bourgeois parties such as 'Kadet' and 'Oktiabrists' was an immediate and automatic result of the October coup. On November 28, the new authorities announced the arrest of the leaders of the 'Kadet' party, the most consistent advocate of democracy in the country. Similarly, it took only a few months to remove the socialist parties— the Mensheviks and Socialist Revolutionaries—from the political scene. The new regime also quickly eliminated the free press. On October 27, only a few days after the coup, all anti-Bolshevik newspapers were closed. The next assault on civil society came in the form of the dismantling of the Constituent Assembly, which had been freely elected by the population of the country after the October revolution. When the Bolsheviks received only 9 million of the 36 million votes, Lenin organised a coup against the Assembly. After the October 25 coup, which was carried out by Red sailors, the Bolsheviks began a decades-long suppression of one of the pillars of any prosperous civil society—its control over the state. Having destroyed all of the political elements of civil society, the Bolsheviks initiated a system of terror that made the entire population tremble, and led to the imprisonment and deaths of thousands of people. It was during the period immediately after the October revolution that the foundations of Soviet society were laid. These foundations included the merging of the party and the state, the creation of the *Nomenklatura* system, the elimination of the distinction between public and private life, and several other policies to be outlined below.

The state's submission to the party was complete, and included all judiciary bodies, the police, and the army. For all practical purposes, the state and the party apparatuses were merged, and all state bodies were considered to be sections of the party. This merger occurred despite the fact that some Soviet politicians (including Stalin in the last years of his life)[33] preferred to emphasise the state as the backbone of Soviet society.[34] Since the early years of the Soviet system, exclusion from the party automatically meant not only the loss of one's job (a practice that remained essentially intact until the 1970s) but also, during the Stalin era, arrest followed by a long prison sentence, or death. The Bolsheviks regarded the persecution and elimination of independent organisations as one of the most important elements of their model for society. Any organisation not completely controlled by the state—from the appointment of its leaders down to the delineation of its program of activity—was dismantled. This policy was strictly observed, whether the organisation was interested in collecting stamps or the collective study of Marxism. The destruction of independent organisations began almost immediately after the revolution, and was completed within about ten years. The Bolsheviks also moved quickly to introduce the *Nomenklatura* system. This system meant that the appointment of all officials in both the party and the state was overseen by a party committee created in the first years of Soviet power.

The distinction between public and private life was swiftly eliminated after the October revolution (at the expense of the latter). As this distinction disappeared, the state began intervening in every facet of people's lives. The Bolsheviks considered it important that people be involved in public activity as much as possible, including during their leisure time. This active public involvement guaranteed the people's maximum contribution to the achievement of public goals, allowed for incessant ideological indoctrination, and minimised people's opportunities to engage in activities hostile to the regime. Another of the new regime's early actions was the creation of the political police (CHEKA). The CHEKA created a network of informers that watched people with even the slightest potential to oppose the new system, even if only in thought.

The Bolsheviks realised that production units (such as plants, colleges, research institutes, theatres, and so on) offered ideal opportunities to extend their control even further into people's lives. In fact, production units were found to be far more efficient arenas of control than were residential blocks, which had also been targeted for such purposes. As a result, collectivism, which was so highly praised by the Marxists and later by Soviet ideologues, was turned into a powerful means of spiritually and materially enslaving the Soviet people. The ruling elite even managed to convince the Soviet people of the superiority of collectivism over individualism.

Starting in 1917, the Bolsheviks began transforming all public organisations that were permitted to exist, such as the Trade Unions or Youth Leagues, into obedient organs of the party. The Bolsheviks' intentions were clear, and the 8th party congress openly declared in 1919 that the party wanted 'to win decisive influence and total leadership in all organisations of working people'.[35] The Bolsheviks made widespread use of political rituals to further the impression that the Soviet political order was based on self-government by the workers and the peasants. Elections of local bodies were transformed into formal games executed under the control of party committees.[36]

From the beginning, the Bolsheviks proclaimed that, as the absolute masters of the country, they were determined to ignore private property and were ready to confiscate anything they chose. They also declared their opposition to spontaneous economic regulation and market forces, and discounted the ability of market forces to guarantee economic progress. The Bolsheviks considered market and other spontaneous forces hostile to a state society, since these forces automatically engendered and reproduced the elements of capitalism, which is independent of the state. In the first years after the revolution, the Bolsheviks laid the groundwork of the Soviet economic order, which remained essentially intact until 1987. From the beginning, they considered the economy to be their property, and believed that unrestrained intervention into economic activity was their natural right. The economic measures instituted by the Bolsheviks in the first years of their regime were dictated not by the special circumstances of the civil war, but by their vision of the society they wished to create. Lenin unequivocally acknowledged this several times.[37] In the beginning, the Bolsheviks' economic policy appeared rather mixed. That is, they seemed willing to give as well as to take. The decree adopted on October 25, the first day of the new regime, gave land to the peasants and drastically increased the number of landowners, thus apparently promoting the independent sector of the economy. Yet, within six months, 'war communism' was introduced, and the government installed a 'food dictatorship': the state claimed a monopoly on selling bread, and all farms were taxed at a level that brought the peasants to the verge of starvation. Not satisfied with this, the Bolsheviks began in 1918 to confiscate individual farms belonging to prosperous peasants (*kulaks*) and began promoting agricultural communes, which were controlled by the state. The regime quickly implemented its policy of nationalising industry and commerce. The regime began in this process in November 1917 by disenfranchising the owners of private enterprises and replacing them with 'workers' control.' Of course, those who accepted the idea of workers' control at face value were swiftly rebuffed by Lenin's government, which insisted that the plants belonged not to any collective of workers, but to the 'whole society,' meaning, of course, the Soviet state.

Apparently dissatisfied with even limited workers' control, which universally led to declines in discipline, the Soviet government accelerated the process of nationalisation. By the end of the civil war, 90 per cent of all industries were nationalised. The establishment in April 1918 of the state's monopoly over foreign trade and over the banks was yet another development in the destruction of the economic sphere of civil society. Having encountered great difficulties in food distribution, the Bolsheviks looked for a solution that would extend state control to, and eliminate private commerce in, this sphere of the economy. The rationing of food in November 1918 made the people's dependence, as well as their terror, complete.[38]

The central government created several bodies to oversee economic affairs. The Supreme Council of Economic Affairs (VSNKh) was created in late 1917, and the State Planning Commission (GOSPLAN) was created in 1921. The local branches of these bodies quickly took control of the country's economic life. In the wake of the revolution, the state adopted a policy of both current and long term planning. The 8th Party Congress (1919) had already discussed 'the planned organisation of social production processes' and 'the maximal unification of all economic activities under the guidance of a single economic plan'.[39] The Bolsheviks immediately gave themselves the right to mobilise labour to achieve various goals. The belief that all people, regardless of age, sex, profession, and health, are free to be drafted according to the state's needs or desires has never left the mentality of the Soviet leadership, although such conscription has been carried out differently during different periods.

With their loathing for freedoms and bourgeois culture, the Bolsheviks began their assault on independent cultural activity early in their reign. They eliminated the independent press and created their own mass media network. In 1919, this network issued 623 newspapers. By the end of the civil war, Lenin had shaped the principles of the regime's cultural policy, which was followed by every subsequent regime until the advent of Gorbachev's glasnost'. This policy included strong ideological control over all mass media and all levels of education, strong ideological control over, and the continuous ideological indoctrination of, all segments of the population, strong control over literature and the arts (which was achieved about ten years after the October revolution), and the creation and maintenance (through brainwashing and terror) of a false image of the real world. From its inception, the new regime distorted reality to present the new society as democratic and as possessing the best elements of civil society. In the years immediately after the revolution, official texts and speeches, although far more truthful than those that would follow, contained numerous lies about the participation of the masses in government and about party members' ability to influence their organisation. Resolutions of the party congresses during this period regularly misrepresented the role of the masses in Soviet society.[40] Lenin actively participated in maintaining a false picture of Soviet society as being ruled by the masses.[41]

From the outset, the Bolsheviks declared themselves enemies of the capitalist West. At the same time, however, they intended to use Western experience in the areas of technology and science to help construct their new society.

IV

With the country in a shambles toward the end of the civil war, Lenin introduced the NEP. In practice, the NEP involved the limited restoration of private initiatives in agriculture and in other sectors of the economy. In industry, the limited restoration of private initiatives included only small enterprises (by the end of the NEP, private businesses could hire up to 100 workers). At the same time, state enterprises were also accorded more autonomy than had been the case in the past. Despite these initiatives, the state continued to interfere in all spheres of economic activity. Lenin, for example, demanded increases in 'the state's intervention in private property relations, and in civil cases in the court'.[42]

While allowing the partial resurrection of civil society in the economy, the Bolsheviks continued their offensive against the autonomy of any organisations that survived during War Communism or that emerged after the civil war. During the NEP, terror against the masses continued. Although it was less intense than during the civil war, it was sufficient to keep the population, including party members, frightened. In 1922, a few hundred prominent Russian intellectuals (including Nikolai Berdiaev and Pitirim Sorokin) were expelled from the country. This action was a clear signal that Lenin's regime would not tolerate dissent in thought. During this period, the Kremlin also initiated show trials against its true political foes. At the same time, the Kremlin created the notorious Glavlit, the official censorship body. Glavlit's duties included not only making decisions about anything being published in the country (including business cards and wedding invitations), but also deciding which library books should be accessible to all readers and which should be sent to secret library departments (called Spetskhran), where only people with special permission and good political reputations could borrow them.

Between 1921 and 1927, the party carried out a consistent struggle against trade unions and against professional organisations of scholars, doctors, agronomists, and rural cooperatives.

V

Stalin finished what had been started by Lenin—he destroyed civil society in the USSR. The current author is among those scholars who resolutely reject the continuity between Lenin and Stalin and who deny that events after 1924 are the logical continuation of the processes started by the Bolsheviks. The ideology forged by Lenin, despite containing significant elements of hypocrisy (such as Lenin's uses of term 'democracy' in his post-revolutionary works), rather accurately reflected the views and the plans of the Bolsheviks. Stalin, however, introduced a radically new feature to the Bolshevik (or

Leninist) ideology: he split the official ideology into two parts—one part addressing the masses and the other addressing the party apparatus and the intelligentsia; that is, the two strata necessary to rule the country. The interaction of the two ideologies was very subtle, and only those privy to 'the inner party,' to use an Orwellian term, could grasp differences and find the genuine commands in Stalin's speeches and party documents.[43]

The ideology directed toward the masses (the 'open ideology') created an image of a society that surpassed not only civil or bourgeois society in the West, but past Russian society as well. This society was depicted as a genuine democracy, with opportunities for people to create all kinds of associations and actualise their talents in all spheres of life. Stalin easily outstripped Lenin in praising the proletarian dictatorship and the Soviet state. According to Stalin, these institutions were a haven of democracy for the majority of the people in the 1920s, and for all of the people by the middle of the 1930s.[44] The second ideology (the 'closed ideology') is dominated by the ideas of absolute power for the party-state apparatus and the elimination of even the slightest freedom in the activities of the people. While the open ideology praised Soviet society as the best in the world, the closed ideology strove for the elimination of all remnants of Marxist and Leninist ideas regarding the withering of the state in socialist society. Instead, Stalin's closed ideology considered strengthening the Soviet state to be the major task of the party, a theoretical innovation justified by the existence of capitalist encirclement.[45] Stalin declared that the party dominated society and had the right to interfere in any activity of any individual or any organisation in the country.[46] This mandate placed the state and society as a whole above the individual, and justified the suppression of the human personality and the condemnation of the so-called all-mankind values (such as kindness, generosity, and compassion). Still, while sending obvious signals to the true holders of power, Stalin was angered by those who publicly equated the dictatorship of the proletariat with party rule, and especially by those who equated party rule only with the leaders. Stalin paid great attention to the preservation of political rituals and vehemently criticised those who ignored the 'rules of the game'.[47]

Beginning in the early 1930s, Stalin initiated a cult of the state, which grew until his last years. Stalin used the Russian monarchy as the basis for this cult, and commanded his historians and writers to praise the strong Russian tsars. Among those so praised were Ivan the Terrible, Peter the Great, and even Nicholas the First, who, for the Russian revolutionaries, was the harshest enemy of freedom. Stalin borrowed significantly from Imperial Russia: he restored the old titles of government bodies (for example, The Council of Ministers instead of the Council of People's Commissars), changed the titles of military and bureaucratic personnel in several Ministries, and introduced uniforms for several categories of civil officials.

After Lenin's death, the Soviet state began to gradually withdraw the economic concessions granted to the private sector. Between 1925 and 1930, practically all private enterprises were either nationalised or dismantled. In 1928, the law that permitted private individuals to lease state enterprises was abolished. By 1931, private commerce had essentially ceased to exist. The collectivisation of 1929–1932 destroyed private farming. By 1939, private farmers and private artisans constituted only about 1.6 per cent of the population, compared with 72.9 per cent in 1928. By 1934, Stalin could boast that the country's private sector had been reduced to minuscule proportions.

Stalin's major political contribution was to establish total fear as a permanent part of life in the country. This goal was achieved through systematic campaigns of terror directed against whatever group was chosen at any given time. Constant supervision of the individual was an important ingredient in the intimidation of the Soviet people. This supervision was performed by an army of informers (data from Eastern Europe suggest that informers constitute almost ten per cent of the adult population) and by millions of Soviet people who eagerly and voluntarily denounced each other, colleagues, and neighbours. Because the absolute majority of Soviet city dwellers lived in communal apartments, the surveillance efforts of the political police were greatly simplified.

The establishment of political rituals was another major development during this period. Substantial effort was expended to present Stalin's regime as democratic and as enjoying all of the political virtues of civil society. The Soviet population was forced to participate in elections with only one candidate on the slate and to join various 'voluntary' organisations supposedly independent of the state. The adoption in 1936 of a new constitution that presented Soviet society as the most democratic in the world at the same time that mass terror was reaching its peak was an unprecedented triumph of political hypocrisy. The 1936 constitution led to the first elections to the Soviet parliament in 1937. In these one-sided elections, 98.6 per cent of the Soviet people voted for the regime's candidates.

By the end of the Stalin era, Soviet society was absolutely cut off from the external world. Written correspondence with foreigners, travel abroad, and emigration were all forbidden, as was access to Western mass media and Western culture (a few exceptions, mostly related to movies, were made). Contact with foreigners visiting the USSR was strictly forbidden.

Stalin totally eliminated any autonomous cultural life in the country. In the late 1920s, he began a program of persecuting Soviet intellectuals that continued until his death. Thousands of intellectuals perished in the Gulag, and those not imprisoned were terrorised to the end of their lives, even if they outlived Stalin by several years. The entire intellectual community was stripped of its autonomy. All organisations of creative people—including the Academy of Science and the unions that represented writers, artists, movie makers, composers, theatre figures, and others—were transformed into docile and obedient servants of Stalin's regime. It seemed that there was nothing these organisations would not do to gain favour. In comparison to the Stalin era, the freedom granted similar organisations in prerevolutionary Russia was substantial. It is remarkable that among the cultural organisations liquidated by the Stalin regime were those that emerged after 1917 with the goal of defending the revolution and promoting Marxism and socialism. These organisations were eliminated because, as a result of the revolution, they gained a measure of independence from the state and the ruling elite. Among these organisations were associations of 'proletarian writers', 'proletarian musicians', 'artists of revolutionary Russia', and others.

Institutions of higher education, including the country's leading universities, were forced to forget their former autonomy. These institutions came under the absolute control of the authorities, who made decisions about the appointment of professors and established rules regarding student admissions. High schools also came under the absolute control of the party and the state. Several official decisions in the early 1930s eliminated any vestige of the autonomy granted high schools during the first postrevolutionary years in reaction to the tsarist school system. Decrees passed in 1931–1935 restored strict state control over elementary and secondary education and declared ideological work to be a major task of teaching. All textbooks had to be endorsed by the central authorities, and social science teachers had to be approved by local party committees. All teachers were engaged in the ideological indoctrination of their pupils, and mathematics classes were considered as appropriate a place for such indoctrination as were history or social science classes. In addition, teachers were required to engage in ideologically-oriented extracurricular activities with their students.

By the mid-1930s, Stalin's regime had gained control over individual thought. This control was achieved by eliminating all sources of information not under the state's direction—even verbal communications were effectively halted. In the end, political jokes survived as the single outlet for free thought. All Soviet institutions, including those in the arts, education, science, the mass media, professional organisations (including those concerned with the narrowest of professional issues such as chess or husbandry), and public organisations, were involved in the daily indoctrination of the Soviet people. Millions of Soviet citizens were recruited as propagandists and were themselves forced to attend countless political courses and schools for retraining.[48] The state also assumed control over the presentation of the past. The publication of Stalin's *Short History of the CPSU* in 1938 set strict standards for describing the Soviet and Russian past, not only in textbooks but in movies, novels, paintings, and sculptures as well. Even remote eras of human history, such as that of ancient Rome, were treated according to Stalin's remarks, even if the remarks were casual. The regime's control over the presentation of contemporary events was equally stringent. By distorting data, withholding data, and prohibiting empirical studies, the regime was able to create its own image of the country.

During the Stalin era, the Soviet people lost not only political freedom, but also freedom of choice in almost every sphere of life, including family and friends, place of residence, professional work, and leisure time. The political police—the NKVD and later the KGB—managed to destroy the private lives of the Soviet people. To a great degree, families became agents of the state, responsible for both the loyalty and, to a lesser degree, the productive activities, of their members. It was common for the state to persecute cruelly the wives and children of those declared 'enemies of the people.' It is understandable, then, why family members were afraid of one another, especially parents of their children. The state regularly interfered in the family life of the Soviet people, both as the guardian of family bonds and as the supervisor of the educational process. It was as normal for party committees to punish people for adultery and for a desire to change spouses as it was to punish them for neglecting their children. The state strongly influenced people's choices of spouses, friends, and lovers. Entire categories of brides, grooms, and friends were considered unacceptable by the authorities and were therefore shunned by those desiring a career in Soviet society. In the 1920s the children of former capitalists and landlords were singled out, in the 1930s the children of the 'enemies of the people' were shunned, and in the 1940s and 1950s those who were prisoners of war and those who lived in the territories occupied by Germans, Jews, Crimean Tatars, and other nationalities were persecuted by Stalin. Friendship, a strong institution in Russian culture, also lost much of its appeal. People generally avoided, and certainly did not assist, those of their friends who found themselves at odds with the authorities.

In the 1930s, the Soviet people lost the right to change residences in the country, and police permission was required to move to another city. Members of collective farms, being true serfs, could not leave their villages without the consent of the collective farm chairman, a genuine landlord. It was equally difficult to change apartments within the same city. Again, people had to receive permission from the local authorities to swap apartments. Throughout Stalin's reign, the Soviet people were not only assigned a job after graduating from a higher school or vocational college, but were prohibited from leaving their job without official permission. Violation of these labour laws meant a prison sentence. Living in a closed society and being monitored around the clock by informants, colleagues, and neighbours, the Soviet people had to be content to entertain themselves in public places controlled by the authorities. Restaurants, for example, were the last safe haven for confidential conversations. Movies, theatres, concert halls, and circuses offered the only programmed entertainment endorsed by the state. Private entertainment, such as an unofficial concert or a poetry recital, was absolutely forbidden.

When Stalin died, Russia was almost totally bereft of any element of civil society. The single significant legal vestige of civil society was the existence of private agricultural plots throughout the countryside. Stalin reluctantly tolerated their existence because these plots, along with a very limited private farm market marginally regulated by the state, prevented the starvation of collective farmers and their families. The illegal elements of civil society in the early 1950s (the criminal world was, of course, outside the state's control) included private tutoring, private teaching of music and foreign languages, domestic help, and limited work for artisans.

Civil society began to revive in the late 1950s, a few years after Stalin's death. *Samizdat* publications, widespread distribution of the tapes of the bards, and unofficial gatherings of intellectuals all heralded the awakening of civil society. Of course, it took almost three decades before this society was acknowledged and legalised by the political establishment.

VI

The destruction of Russia's civil society had a tremendous, partially irreversible impact. Soviet society entered the Gorbachev era with a severely decayed social fabric, and with only major two actors in play—the political elite and the atomised, isolated Soviet people. Between these two actors stood a few organised institutions, which were totally alienated from most people and were not thought to be interested in defending the interests of the people.

Moreover, after seven decades without any genuine civic activity, the Soviet people had lost their knack for authentic collective action. In 1985, for example, peasants, members of kolkhoz, and collective farmers were unable to complete even the modest collective task of repairing one mile of road, a failure vividly described by several Soviet authors. Various sociological and anecdotal Soviet sources, including novels and movies appearing in the 1970s and 1980s, depicted the Soviet people's deep aversion to collective action.[49] Thus, when the role of the state began to decline during 1985–1990, the nascent civil society was unable to fill the resulting vacuum of power and action. As a result, anarchy and chaos spread through several facets of Soviet life. With decades of arbitrary power behind them, the Soviet people were very cynical regarding any political institutions, including new, democratic ones. In 1990, the majority of the population remained distrustful of not only the Communist party and the government but the new democratically elected parliaments and local governments.

The destruction of civil society in the economic sphere also had disastrous consequences. The command economy destroyed almost all sense of entrepreneurship in society, and it severely damaged the people's trust in law and in the state's willingness and ability to honour its commitments toward private business and private owners. Thus, when Gorbachev's regime began its privatisation efforts, it was difficult to entice peasants to become private farmers or to induce people to start small businesses in the service sector.

Moreover, those who did decide to enter the private sector questioned the stability of official policies and conducted their business under the assumption that the state could confiscate their property at any moment.

Family and friendship were the only social institutions to survive the destruction of Soviet civil society. These institutions now form part of the foundation of a new civil society in Russia. Still, it will be many years before the Soviet people become members of a full-fledged civil society.

Notes

1   The influence of the Bolsheviks' prerevolutionary ideology on their postrevolutionary behaviour has been discussed in Barrington Moore, Jr, *Soviet Politics—The Dilemma of Power* (Cambridge: Harvard University Press, 1950) pp. 9–10.

2   See Карл Маркс and Фридрих Энгельс, *Собрание сочинений* (Moscow: Institute of Marx-Engels-Lenin) Vol.XIII, p. 6; Карл Маркс and Фридрих Энгельс, *Фейербах. Противоположность материалистического и идеалистического мировозрении* (Moscow: Politizdat, 1966) p. 51. Soviet authors also recognize the existence of both concepts in 18th and 19th century literature. See Владимир Нерсесянц, (ed.), *История политических и правовых учений* (Moscow: Izdatel'stvo 'Iuridicheskaia Literatura', 1988) p. 475.

3   Marx and Engels insisted that, in a capitalist society, the individual is alienated from both the state and from civil society. This alienation, they theorised, results from the conflict between public and private life, between 'general' and 'particular' concerns, and between civil society and the political superstructure—all conflicts that could be eliminated by a social revolution.

4   Л.Д. Троцкий, *Перспективы Русской Революции* (Berlin: Ladyzhnikov, 1917) p. 50.

5   В.И. Ленин, *Собрание сочинений* (Moscow: Politizdat, Fourth edition) Vol. XXV, p. 359.

6   Ibid., Vol. XXV, p. 445.

7   Ibid., Vol.XXV, p. 401; see also pp. 418–419.

8   Троцкий, p. 14.

9   Ленин, *Собрание сочинений*, Vol. XXV, p. 387.

10   Ibid., Vol. XXX, p. 93.

11   See Robert Dahl, *Polyarchy* (New Haven: Yale University Press, 1971).

12   Lenin, Trotsky, Bukharin, and other leading Bolsheviks were absolutely intolerant toward their opponents, a tradition inherited from their spiritual fathers, Marx and Engels, whose works brimmed with venomous and virulent tirades against highly respected scholars and politicians. Lenin's *Materialism and Empiriocriticism* (1908) and *The Proletarian Revolution and Renegade Kautsky* (1918), Bukharin's *The Economics of*

the *Transitional Period* (1920) and *On the Liquidation of our Ideas* (1924), and Trotsky's *Perspectives on the Russian Revolution* (1905/6), are as prejudiced toward their opponents as are Marx's *Capital* (1867) or Engels's *Anti-Dühring* 1878).

13 Троцкий, p. 35.

14 Lenin's belief in the role of a revolutionary minority was similar to that of the Russian populists, his political mentors and enemies, although on the surface he criticised their views. The populists, like Carlyle, believed in the decision role of prominent personalities in history. Unlike the populists, however, Lenin believed that the revolutionary minority needed to know the laws of history and should therefore look for support not among peasants but among the proletariat. Lenin also believed that single terrorists could not crush the state machine. Rather, he believed that the job could only be accomplished through a Marxist-led mass revolution.

15 В.И. Ленин, 'Государство и революция', in В.И. Ленин, *Избранные произведения* (Moscow: Politizdat, 1966) Vol.II, pp. 227–324.

16 Ленин, *Собрание сочинений*, Vol.XXV, p. 422.

17 В.И. Ленин, *Полное собрание сочинений* (Moscow: Politizdat, Fifth edition) Vol.XI, pp. 13, 39; Ленин, *Собрание сочинений*, Vol.XXV, pp. 394–395.

18 Ленин, *Собрание сочинений*, Vol.XXV, p. 365

19 Ibid., Vol.XXV, p. 433

20 In his posthumously published novels, Vasilii Grossman, the great Soviet writer, vividly portrayed Lenin as anything but a supporter of freedom. Grossman's novel *It Flows* (1989) was the first *glasnost*'-era text to reject the official line of support for Lenin. *It Flows* made a strong impression on the Soviet people and began the revision of Lenin's image in the Soviet press. 'Lenin's intolerance, unshattered desire to achieve goals, contempt for freedom, cruelty toward those who think in other ways, and ability to sweep from the face of the earth not only fortresses but also districts and whole provinces that challenged his convictions— these features did not appear in Lenin only after October. These featured were typical for Volodia Ul'anov. These features had deep roots' (Василий Гроссман, 'Все течет', *Октябрь*, no.6, June 1989, pp. 30–108, at p. 94).

21 Н.И. Бухарин, *Избранные Произведения* (Moscow: Politizdat, 1988) p. 13.

22 Ленин, *Полное собрание сочинений*, Vol.XLV, p. 95.

23 Ibid., Vol.XLV, p. 370.

24 Н.И. Бухарин, *Путь к Социализму в России* (New York: Omicron Books, 1967) pp. 115–116.

25 Ibid., p. 102.

26 *Коммунистическая Партия Советского Союза в резолюциях и решениях съездов, конференций и пленумов ЦК* (Moscow: Gospolitizdat, 1953) Vol.I, pp. 527–530.

27 Ленин, *Полное собрание сочинений*, Vol.XXXIV, pp. 287–339; vol.XLIV, p. 147.

28   Ibid., Vol.XXXVII, pp. 253, 265–266. Until 1988–1989, Lenin had been
      considered by liberals, especially those close to the party, to have been a
      true democrat easily distinguished from Stalin. Liberals maintained this
      position during the early years of *glasnost'* and were supported by
      Gorbachev, who also tried to present Lenin in this light (see Ф.
      Бурлацкий, 'Брежнев и крушение оттепели: Размышления о
      природе политического лидерства', *Литературная газета*,
      14 September 1988, pp. 13–14). Mikhail Shatrov, in his historical plays
      about the events of 1917–1924 (especially *Further, further, further...*),
      was the most eloquent propagandist of this theme. Shatrov's plays
      described the liberal, true Leninist (or Bukharinian) and the
      bureaucratic (Stalinist) alternatives following the October revolution
      (see Михаил Шатров, 'Дальше ... дальше ... дальше', *Знамя*,
      no.1, January 1988, pp. 3–53; and the interview with him in *Огонек*,
      no.45, 1988, p. 16; Ю.Н. Афанасьев, 'Ответ историка', *Правда*, 26
      July 1988; Ю. Буртин, 'Возможность возразить', in Ю.Н.
      Афанасьев (ed.), *Иного не дано* (Moscow: Izdatel'stvo 'Progress',
      1988) pp. 468–490; А. Бутенко, 'О революционной перестройке
      государственно-административного социализма', in Ю.Н.
      Афанасьев (ed.), *Иного не дано* (Moscow: Izdatel'stvo 'Progress',
      1988) pp. 551–568; and В. Кисилев, 'Сколько моделей
      социализма было в СССР?', in Ю.Н. Афанасьев (ed.), *Иного не
      дано* (Moscow: Izdatel'stvo 'Progress', 1988) pp. 354–369). Several
      Western socialists as well as others shared this view, suggesting that the
      development of Lenin's ideas would have lead to democratic socialism, or
      to socialism with a human face (see Stephen F. Cohen, *Bukharin and the
      Bolshevik Revolution: A Political Biography 1888–1938* (London:
      Wildwood House, 1974)). It was not until 1988 that Soviet intellectuals,
      Westernizers, and Russophiles had the opportunity publicly to debunk
      this myth, arguing instead for continuity between Lenin and Stalin.
      They described Lenin as anything but an admirer of true democracy and
      civil society, even though he did change some of his economic views in the
      last years of his life. (Л. Баткин, 'Возобновление истории', in Ю.Н.
      Афанасьев (ed.), *Иного не дано* (Moscow: Izdatel'stvo 'Progress',
      1988) pp. 154–191; М. Гефтер, '"Сталин умер вчера ..."', in Ю.Н.
      Афанасьев (ed.), *Иного не дано* (Moscow: Izdatel'stvo 'Progress',
      1988) pp. 297–324, at p. 311; И. Клямкин, 'Почему трудно
      говорить правду?', *Новый мир*, no.2, February 1989, pp. 204–238;
      В. Селюнин, 'Истоки', *Новый мир*, no.5, May 1988, pp. 162–189; А.
      Ципко, 'Превратности чистого социализма', *Наука и жизнь*,
      no.12, December 1988, pp. 40–48). Some of Lenin's detractors went even
      further and declared Marx and Engels to be the ultimate cause of Lenin's
      hostility toward civil society and democracy. Aleksandr Tsipko, a rather
      unrenowned philosopher, was the initial proponent of the image of Lenin.
      In a series of articles in *Наука и жизнь* (Science and Life), he discussed
      'the main truth' of the direct connection between the Stalinist system
      and 'the Marxist project of society', which was based on unrealistic
      assumptions such as 'a non-commodity and non-money economy, social
      property, the exaggeration of the role of theory in social development, and
      the neglecting of democratic principles, and so on' (Ципко, 'О зонах
      закрытых для мысли', *Наука и жизнь*, no.11, November 1988, pp.

45–55; 'Превратности чистого социализма', *Наука и жизнь*, no.12, December 1988, pp. 40–48; 'Эгоизм мечтателей', *Наука и жизнь*, no.1, January 1989, pp. 46–56.

29   Ленин, *Полное собрание сочинений*, vol.XLIV, p. 497.

30   See, for instance, the decision of the 13th party conference in *Коммунистическая Партия Советского Союза в резолюциях и решениях съездов, конференций и пленумов ЦК*, Vol.I, pp. 774–775, 777.

31   When Lenin came under public attack in 1989–1990, Gorbachev and his loyalists emphasized the difference between the Lenin of 1921–1923 and the Lenin of earlier periods, particularly in regard to the installation of War Communism as a desperate effort to save his crumbling authority over Soviet society.

32   Ленин, *Полное собрание сочинений*, Vol.XLIV, p. 370.

33   After the war with Germany, Stalin publicly downgraded the role of the party and highlighted the role of state. He regularly signed joint decisions of the party and the government as the Chairman of the Council of Ministers but not as the leader of the Party (he even abandoned the title of General Secretary, and when absolutely necessary, referred to himself as merely a Secretary of the Party).

34   In the 1960s and 1970s, Soviet social scientists close to the party but also influenced by new, more liberal, trends began to debate the relationship between the state and party apparatuses, a previously taboo issue. Some of these social scientists, trying to close the gap between the Soviet reality and the dominant ideology, tried to highlight the commonalities of the two apparatuses and to treat the party as a 'normal' part of the Soviet state. Conservatives, however, afraid to tamper with old dogmas, insisted that the party was no more than a public organization running the state at the request of the people, just as in any other 'normal' country in the world.

35   *Коммунистическая Партия Советского Союза в резолюциях и решениях съездов, конференций и пленумов ЦК*, Vol.I, p. 446.

36   It is remarkable that party congress resolutions after October 1917 almost never mentioned procedures for electing Soviet bodies. It was as if these elections were beyond reproach (see *Коммунистическая Партия Советского Союза в резолюциях и решениях съездов, конференций и пленумов ЦК*, Vol.I, pp. 413–416, 514–572, 599–900).

37   Ленин, *Полное собрание сочинений*, Vol.XLIV, pp. 157, 208.

38   On Lenin's use of bread rationing as a political weapon, see Владимир Солоухин, 'Читая Ленина', *Родина*, no.10, October 1989, pp. 66–70.

39   Ленин, *Полное собрание сочинений*, Vol.XLII, pp. 153–154; *Коммунистическая Партия Советского Союза в резолюциях и решениях съездов, конференций и пленумов ЦК*, Vol.I, p. 421; see also Николай Запкин et.al. (eds)., *Планирование экономического и социального развития СССР* (Moscow: Izdatel'stvo 'Mysl', 1983) pp. 12–18.

40   See *Коммунистическая Партия Советского Союза в резолюциях и решениях съездов, конференций и пленумов ЦК*, Vol.I, *passim*.

41   Ленин, *Полное собрание сочинений*, Vol.XXXIX, pp. 419–420.

42   Ibid., Vol.XLIV, p. 412.

43   On the two official ideologies, see Vladimir Shlapentokh, *Soviet Public Opinion and Ideology* (New York: Praeger, 1986).

44   И.В. Сталин, *Вопросы Ленинизма* (Moscow: Politizdat, 1952) pp. 33–36, 555.

45   Ibid., pp. 642–646.

46   Ibid., p. 126.

47   Ibid., pp. 126–127, 133, 138.

48   See Shlapentokh, *Soviet Public Opinion and Ideology*.

49   See Vladimir Shlapentokh, *Public and Private Life of the Soviet People* (Oxford: Oxford University Press, 1989) pp. 129–138.

6

Mono-organisational Socialism and the Civil Society

T.H. RIGBY

I

In February-March 1990 the predominantly conservative Central Committee of the Soviet Communist Party agreed to abdicate its constitutional monopoly of power, and this was endorsed four months later by the no less conservative Twenty-eighth Party Congress. The reasons for such a rare collective sacrifice of authority and privilege will long be debated, but need not detain us here. It is what was at stake that I wish to draw attention to, namely not only *who* might rule the state, but *how* the state, and indeed the whole *social system*, would be run. For the key passage, now deleted, in article 6 of the USSR constitution, referred to the Communist Party as 'the leading and directing force of Soviet society and the nucleus of its political system, of all state organisations and all social (*obshchestvennye*) organisations'. This was the cornerstone of the long-entrenched system of mono-organisational socialism, on which more later, and it was manifestly incompatible with any concept of a 'civil society'.

The word 'any' is used advisedly. From Hobbes and Locke to Gramsci and Habermas, the 'civil society' has been diversely defined and evaluated, and this diversity, as Kukathas and Lovell show in Chapter 1, is not least apparent in the revolutionary tradition that led through Marx to Lenin's Bolsheviks. Nevertheless the most persistent central component in understandings of the civil society is the salience of socially relevant activity and relationships which are more or less autonomous of the state, and it is precisely this which is inconsistent with a mono-organisational system.

Small wonder, then, that the critical intelligentsia in countries living under such mono-organisational systems were to take up the civil society as both an analytic concept and a project, particularly in Poland, where it came into prominence as early as the 1970s.[1] In the Soviet Union itself, it began to figure significantly in political discourse in the late 1980s. The reform economist (and later Deputy Premier) Leonid Abalkin directed attention to it in his speech to the 19th CPSU Conference in June 1988, when speaking of the goals of democratisation and the law-bound (*pravovoi*) state. Describing the latter as one of the most important current issues, he added:[2]

> But of course the law-bound state is only one part of the civil society with its laws, relationships and linkages, which are by no means all state relationships and which give rise to a variety of forms of associations, self-motivated activity (*samodeiatel'nosti*) and associative work-groups (*ob"edineniia trudovykh kollektivov*).

Abalkin's use of the civil society concept here seems to owe little to the Gramscian approach which was perhaps the dominant one in Eastern Europe. It is, on the other hand, very pertinent to the analysis offered in this chapter, and the same applies to an influential article on the future of socialism in the USSR by A.P. Butenko of the Institute of the Economy of the World Socialist System, which appeared in *Pravda* in August 1989, and almost simultaneously as the concluding section of his book *Contemporary Socialism*. As the first of three major questions bearing on the shape of a future Soviet society, Butenko asks 'what should the civil society be like under socialism, what should be its basic parameters?':

> As we know, Stalinism, having achieved the total subordination of all citizens to the despotic power of Stalin and his state apparatus, virtually eliminated the civil society as a system of links between independent citizens. Post-Stalin developments failed to provide here any qualitative change. Therefore the restoration of a civil society characteristic of the new order (*stroi*) is one of the cardinal tasks of *perestroika* and an important feature of the contemporary vision of socialism.

> Under present conditions the civil society must provide first and foremost the economic foundations for the freedom of each individual, of each citizen. Without this, socialism as such is impossible, and there is no place for real socialist democracy.

Developing this last point, and characterising as utopian the attempt to retain and adapt bourgeois freedoms and democracy while placing the whole economy in the hands of the state, Butenko states that the existing two-form system of socialist property (state and kolkhoz-cooperative) must give way to a multi-form system ('national, kolkhoz-cooperative, municipal, and also individual and personal property, etc.')—a listing that was to look quite conservative within a few months.[3]

Gorbachev himself has been sparing in his use of the concept, although his constant emphasis on the 'law-bound state' and on the need to free society from enslavement to the 'command-administrative system', along with his *actions* to this end, indicate a commitment to the substance of it. His main interest, however, is evidently its role in the *political* transformation he is seeking to effect, which, as he put it in his important theoretical article 'The Socialist Idea and Revolutionary Restructuring',[4]

> presupposes both a rational demarcation of 'spheres of influence' between state structures and various social structures, the institutions of civil society, and at the same time the 'germination' of self-governing principles in Soviet statehood, which will be fostered by the whole system of the soviets of people's deputies.

My chief concern in this chapter is precisely with the *substance* of the civil society in the Soviet Union, rather than its theoretical uses,[5] but one further influential example of the latter should be noted before we move on. Igor Kliamkin and Andranik Migranian, also of the Institute of the Economics of the World Socialist System, have argued in a series of papers that a direct transition from totalitarianism to democracy in the USSR is likely to prove impossible, and a transitional phase of enlightened authoritarianism may be necessary, in order to hold things together while the noisily emergent civil society becomes stabilised, otherwise chaos could ensure and provoke a return to the *status quo ante*.[6] Understandably, these views have been hotly contested on historical, theoretical and political grounds,[7] but their pertinence in the context of the social and ethnic turbulence of 1989-90 is obvious.

Western scholarship has until recently made little use of the civil society concept as a tool for analysing political and social change in the USSR, although it has been employed to good effect in a few descriptive accounts, notably by Gail Lapidus.[8] S. Frederick Starr was among the first to argue that such factors as rapid urbanisation and mass post-elementary education have been preparing the social basis for a possibly distinctive Soviet form of civil society.[9] Richard Sakwa presented a stimulating paper entitled 'Civil Society and Commune Democracy' to the Fourth World Congress on Soviet and East European studies in July 1990. Judging by the current interest in the topic, further valuable work on the topic is doubtless under way, but it cannot be said that there is yet a body of relevant writing offering us a ready-made conceptual framework for guiding our research and interpretation.

II

For the purposes of this chapter I define 'civil society' as consisting of those structures and processes through which individuals and groups interact autonomously of the command structures of the state in pursuit of their particular concerns. This definition should help us to identify the distinctive relevant aspects of Soviet society, while being adequate for more general comparative purposes. Some points of amplification are necessary. First, 'autonomy' I treat as a relative rather than an absolute quality. Secondly, the civil society as defined will obviously comprise a traditional and communal (*Gemeinschaft*) dimension in addition to the contractual and associative (*Gesellschaft*) one which is commonly identified with the civil society. This reflects my view that the mutual reinforcement of these two dimensions is in practice essential to any flourishing civil society. It is obviously a controversial view, but I do not wish to digress to argue the case for it here, since in what follows I shall be focussing for the most part on the relatively unproblematical *Gesellschaft* dimension. And finally, my definition draws a line between the civil society and specifically the *command* structures of the state, not between the civil society and the political order generally. This reflects my view that if the civil society is to flourish it must not only be in symbiotic relationship with the political order, but must substantially *colonise* it and remake it in its own image. Parliamentary government is the quintessential consequence of successful colonisation of the political order by the civil society.

Our subject requires a historical perspective and we must start with the pre-revolutionary Russia onto which the mono-organisational system was grafted. During the nineteenth century the common Western image of Russia was of an 'oriental despotism', a nation not of citizens but of slaves.[10] It is a simplistic and one-sided view even for the period before the reforms of the 1860s, but it is not wholly misleading. In any case structures and processes of the contractual, *Gesellschaft* kind were relatively few and they had very limited autonomy *vis-à-vis* the command structures of the state. The abolition of serfdom in 1861 did not directly change this, since peasant holdings were transferred to the ownership and control of the village commune rather than the individual peasant. But it was accompanied by two other reforms that were of great relevance to the growth of the civil society: the introduction of a relatively modern and enlightened judicial system and the establishment of elective local and provincial councils. The break with the past was only partial. The elections were not all that democratic, the councils' powers *vis-à-vis* the provincial governors were limited, and the police still had powers of administrative arrest and banishment independent of the courts. There were neither legitimate political parties nor a national legislature.

All the same, Russia was hardly an 'oriental despotism' at the end of the nineteenth century. And meanwhile urban society was being transformed by the growth of commercial and industrial capitalism, which was extraordinarily rapid from the 1890s on. The 1905 revolution brought what could have proved the decisive breakthrough to a flourishing civil society: quasi-parliamentary government with a multi-party system, a relatively high level of freedom of expression and freedom of association, and a profusion of autonomous organisations of all kinds.[11] The overthrow of the monarchy in February 1917 seemed all that was needed to complete the process. But then came October.

When Lenin and his Bolsheviks seized power they had the most sublime of goals: a society totally rebuilt without exploitation and oppression, in which humanity could at last taste true freedom. They believed that to this end they would themselves have to take total direct control over all aspects of it. They called this 'the dictatorship of the proletariat' and made no attempt to deny that this amounted in practice to dictatorship of the Communist Party leadership, since they were the ones best able to lead the way to the new society. This dictatorship was not to be restricted by laws of any kind or by moral scruples of any kind.[12]

It is obvious that there was no place in such a concept for traditional institutions, for the play of market forces, for autonomous organisations or associations of any kind, or for any concept of democracy that might obstruct the 'dictatorship of the proletariat'. In short, it was implacably hostile to all that pertained to the civil society, and this hostility, as Lovell and Kukathas remind us, was firmly grounded in classical Marxism. In consequence, every field of social activity was soon to become the monopoly of an officially designated organisation run by a hierarchy of command that culminated in the party leadership, and the whole complex of organisations to be welded into a single organisational structure by the command hierarchy of the party apparatus. The party did not just coordinate their policies, it now exercised on their behalf the key functions of any organisation, namely determining their goals, their structures, and their leading personnel. The system could fairly claim to be a socialist one, since all economic entities were in public hands, but it was a socialism the most distinctive feature of which was that the whole life of society was incorporated into a single organisational structure. That is why I consider the most appropriate term for it to be 'mono-organisational socialism'. And the requirements of such a system obviously included a monopoly of all public communication and information by official agencies, and an extraordinarily high level of coercive control.

Mono-organisational socialism started to take shape in the very first months of Bolshevik rule and blossomed under 'war communism', but by 1921 Lenin began to have serious doubts about it, and his New Economic Policy would probably have led Soviet society in a different direction if he had lived to preside over it, although there are disagreements about this that may never be resolved. Stalin, *pari passu* with the consolidation of his power, went on to complete the building of the mono-organisational system, also infusing it with his own obnoxious variant of personal tyranny. The tyranny died with the tyrant in 1953, but the mono-organisational system survived, and changed very little until three or four years ago.[13]

III

Russia's civil society was now dead: it had been swallowed up by the mono-organisational party-state. But was it completely dead? Very nearly so, I think all would agree. And yet some flickers and echoes of life remained, even in the darkest days of Stalinism: vestigial elements of the civil society. The remainder of this chapter revolves around the nature of these vestigial elements and what subsequently happened to them. They were of three kinds, which I will call overt active elements, overt symbolic but inactive elements, and covert active elements.

Overt Active Elements. In the economy there was a limited market in labour, despite a good deal of compulsory job-allocation and restrictions on job-transfer, especially between 1940 and 1950; the household consumption sector was largely supplied through retail marketing, even though administrative distribution was also important, and market choice was only limited; and the family plots kept alive an element of private enterprise in the farm sector.

Large areas of inter-personal relations, from marriage and divorce to transfer of personal property, were determined by mutual agreement, subject to the civil law rather than administrative direction. Civil law-governed contract also had a residual role in inter-organisational relations.

Overt Symbolic But Inactive Elements. Not all official organisations were formally incorporated into the state. Quite a few were in form voluntary—the Russian term is *obshchestvennye organizatsii*, which is variously translated into English as 'public', 'voluntary', or 'social' organisations. These included trade unions, the Komsomol (Youth League), the unions of writers, composers, and so on, sporting associations, and quite a few others. Some of these had pre-existed the mono-organisational system and been taken over by it, while others had been set up later by the party. In any case they were just as much 'official', and just as much subject to party direction, as were agencies and enterprises formally belonging to the state. But they did keep alive an echo, as it were, of the civil society: a notion of the voluntary association as a social form alternative to state organisations.

But the most important symbolic but inactive vestige in the mono-organisational system was democracy. The party itself, the state (in the form of the soviets), and the voluntary organisations, all had their democratic rules and institutions, providing for the election from below of leaders, committees and representatives, responsibility of their executives to elective bodies, and so on. And we should not forget that democracy had originally formed a genuine element in the Bolshevik tradition, despite Lenin's centralism, while the soviets were born in an explosion of democracy, rough and ready though it was. It was the evolution of the 'dictatorship of the proletariat' into mono-organisational socialism that emptied the democratic forms and language of democratic content. By Stalin's time, of course, all members of committees, soviets and other bodies were being selected administratively, like their leaders, under the *nomenklatura* system, they were completely under the control of their centralised hierarchies of command, and their brief and infrequent meetings did little more than perfunctorily endorse official decisions. The democratic forms, apart from serving to mobilise some millions of persons to give unpaid help in official programs, were now primarily a device for legitimating the power of the apparatus—the homage of bureaucratic vice to democratic virtue. And like all such exercises in institutionalised hypocrisy, which serve to affirm a value or ideal in the very process of betraying it, the daily travesty of democracy helped to nourish the soil for its eventual revival.

Covert Active Elements. Most obvious here were the shadow economy and clientelist groupings and networks, both of which flourished from the earliest days of the mono-organisational system. No large-scale organisation can function without a complex set of informal relationships, processes and norms which supplement and partially supplant the formal ones. In Soviet-type societies the personal networks and shadow economy constitute the informal organisation of the mono-organisational system. They superimpose an unofficial contractual dimension onto the system's official command-structure. The peculiar salience of this informal organisation in mono-organisational systems seems to be due to the comprehensive scope of these systems and the absence therefore of alternative structures and processes through which individuals and groups can pursue their special concerns.

Another active vestige of the civil society was the covert vestigial market in ideas—embracing all forms of cultural expression: scientific, artistic, philosophical, religious etc. Even at the height of the Stalin era, when orthodoxies were imposed and policed in every sphere of intellectual life, and the prescribed role of the scholar or artist was to carry out an assigned task in conformity with approved formulas, the shadow market in ideas was never totally suppressed. Indeed here and there it enjoyed a degree of toleration, especially in some fields of the natural and applied sciences. Paradoxically, it flourished best among the enslaved scientists of the *sharashka*, Solzhenitsyn's 'first circle' of the 'Gulag Archipelago'.

IV

The generation that passed between Stalin's death in 1953 and Gorbachev's election as General Secretary in 1985 saw no major changes in the essentials of the mono-organisational system, but important differences emerged in the way it operated, which helped all of the vestigial elements of the civil society to gather strength.

So far as the *overt active elements* are concerned, there was, first, a marked expansion in the household consumption market, especially for consumer durables, and to a lesser extent in the housing sector. There was also a blossoming of the 'market in ideas'. Although all the old ideological, organisational and police controls remained in operation, a greater range of views and approaches was permitted, not only in the natural sciences but in the social sciences and humanities and in the arts. They were now permitted because the post-Stalin leadership had become aware of the great economic and potentially political costs of continued dogmatism and intellectual isolationism. There was even some muted public controversy over certain social issues, in which various concerns were given a modest airing.[14]

The *overt symbolic elements* showed occasional signs of flickering into life, especially during the Khrushchev period, when there were cases of voluntary organisations actually pressing members' concerns in the face of official disapproval, and of people refusing to elect the official candidates for office or using the meetings of various bodies to advocate their special interests.[15]

But the most interesting developments came in the covert active elements. I am not thinking so much of the shadow economy and clientelist networks, although these also thrived mightily, especially during the Brezhnev years. Of far greater importance for the future of the civil society was the profuse blossoming of what I have called the covert 'market in ideas', a blossoming vastly greater than what was apparent publicly. The key facilitating factor here was the curbing of the political police after Stalin's death. Deprived of its powers of arbitrary arrest and of inflicting punishment by its own tribunals, powers which it had used on a mass scale, the KGB was still authorised to maintain saturation surveillance of people's behaviour and opinions, to harass and threaten erring citizens and where it deemed it necessary to bring them to trial in the politically compliant regular courts. But all the same people gradually found they could get away with a great deal in the way of unorthodox opinions and behaviour in private—from rock music to listening to western radio broadcasts, from abstract art to passing on forbidden books or *samizdat* materials. The rehousing program helped here, because tens of millions of city dwellers now acquired some real privacy as they moved from so-called communal apartments to little family flats. The Soviet population was acquiring 'freedom of speech in one kitchen'. The result was that a kind of 'shadow culture' emerged, in many ways richer and more valued than the official culture.

People participated in this 'shadow culture' not just as individuals. For the most part it was shared within the intimate circle of family and close friends, but sometimes embraced wider groups of acquaintances who gathered in each other's flats to pursue some common recreational interest or shared concern. Any regular gatherings of this kind would soon come to the attention of the KGB, which would find ways of establishing whether anything ideologically or politically subversive was afoot. If not, it would usually leave them alone, but if there was it would proceed to warnings, to harassment, and eventually, if necessary, to arrests. This amounted to a conditional *de facto* tolerance of informal associations, one end of which evolved into what came to be called the dissident movement. The dissident groups had a long history but their heyday was from the mid 1960s to the late 1970s, by which time the KGB had reduced them to a remnant. Although their active membership probably never numbered more than a few thousand, there were perhaps millions who were influenced by them, and their intellectual and moral impact on later developments was incalculable.[16]

The vestigial elements of the civil society, whose fluctuating fortunes I have sketched out above, await an extended analysis, but their existence and relevance to the resurgence of the civil society under Gorbachev has been noted by other authors as well. Richard Sakwa has characterised what I call the 'covert' elements as 'the uncivil society',[17] and Evgenii Ambartsumov has commented on them as follows:[18]

> One cannot say that no civil society whatsoever took shape in our country (*u nas*). But finding itself in forced opposition to the state, it grew deformed, acquiring along with normal interpersonal and intergroup relationships ugly and pathological ones as well.

What is, however, obvious is that these 'deformed' and 'uncivil' elements could never be more than 'vestiges' of the civil society so long as the mono-organisational system was in place. Might, then, the ideal of a civil society have been in Gorbachev's mind when he launched his *perestroika* in 1985? I see no evidence for that whatsoever, although it may have been a gleam in the eyes of certain of his advisors, and his commitment to the 'law-bound' state was probably a long-standing one. The unravelling of the mono-organisational system has to be understood as a complex political process involving a kaleidoscopic interplay of motivations and forces. It is not my task here to recount and analyse this process, but rather to outline how elements of the civil society both fostered and were fostered by the unravelling of the system.[19]

The term *perestroika* (rebuilding, reconstruction, reorganisation) is one of those resounding but vague slogans favoured by politicians, especially when most people see the need for change but cannot agree on what changes they want or how deep they should go. It can cover a 'hidden agenda' or the lack of one. In practice Gorbachev's *perestroika* has gone through three phases: 'within-system' changes of structures and policies (1985-mid 1986); changes of important elements of the system, but not its key elements (late 1986-1989); changes in its key elements (1990-). Conflating the first two phases, let us look at how the process unfolded up to the beginning of 1990. This was a period of only modest economic reforms but of accelerating and ultimately profound changes in the cultural and political spheres.

In the economy the first tentative move towards systemic reform was the November 1986 law permitting individuals to engage in a variety of productive and service activities, although this was widely seen as aimed at little more than legalising (and taxing) a segment of the second economy. A June 1987 Law on State Enterprises potentially conferred on their managements a high level of commercial autonomy, but this was largely negated by a system of compulsory state orders. The most radical measure of this period, in terms of its short-term impact, was the May 1988 Law on Cooperatives. Within a year there were 100,000 production and service cooperatives in existence employing over two million members. However, they did not greatly benefit the mass consumer and generated a good deal of jealously and resentment. In agriculture the old system of collective and state farms remained intact, and modest measures allowing individual and cooperative leaseholdings had little impact owing to the caution of the farming population and the passive resistance of local party and government officialdom. Genuine economic radicalism was to be found chiefly in the sphere of ideas, where proposals pushing beyond 'market socialism' to quasi-capitalism were mooted more and more openly.[20]

It was in the dramatic widening of freedom of information, expression and association—surely key components in any civil society—that *perestroika* made its greatest impact during this period. This widening was very tentative up to the end of 1986, when Gorbachev made his remarkable telephone call to Academician Sakharov inviting him to return from exile in Gorki and resume his professional and public life. Hundreds of imprisoned dissidents were released and it was made clear that the non-violent activities of the kind for which they had been sentenced were now not only acceptable but actually valued as an aid to *perestroika*. Throughout 1987 and 1988 censorship and other controls over the media, the arts and public expression generally were progressively relaxed. The unofficial culture of the pre-Gorbachev era emerged from the shadows. Unofficial clubs and associations also came out in the open and multiplied rapidly; there were at least 60,000 of them by the end of 1988, perhaps a quarter of which were concerned with public issues of one kind or another. Many of them acquired printing facilities and some held public meetings and processions which would have been automatically crushed by the police just two years earlier. Freedom of information, of expression and of association were far from absolute, but in international and historical comparison they now looked very substantial.

Along with these public freedoms, democratisation also began to take off in 1987, although it developed more slowly. It had two aspects: on the one hand the change from elections as the ritual endorsement of bureaucratically chosen candidates to elections as a genuine choice between alternative candidates, including 'unofficial' ones; and on the other hand the conversion of the soviets, party conferences and committees and so on from mouthpieces of the bureaucracy into genuine decision-making or at least decision-influencing bodies. The first great breakthrough was the election campaign to the Congress of People's Deputies in March 1989 and the subsequent development of the Congress and the Supreme Soviet chosen by it into a regularly functioning parliament.

V

My central proposition here is that these developments, both the new freedoms and the progress towards democracy, would neither have moved so quickly nor gone so far, if indeed they could have occurred at all, had it not been for the pre-existing vestigial elements of the civil society discussed above, that is, without the forms and rhetoric of democracy immediately available to fill with democratic content, and without the experience of 'freedom of speech in one kitchen', of informal groups, of the 'shadow culture', which could then be played out on the wider public stage when the ideological, organisational and coercive controls of the regime were relaxed.

By the beginning of 1990 Soviet society had discarded several key components of the mono-organisational socialism which had prevailed there for two generations, and was beginning to free itself of the most fundamental of them—the directing and coordinating role of the party apparatus, its effective incorporation of all other social entities into a single organisational whole by virtue of its choice of their goals, their structures, and their leading personnel.

The breakthrough to relative freedom of information, expression and association had cost the apparatus its right to constantly direct and supervise all public communications and organised activity. Then, in keeping with decisions of the 19th Party Conference in June 1988, party committees were told to stop issuing directives to economic agencies as well, and three months later the Politburo ordered drastic cuts in the party apparatus that would deprive them of the capacity to do so. The party was now told it must cease being the key component of the 'command-administrative system', and concentrate its resources on the political role of framing national policy and winning the necessary popular support to have it implemented. The February-March 1990 decision that the party should abdicate its constitutional right to rule without opposition, with which I began this chapter, was therefore the culmination, not the beginning, of a process. And the central meaning of this process is not that the party is losing the privilege of facing the electors unopposed, but that it will no longer provide the essential cement of the mono-organisational system. This removed the chief obstacle to the revival of the civil society.

It removed the chief obstacle, but it did not remove all obstacles. Two major ones remained. The first was that the Stalinist command economy was still largely intact, and it was obvious to all that only a radical shift towards a market economy could ensure the level of individual autonomy essential to a stable civil society. When this radical shift was duly launched, in September 1990, it was of course motivated primarily by the critical state of the Soviet economy itself, but political considerations, including the ideal of a civil society, undoubtedly inspired many of the scholars, writers, journalists and political activists who contributed so vitally to the climate that made radical economic reform possible, if not inevitable. In any case, at the time of writing the prospects for a successful marketisation of the Soviet economy remain uncertain.

The other main obstacle was the existence of powerful forces within the party, military, police and bureaucratic elites, as well as part of the intelligentsia and the general population, who are hostile to all that goes to make the civil society, and who could still get the upper hand, especially in the event of a widespread breakdown of public order provoked by ethnic violence, strikes in the energy or transport sectors, food shortages, etc. Whether or not the fears of such an outcome were justified, they seemed virtually universal among liberal-minded Soviet citizens in the second half of 1990. If there were a conservative coup it could lead to the restoration of the

mono-organisational system in the form of a shabby and repressive
'barracks socialism', although a more limited autocratic regime
seems more likely. Either alternative could mean a second false dawn
for Russia's civil society, and one could only hope it would not be
followed by such a long, dark night as the false dawn of 1905–1917.

Notes

1   See John Keane (ed.), *Civil Society and the State: New European
     Perspectives* (London: Verso, 1988) Part Three, especially Z.A.
     Pelczynski, 'Solidarity and the "Rebirth of the Civil Society in Poland,
     1976–81"', pp. 361–380; and Robert F. Miller (ed.), *The Development of
     Civil Society in Communist Systems* (Sydney: Allen & Unwin,
     forthcoming).

2   XIX Всесоюзная конференция Коммунистической партии
     Советского Союза: Стенографический отчет (Moscow:
     Izdatel'stvo politicheskoi literatury, 1988) Vol.I, p. 118. On the nexus
     between the law-bound state, the civil society, and individual freedom, see
     В.С. Нерсесянц, 'Правовое государство: история и
     современность', Вопросы философии, no.2, 1989, pp. 3–18 at p.
     12.

3   А. Бутенко, 'Каким быть социализму?', Правда, 8 August 1989,
     p. 3 and А. Бутенко, Современный социализм (Moscow:
     Izdatel'stvo politicheskoi literatury, 1989) pp. 295–296. The ambiguities
     in Butenko's linkage of the civil society with socialism are as nothing
     compared with economist E.A. Ambartsumov's somewhat earlier
     gyrations. See Е.А. Амбарцумов 'О путях совершенствования
     политической системы социализма' in Ю.Н. Афанасьев (ed.),
     Иного не дано (Moscow: Progress, 1988) pp. 77–96, especially at pp.
     84–85.

4   М.С. Горбачев, 'Социалистическая идея и революционная
     перестройка' Коммунист, no.18, December 1989, pp. 3–20 at p. 17.

5   Roderic Pitty offered a valuable review and analysis in his paper 'Civil
     Society and Socialist Rhetoric in the USSR', presented to the 1989
     conference of the Australasian Political Studies Association.

6   See А. Мигранян, 'Механизм торможения в политической
     системе и пути его преодоления' in Ю.Н. Афанасьев (ed.),
     Иного не дано (Moscow: Progress, 1988) pp. 97–112; А. Мигранян,
     'Долгий путь к европейскому дому', Новый мир, no.7, July
     1989, pp. 166–184; and И. Клямкин and А. Мигранян, 'Нужна
     "Железная рука"?', Литературная газета, 16 August 1989, p. 10.

7   See, for example, Леонид Баткин, 'Мертвый хватает живого',
     Литературная газета, 20 September 1989, p. 10.

8   Gail W. Lapidus, 'State and Society: Toward the Emergence of Civil
     Society in the Soviet Union', in Seweryn Bialer (ed.), *Politics, Society
     and Nationality inside Gorbachev's Russia* (Boulder: Westview Press,
     1989) pp. 121–149.

9   S. Frederick Starr, 'Soviet Union: A Civil Society', *Foreign Affairs*, no.70, Spring 1988, pp. 26–41. See also Moshe Lewin, *The Gorbachev Phenomenon: A Historical Interpretation* (Berkeley: University of California Press, 1988), and H. Gordon Skilling, *Samizdat and an Independent Society in Central and Eastern Europe* (London: Macmillan, 1989) especially Chapter 7.

10   This image was not purely an esoteric scholarly one, but was constantly to be found in more popular literature. See, for example, The Reverend George Trevor, *Russia Ancient and Modern* (London: The Religious Tract Society, 1862) pp. 308–312.

11   For further discussion and reference to relevant sources on the ambiguous legacy of pre-revolutionary Russia, see T.H. Rigby, *The Changing Soviet System: Mono-organisational Socialism from its Origins to Gorbachev's Restructuring* (Aldershot: Edward Elgar, 1990), pp. 10–17.

12   See Leszek Kolakowski, *Main Currents of Marxism* (Oxford: Oxford University Press, 1978) Vol. II, pp. 467–527, especially pp. 515–517.

13   See Rigby, *The Changing Soviet System*, Chapter 4.

14   Western sovietologists produced a vast literature relevant to this section. See especially A. H. Brown, *Soviet Politics and Political Science* (London: Macmillan, 1974), H. Gordon Skilling and Franklyn Griffiths (eds), *Interest Groups in Soviet Politics* (Princeton: Princeton University Press, 1971), and Susan Gross Solomon, *Pluralism in the Soviet Union* (London: Macmillan, 1983). I attempted an account of relevant developments in the Khrushchev period in J.D.B. Miller and T.H. Rigby (eds), *The Disintegrating Monolith: Pluralist Trends in the Communist World* (Canberra: The Australian National University, 1965) pp. 17–45.

15   See, for example, Ernest J. Simmons, 'The Writers', in H. Gordon Skilling and Franklyn Griffiths (eds), *Interest Groups in Soviet Politics* (Princeton: Princeton University Press, 1971) pp. 253–289 at pp. 270–271; and T.H. Rigby, 'Party Elections in the CPSU', *Political Quarterly*, vol.35, no.4, 1964, pp. 420–443, at pp. 435–439.

16   See Ludmilla Alexeyeva, *Soviet Dissent: Contemporary Movements for National, Religious and Human Rights* (Middletown: Wesleyan University Press, 1985); and Rudolf L. Tökés (ed.), *Dissent in the USSR: Politics, Ideology and People* (Baltimore: The John Hopkins University Press, 1975).

17   Richard Sakwa, 'Civil Society and Commune Democracy during Perestroika', Paper presented to the Fourth World Congress of Soviet and East European Studies, Harrowgate, 1990, p. 9.

18   Амбарцумов 'О путях совершенствования политической системы социализма', p. 85. See Skilling, *Samizdat and an Independent Society* for a valuable analysis of similar developments in Central and Eastern Europe.

19   I examine these matters at greater length and cite relevant sources in *The Changing Soviet System*, Chapter 9. See also Archie Brown (ed.), *Political Leadership in the Soviet Union* (London: Macmillan, 1989); Alec Nove, *Glasnost' in Action: Cultural Renaissance in Russia* (Boston: Unwin Hyman, 1989); and Stephen White, *Gorbachev in Power* (Cambridge: Cambridge University Press, 1990).

20   The best account of economic changes and debates during this period is
     Anders Åslund, *Gorbachev's Struggle for Economic Reform: The Soviet
     Reform Process 1985–88* (London: Frances Pinter, 1989).

7

Civil Society and Systemic Legitimation in the USSR

LESLIE HOLMES

I

Although I do not wish to become over-embroiled in semantics, the very heated debates there have been in recent times concerning the meanings of 'civil society',[1] 'legitimation', and even 'system' mean that any analysis of these in the USSR, or anywhere else, must start with a definition of terms.

Of the three terms, 'civil society' is perhaps the most difficult both to define in the abstract and to identify in 'the real world'. According to Antony Black,[2] the term 'civil society' entered European usage approximately six centuries ago, reviving an interest of Cicero's in first-century B.C. Rome. In its medieval usage, the term implied civil relations within society and a proper legal code. It also covered *both* society *and* the state. By the late-18th century, the term had begun to develop a pejorative connotation for many analysts. For Marx, for instance, 'civil' society was in reality the hypocritical and egocentric bourgeois society, in which individuals and groups sought to circumvent the laws and the ethical code of the state—ultimately by dominating the state. In this more recent conception, there is a clear distinction between civil society and the state, although they are in a very close relationship. Let me now turn to a far more recent and more local perspective.

At a conference on civil society and communist systems held at the Australian National University on 9 March 1990, Eugene Kamenka argued that ultimately the term 'civil society' as we tend to use it is not clearly distinguishable from 'society'; for this reason, he—and others at the conference, such as Barry Hindess—suggested that we might simply use the term 'society'. Whilst having some sympathy with this position, and whilst recognising the considerable problems involved in defining the parameters of 'civil' society, I would argue that there is still some mileage in the term. Expressed very crudely, it seems to me appropriate to distinguish between *three* closely related but discrete phenomena. The first is just 'a society', which can be defined as the sum-total of a complex set of interactions of individuals, structures, functions, ideas and mores, that is sufficiently distinguishable from other aggregations to be recognised as an entity both by (at least most) of the people comprising it and by external agents, notably other societies. Such an entity has its own internal dynamics and is obviously a living phenomenon. Nevertheless, by talking merely of 'society', we are—it is argued here—not making any statements about levels or types of politicisation of society. For instance, there is nothing implicit here about the relationship with the state. Borrowing and adapting an idea from Marx, I would want to use the term 'society' in the sense of an entity *in* itself, without any reference to its own self-awareness in a political sense (that is, *for* itself). At the other end of the spectrum is the overtly highly politicised society, which can be called 'political society'. But this term can be both ambiguous and misleading. In communist systems, for instance, societies might appear to be highly 'politicised', but in a way that is so fundamentally different from what is normally understood by this term in liberal democracies that to apply the term to both kinds of system blurs or even completely overlooks some important differences. Most notably, a 'politicised' society in a communist system *may* mean no more than that the citizens (most of the members of society) are subject to constant, intensive and overt (purposive) socialisation. People might communicate in 'the language of communism', yet do not (dare?) fundamentally to question the nature of the system and therefore could be argued to have a shallower normative attachment to it than in a situation in which people *are* 'encouraged' to think critically about their system and, having done so, *believe* they are better off with that system than with any alternative.[3] Expressed another way, I wish to distinguish between a situation in which citizens are basically imbibers—being subject to political values, ideas, etc. from the state (in communist systems, the party-state complex) and one in which citizens to a perceptible degree play, or have the legitimate right to play, a meaningful, *self-motivated*, *self-directed*, and *self-regulating* role. For a full-blooded political society to exist, this distinction between externally directed and self-directed activity is critical—only where the latter pertains is there, in my opinion, political society in its true sense; the former arrangement, for the sake of clarity, could be called 'politically directed society'.

So where does 'civil' society fit in? As used by Kukathas and Lovell in chapter 2, the term is virtually coterminous with 'the market' writ large:

> ... civil society is a complex of institutions and practices which make up 'the market', as well as associations of individuals who join together to pursue all sorts of goals beyond narrowly economic ones.

By including the modifier 'narrowly' in the latter part of this definition, Kukathas and Lovell are—at least implicitly—suggesting that civil society *is* basically concerned with economic activity that is autonomous of the state. If this were all there were to civil society, much of the rest of this paper would be concerned with the uncoupling of the economy in the USSR. Whilst this will and should constitute a major dimension of the discussion, I would argue that civil society cannot be reduced to, essentially, autonomous economic activity.

For T.H. Rigby, civil society clearly relates to 'the political sphere' as well as to 'the socio-economic sphere'. His definition, given in chapter 6—[4]

> ... it consists of those structures and processes through which individuals and groups interact autonomously of the command structures of the state in pursuit of their particular concerns

—is clearly a broader one than that of Kukathas and Lovell, and it is significant that there is no explicit reference in Rigby's definition to the economic sphere. Of course, one *can* argue that, ultimately, everything is reducible to economics—or, at least, self-interest, with economic activity in its broad sense being the most visible manifestation of this. But one can equally well argue that, ultimately, everything is reducible to politics (power-relations) or to the sexual drive (eros) or to the fear of death (thanatos). Such holistic and reductionist approaches have some intrinsic interest, but are, at the end of the day, matters of faith, unverifiable, and certainly hinder complex, multi-factoral analyses that might bring us closer to 'the truth' than such reductionist arguments. Partially for this reason, I would opt for Rigby's broader approach than for the approach of Kukathas and Lovell, *especially* for analysing the USSR. In particular, I would fully endorse the point Rigby makes that—at least for analysing Soviet-type societies—one should not draw a sharp line between 'civil society' and 'the political order' but 'between the civil society and specifically the command structures of the state'.

Implicit in this approach is the concept of *autonomy*; this is the concept most obviously juxtaposed with 'the *command* structures of the state'. I would argue—as already intimated above—that the emergence of 'civil society' relates to the development of autonomous, self-motivated, self-directed, self-regulated and legitimate activity by individuals and groups of individuals. Such activity can relate to the economy, to religious and philosophical beliefs—indeed to any sphere of human activity. It certainly *can* relate to *political* activity, as long as this is understood to be self-motivated and self-regulated by citizens rather than activity directly or indirectly motivated and controlled by the party-state complex. Indeed, one does not have to be a Marxist to accept that the notion of autonomous economic activity emerging without overt or implicit political activity is unrealistic. If, as seems almost certain, competitive market-relations become a salient feature of Soviet society, then they will, inter alia, mean a substantial reduction in the steering role of the party-state complex—in short, a reduction in the role of the state in its broad sense. This *is* political, so that to concentrate solely, or predominantly, on economic activity is being unduly and inappropriately self-limiting.

Whilst 'civil society', as the term is used here, is clearly distinguishable from just 'society'—civil society is, in terms of our earlier analogy, society *for* itself—it might be less obvious in what way it is distinguishable from political society. Two points need to be made in answering this. The first is to remind the reader of the distinction I have drawn between 'politically-directed society' and 'political society in its full-blooded sense'. The former is logically incompatible with civil society,[5] whilst the latter is only one part of civil society. Thus, just as I reject the notion of civil society being essentially equivalent to economic activity that is autonomous of the state, so do I reject the notion that civil society is essentially equivalent to self-motivated and self-directed political activity that is essentially autonomous of (though by no means necessarily non-interactive with) the state. In my view, civil society includes *both* these activities and more. In other words, 'political society in its full-blooded sense' is one part of civil society.

Purely for the sake of analysis, and being fully aware of the limitations and dangers involved in elaborating the component parts of analysis, I shall in this paper very briefly consider five major dimensions of civil society:

i   Political activity that explicitly challenges the party-state's policies;

ii   Political activity that explicitly challenges the political system;

iii   Economic activity that explicitly or implicitly challenges the party-state's policies and, eventually, the political system (even if such activity has initially been sanctioned by that system);

iv   Overt interest in and involvement with value-systems that are in conflict with those of the party-state complex (notably religion);

iv   The uncoupling of the legal system from the party-state complex.

Before I move on to this part of the analysis, the terms 'legitimation' and 'system' have still to be defined.

For the purposes of this paper, legitimation refers to the *process* whereby a political order seeks to acquire legitimacy. A 'political order' can be disaggregated into two component parts—the system and the regime. Elsewhere I have argued at length that the distinction often (implicitly or explicitly) drawn between 'system' and 'regime' is for most purposes too stark.[6] Whilst regimes will often attempt to legitimate both the system and themselves, they will normally opt for the latter if a choice has to be made. Nevertheless, they will also generally attempt to modify the system at the same time as they seek to enhance their own legitimacy. In this approach, therefore, the system—in the case of the USSR, a Marxist-Leninist system with a communist telos—is perceived as an entity that can and does change over time. It is, expressed another way, in a dynamically interactive relationship with the regime. Whereas 'the system' here refers to the official political structures, processes and goals in a given country, the regime is the particular leadership team that takes upon itself the running and interpretation of the system at any given point in time. It is argued in this essay that this symbiotic relationship between the system and the regime operates within a limited context, not indefinitely. In other words, there is a limit to how far the regime can remould a system; at a certain point, the system has changed so much in terms of structures, processes and goals that it ceases to be recognisable even as an 'updated' or 'modified' version of the original concept. The familiar analogy of water and steam (or ice!) is appropriate here. It is argued that marginal modification to the system can be made over time—the water can heat up one degree at a time, and thus be different (warmer) from its earlier state; but at a certain point—100 degrees Celsius—it ceases to change merely quantitatively and is transformed qualitatively. This image will be particularly appropriate to the subsequent discussion of the emergence of civil society and systemic legitimation in the USSR.

Having defined our terms, we can now consider the dynamics of system legitimation in the USSR; this will be followed by a discussion of the emergence of civil society, the implications of this for system legitimation, and a concluding section in which the inherent contradictions of the process identified will be highlighted.

II

In any political order, power is exercised predominantly in one of two ways—coercively or on the basis of legitimation (that is, normatively).[7] By using the word 'predominantly', I am intending to highlight the fact that power is *always* exercised in *any* system on the basis of *both* coercion and legitimation; one is talking, therefore, about the relative balance between these two elements. Bearing this point in mind, the dynamics of the Soviet exercise of power can be considered. The ensuing argument is, of course, postulated on the assumption that there *is* a dynamic; if this is not accepted, the argument becomes largely invalid.

In the early days of Bolshevik rule, the leaders were primarily concerned with consolidating power and defining the system; Marx, after all, had not specified in any detail what kind of political arrangements would follow a *timely* socialist revolution, let alone a premature one. Once the system was consolidated and more or less clarified, coercion became the major way in which power was exercised. By the 1930s, the most extreme form of coercion—state terror—had become salient. Even at this stage, there were *some* attempts at legitimation, of course—to a limited extent in terms of what Rigby has called 'goal rationality' (the proclamation of socialism in 1936 is an example of this), to some extent in terms of official nationalism (for example the concept of 'socialism in one country', and describing Soviet involvement in the Second World War as 'The Great Patriotic War') and to no small degree in terms of charisma (the personality cult that was constructed around Stalin). By the 1950s, and with a new leadership team that appeared to want to exercise power more in terms of normative acceptance than of coercion, the relative balance between coercion and legitimation began to change. Without doubt, the major *symbol* of this was the 'Secret Speech' of February 1956, in which so much of Stalinism was rejected. There was an even greater emphasis at this time on goal-rational (teleological) legitimation—the Communist Party of the Soviet Union (CPSU) Party Programme of 1961 is a prime symbol of this. But there also gradually emerged a greater emphasis on eudaemonic legitimation. One early sign of this was Malenkov's stress on the consumer in the period 1953–1955. But eudaemonism was not the *dominant* form of legitimation at this time; in addition to goal-rationality—of which competition with the West was another important symbol—there was also a growing, if limited, emphasis on Khrushchev's charisma. Whilst the Khrushchevian personality cult never reached the proportions of Stalin's, it would be unwise to overlook Khrushchev's own attempts at charismatic legitimation.

Following Khrushchev's ouster, there were certainly signs that coercion was still a major dimension of the Soviet political order, notably in the treatment of both dissidents and unofficial nationalists. But the Brezhnev era—particularly in the early stages—also witnessed some important signs of further moves towards eudaemonic legitimation. Perhaps the most significant symbols of this were the two major economic reforms of 1965—of agriculture in March, and of industry and planning in September. The subsequent putative emphasis on the consumer at the expense of the capital goods sector in the 1971–75 plan, and the replacement of the concept of the economic plan with that of the economic and social plan, were further signs of the regime's attempt to legitimate both itself and the system in terms of eudaemonism.

Unfortunately, eudaemonism was far from successful. The reforms did not bring the intended improvements in living standards, for a variety of reasons. One of the most important was that the bureaucracies that were to implement the reforms were also to be negatively affected by them; given both certain ambiguities in the leaders' own policies—commentators have noted the different goals and approaches of Brezhnev and Kosygin, for instance—and the desire on the part of the leadership to show their staffs, at least, that the coercion and arbitrariness of the past were not to be a feature of their rule (which largely explains the 'stability of cadres' policy),[8] the bureaucracies were able to a considerable extent to nullify the attempts at eudaemonism-related reform.

The later Brezhnev era was a period of waiting; applying the words of Abel Aganbegian, 'we waited, we slept'.[9] Of course, both coercive and legitimation-based forms of power continued to be exercised, but there was, to no small extent, a sense of expectation. The regime really had 'stagnated'—Gorbachev's term is an apt one—

but it had not yet fundamentally lost its way. Old ways of thinking and doing things were not *seriously* being questioned in the centres of power.

But the 1980s witnessed a growing crisis in the USSR. Following the continuation of a sense of limbo that the Andropov and Chernenko eras represented, by the mid-1980s those who had most power in the system had realised that the state of limbo could not and should not continue. 1980 had come and gone, and no-one was cynical enough to claim that the bases of communism had been laid. With an economy that was not merely slowing down, but was actually falling behind in its competition with the West, an emphasis on goal-rationality would have seemed inappropriate. The new (Gorbachev) regime could have returned to a predominance of coercion, but the new leaders were too sophisticated not to realise that this becomes an increasingly brittle and dysfunctional form of power. For one thing, and as Solzhenitsyn highlights so well in *The First Circle*, an economy will not function as well if the overall system operates mainly through coercion as when it operates on a more normative basis.

Rather than return to coercion, Gorbachev sought to base his regime's legitimacy on eudaemonism, and in the first couple of years of his 'reign', economic *perestroika* was a top priority. *Inter alia*, this had major implications for foreign policy, since Gorbachev appreciated that Soviet adventurism and expansionism was one reason why Soviet consumers had fared so badly; this was a major reason for the emergence of 'new thinking' in foreign policy. But a winding down of Soviet involvement in so many parts of Europe, Asia, Africa and even Latin America was only one part of restructuring. Gorbachev also realised that the concept of the centrally-planned economy itself was in desperate need of a major overhaul. Gorbachev realised that there would have to be a fairly major 'uncoupling' of the economy if there were to be any real hope of major improvement; this point will be elaborated in the next section.

In my view, Gorbachev appreciated at the time he took power that one of the major reasons why reform—the success of which was crucial to the fate of eudaemonic legitimation—had largely failed was that the bureaucracy was conservative. Unlike the Brezhnev-Kosygin team, therefore, he did not opt for a major economic reform policy early in his tenure. Rather, he decided to attack the bureaucracies first; only by doing this could he hope to be in a position further down the track to introduce reforms that—this time—would be properly implemented. The basis for his attack had been laid by Andropov, who had launched a major anti-corruption campaign almost as soon as he had taken office. Gorbachev pursued this, although he placed somewhat less emphasis on state bureaucrats and considerably more on party apparatchiki than his hero and former mentor had done. He also engaged in various *structural* reforms; the major changes made in the administration of agriculture since 1985 suggest, however, either that Gorbachev had not really thought through his restructuring or else had decided to adopt some policies quickly and to modify them subsequently in the light of experience.[10]

To some extent, in attacking the staffs Gorbachev had a vision of taking the USSR into a particular form of legal-rationality. Theorists from Weber to Poggi have argued that this is the only form of legitimation really appropriate to the modern state, and the early signs of movement in this direction did suggest that the USSR might at long last be in transition to full modernity.[11] The emphasis on *glasnost'* and *demokratizatsiia* were symbols of this new move, and there were numerous concrete signs that Gorbachev's commitment to these ideas was real enough. Eventually, in May 1988, Gorbachev made his first explicit reference to the need for a socialist legal state (*sotsialisticheskoe pravovoe gosudarstvo*),[12] Having moved through charisma, goal-rationality and eudaemonism as the predominant modes of legitimation—with official nationalism as a minor mode— the Soviet regime had reached the stage at which power was to be exercised primarily through legal-rationality, with minor emphasis on new traditionalism,[13] and even, perhaps, charisma.

Before examining the inherent contradictions in these moves, let us now briefly consider how this dynamism of legitimation related to the emergence of civil society in the USSR.

III

Two of the most significant points to be made about the emergence of civil society in the USSR in recent times are that (i) it was initiated and has to no small extent—at least until only recently—been guided and timed *from above*; but just as the leadership believed it could introduce a limited form of legal-rationality, it also believed it could limit and control a form of civil society, and (ii) the Soviet leadership has now largely lost control because of fundamental contradictions in the way civil society has emerged, and because both legal-rationality and civil society are basically incompatible with a Leninist system.

Much of the discussion of these two points is more appropriate to the final two sections of the paper; they are made here simply to contextualise what follows—to alert the reader to the underlying tensions that exist in the developments. Let us now very briefly— unfortunately space precludes a detailed analysis—examine civil society in terms of the five variables listed earlier.

Political activity that challenges the party-state's policies has, of course, existed throughout the period since 1917; what follows can only be an over-generalised brushstroke of a complex phenomenon (although I believe it more or less approximates to perceived reality). Nevertheless, such activity has expanded and changed dramatically (that is, there have been both quantitative and qualitative developments) in recent times, to a considerable extent because of the policy of glasnost'. The expansion and change has taken a number of forms. First, and arguably most significantly, challenges to policies have now become far more legitimate in terms of what the party- state authorities will tolerate. Whilst it is true that many officials— especially CPSU apparatchiki—have publicly expressed concern at the openness of debate, the aggregate position of the party-state complex has shifted markedly. Second, and following on closely from the first point, the nature of legitimate challenges has changed. In the past, as the USSR moved from the highly-centralised, quasi- totalitarian control of the Stalin era to the limited pluralism of the 1970s, there emerged a process of widening consultation before the adoption of policies. But two of the most important aspects of this consultation were that the leaders chose whom they would consult (usually specialists in the given policy-area), and that such specialists overwhelmingly made proposals rather than demands. By the late- 1980s, the leadership had recognised a much broader conception of pluralism, in which groups generally—not just specialists—could make demands more or less legitimately. Changed leadership attitudes towards strikes, the rights of ethnic minorities, and issue- oriented groups such as environmentalists are examples of this. Third, the range of issues publicly discussed has widened—partly because people are now more aware, as a direct result of glasnost', of far more instances of state mendacity, incompetence and hypocrisy than they ever were.

Political activity that challenges the political system itself has not yet been fully accepted by the regime, although the situation is developing at an extraordinary pace. Of course, one can often see *implicit* criticisms of the system in challenges to the party-state's policies, and in this sense the distinction I have drawn is in some senses too sharp. Nevertheless, many groups do now very explicitly challenge the system in a far more open way and on a broader scale than in the pre-1985 or even in the pre-1988 period and this needs to be highlighted. By mid-1990, for instance, there were at least 140 popular fronts (mostly based on specific geographical units and/or ethnic groups), a number of issue-oriented groups that linked their concerns with the nature of the Soviet system (for example environmental groups such as the Social Ecological Union) and even several organisations describing themselves as political parties (such as the Democratic Party of the USSR, established in August 1989; the Liberal Democratic Party, established in March 1990; the Social Democratic Party of Russia, established in May 1990).[14]

Although I have earlier drawn a fairly clearcut distinction between the regime and the system, it is appropriate to disaggregate the latter one step further. Thus we are talking not only about a communist system—with its democratic centralism, Marxism-Leninism, and so on—but also a Soviet federal system. *Both* of these are now explicitly attacked; often one group will launch an attack against both component parts. It would seem that the authorities are at *present* more tolerant of attacks on the first part than on the second, largely because the authorities want some control over the dismantling/breakup of the Soviet 'internal empire'. The term 'not ... fully accepted' was used earlier partly because of the limitations on public associations contained in the draft law first adopted by the Supreme Soviet in May 1990,[15] and partly because of the nature of Moscow's reaction to the Lithuanian declaration of independence in March 1990 (and the declaration of most Soviet republics in the following months). Regarding the latter, for instance, clearly the Kremlin was miffed, and it took measures against Vilnius. On the other hand, the Lithuanians' statements and behaviour were not taken as *so* intolerable that the Gorbachev team was prepared to use outright coercion. Even if the *reasons* why the Soviets did not use more explicit (military) force against the Lithuanians in the first half of 1990 and against other republics subsequently relate to Moscow's anticipation of negative Western reactions, the fact is that the Soviet leadership was less willing to use outright force against such radical challenges than it would have been just a few years ago. In this sense, the political aspects of civil society are rapidly emerging, but are still—as of mid-1990—subject to some restrictions by the state.

The moves towards economic uncoupling are several, and again can only be briefly outlined here. As T.H. Rigby has pointed out in chapter 6, the 1986 law permitting small-scale, private, mostly service-oriented economic activity was not particularly significant, in that it was largely intended to help the state by subjecting a substantial proportion of the already existing underground economy to taxation. This was followed by yet another attempt—in June 1987—to devolve much decision-making to state-run enterprises. A far more radical and significant step was taken with the 1988 law on cooperatives. This has been a controversial policy, and its implementation has enjoyed very mixed results. According to official statistics, there were almost 200,000 cooperatives in the USSR by the end of 1989, employing almost 5 million people.[16] But the cooperatives are just one (albeit important) symbol of the *general* move in the USSR towards a competitive and largely privatised market economy. At the time of writing (October 1990), almost all parts of the party-state complex had accepted that moves in such a direction were inevitable, even desirable, and Soviet President Gorbachev had been working closely with Academician Aganbegian to finalise a plan that would be a compromise between the radical proposal of Stanislav Shatalin and the far more cautious proposal of Soviet prime minister Nikolai Ryzhkov and his advisor Abalkin. Despite being a compromise, this plan was far closer to Shatalin's proposal than to Ryzhkov's. If this—or something like it—is implemented, the party-state complex will have accepted the most extensive uncoupling of the economy since the Bolsheviks took power. In turn, this would represent an enormous step on the road to the autonomous economic activity so many commentators see as either an, or even the most, important aspect of civil society. On *one* level, this move to a competitive, largely privatised economy might serve as the basis for a *relatively* smooth transition to post-communist modernity, even as it undermines overall system legitimacy. If, in the medium term, it both increases the supply of consumer goods and, over a longer period, serves as a base for the emergence of a real market and overwhelmingly privatised economy in the USSR, then the Soviet Union (or whatever the post-empire country is called) might be legitimated largely in terms of eudaemonism.

As in the countries of Eastern Europe, this question of the emergence of a market is critical to the future of the USSR. The Soviet authorities are certainly adopting many measures to make it more possible. In addition to the cooperatives, for instance, the rapidly changing legislation on joint ventures since 1987 and the probable emergence of Special Economic Zones in Vyborg, Nakhodka and elsewhere are but two examples. Given that such autonomous economic activity is accepted as a necessary component of a real civil society, its progress will be a key indicator of the state of civil society in what is presently the Soviet Union. But it does present profound challenges to the communist system. Before elaborating these, let us briefly consider two other dimensions of civil society—autonomous religious activity and the growing autonomy of the legal system.

Whilst Soviet official policy towards religion has varied considerably since 1917—depending both on the particular period and the particular church or sect—Marxism-Leninism has always been a humanist ideology that can at best reluctantly tolerate what its adherents see as a basically metaphysical belief-system. But here, too, radical change is afoot in the USSR. Not only has the oppression of religious groups almost ceased, and once forbidden churches either *de facto* or *de jure* recognised (for example the Ukrainian Autocephalous Orthodox Church, which held an organisational council in June 1990), but certain fundamental religious rights have now been formally recognised. Thus, following its positive response to a similar draft in May 1990[17], the Supreme Soviet in October 1990 almost unanimously (by 341 votes to 2) gave approval to a law that forbids the state from restricting the study, financing or propagandising of any religion and that recognises churches as juridical persons with property rights; this latter point relates to the earlier argument about privatisation of the economy, of course. Moreover, members of the armed forces will, when off duty, now be permitted to attend all forms of church service.[18] And a 1929 resolution of the Russian Soviet Federative Socialist Republic is to be rescinded so that churches will now be able to organise social and charitable work. In sum, religion is being legitimised by the Soviet state—yet another sign of the emergence of civil society.

Much of the recent change in Soviet legal theory and practice could be argued to represent greater 'within system' autonomy, here meaning that there has been a move towards greater 'separation of powers' within the party-state complex. If this were all that the changes represent, they would be of marginal relevance to a study of emerging civil society. But in addition to calls and moves to make the judiciary more independent of the CPSU, for instance, there have been moves to upgrade the citizen's rights *vis-à-vis* the system—which many analysts, myself included, would see as another aspect of the development of civil society. Amongst the numerous changes that have occurred and are occurring in this area, it seems appropriate to focus on the changing attitudes towards those accused of having committed crimes (exemplified by the moves underway to end the situation in which a defendant is in essence considered guilty unless proven innocent and the increasing role and autonomy of defence lawyers); the moves to demystify the KGB and to make it more publicly answerable; and the laws that have been passed enabling the citizen, for the first time, to lay formal charges against party and state officialdom.[19]

IV

It was argued earlier that the Soviet system needs to be disaggregated—into its 'communist' and its 'Soviet federal' components. At first sight, the emergence of civil society would appear to have greater implications for the former than for the latter; indeed, it might even appear that it should have *no* direct implications for the latter. But I would argue this is not the case. I would maintain that patterns of nationalist unrest relate at least partially—often largely—to economic performance. Since patriotism exists in most societies most of the time, and since the existing borders of countries and particular ethnic configurations of many of the world's states are *relatively* recent, one needs to explain why nationalism becomes more of a force at some periods than at others. Whilst economic performance is certainly not the *only* factor—leadership and possibilities for achieving change are two other significant variables—it *is* important. In this sense, it could be argued that if the emergence of a market-dominated economy were to lead to markedly improved economic performance, then eudaemonic legitimation would be more effective and system legitimacy would increase.

Unfortunately for the Soviet leadership, it is not quite as relatively simple—the development of a market is always difficult—as the above scenario might imply. In uncoupling the economy and moving towards a market, the 'communist' component of the system moves increasingly into an identity crisis. Moreover, communism as a system—with its emphasis on vanguardism, voluntarism, and *de facto* personalisation of power—is fundamentally incompatible with real legal-rationality, a *sine qua non* of modern civil society. One of the key features of legal-rational legitimation is the depersonalisation—perhaps impersonalisation—of politics, in the sense that the system cannot be seen to depend on particular individuals. The Soviet leadership seems not to appreciate this (or, perhaps, not to want to acknowledge this). Gorbachev's recent moves to strengthen the state and, in particular, his role as President of that state, testify to this.

His moves towards legal-rational legitimation were always, as mentioned above, intended to be *limited*. They were taken to overcome the conservatism of the bureaucracy and to gain a certain amount of mass legitimacy as a way of buying time; their ultimate aim was never a fully modern state in the Western sense, but an efficient, well-performing communist state—albeit an updated, more pluralistic communist state. Eudaemonism was always, I would argue, the ultimate goal; limited legal-rationality and the tolerance of aspects of a civil society were seen as a means to this end, not an end in itself. But the leadership misjudged how serious the problems in the economy were. Given this, civil society has *now* acquired a momentum of its own. The 'communist' system is in crisis, which, in my opinion, will result fairly shortly in collapse. The Soviet leadership has tried to move towards more 'modern' dominant modes of legitimation, but, in the process, has undermined the basic principles of communism. It looks increasingly like a system in which all the negative features of capitalism—inflation, unemployment, insecurity—are being officially accepted, but in which the comparatively positive features are barely present.[20] Because of this, I cannot agree with the argument—expressed, for instance, by Margot Jacobs[21]—that the emergence of civil society may relieve the Soviet state of some of its burdens and thus buttress it. Even if this were to happen peacefully, such qualitative changes would have taken place in the Soviet communist system that it would cease to be recognisable as such, and would hence be in a systemic legitimation crisis.

V

It has been argued in this essay that, in its early stages, the emergence of civil society in the USSR was largely controlled by the state. That state felt that both coercion and a number of previous modes of legitimation were now largely dysfunctional and outdated. Eudaemonism was the ultimate aim, but the state had to move into a form of legal-rationality in order subsequently to bring about a situation in which eudaemonism might be possible as the dominant mode of system legitimation. Unfortunately, it was postulated on the assumption that the economy would 'pick up' relatively quickly. That assumption was wrong, and the state has had to tolerate further moves into legal-rationality and the uncoupled economy. In doing so, it moves increasingly into an identity crisis—a total crisis of systemic legitimation. The state could try reverting to coercion— as the Chinese state did in June 1989. But the crisis is deeper in the USSR than in the PRC.[22] Moreover, it is not clear to me that the civilian politicians would be *able* to mobilise their own coercive apparatuses against the masses; the military has every reason to feel alienated by Gorbachev's policies and attitudes, and might prefer to take power than to save the civilian communist politicians.

Civil society now has a momentum of its own in the USSR—the leadership can no longer limit it. Although, in theory, it might appear that communism is the only component of the system that can no longer be legitimated, I would argue that the Soviet federal component is so inextricably linked with communism that it, too, can no longer be legitimated. Moreover, whatever the post-communism arrangements look like, it will be some time before an identifiable *system* emerges. In this sense, not only does the emergence of civil society negatively affect communist systemic legitimation, but it seems that there will, for a while, be no proper system legitimation since there will be no identifiable 'system'.

One final point is that it is not at all clear what kind of system that aggregate we are tending to call civil society in the USSR (or its successor) will *want*. As in Eastern Europe, so in the USSR the abandonment of communism will be far more a (negative) rejection of the current system—with its mendacity, hypocrisy, corruption, elitism and incompetence—than the (positive) adoption of some alternative. Too many possibilities present themselves for me to discuss here; I shall therefore briefly consider two polarised possibilities. On the one hand, it should be acknowledged that there is *some*—albeit not great—possibility that the transition to post-communism in the USSR will be *relatively* peaceful; it should not be forgotten that 'the' revolution in Eastern Europe took many forms, and that the violence of the Romanian rejection of Ceausescuism was countered by the relatively very smooth transition in Hungary. On the other hand, if the rapidly emerging civil society leads not only to a transformation of communism into post-communism, but also from a federal system to a series of sovereign states, we might well have to witness a series of wars akin to the one that has already emerged between Armenia and Azerbaijan (or, indeed, different parts of Yugoslavia). The collapse of the Soviet federal communist state may not only signal the collapse of the system—and hence render the issue of systemic legitimation redundant—but may, as intimated by William Maley in chapter 10, also be accompanied by the emergence of a series of most *uncivil* societies. In that the emergence of a markedly improved economic situation in the USSR is the main hope for avoiding, or at least containing, such a situation, the rapid and successful emergence and performance of the economic component of civil society becomes all-important. In this particular sense, at least, I can agree with Kukathas and Lovell's focus on the economic aspect of 'civil society'.

Notes

1   For a relatively early analysis in the context of the USSR see S. Frederick Starr, 'Soviet Union: A Civil Society', *Foreign Policy*, no. 70, Spring 1988, pp. 26–41.

2   See Antony Black, *Guilds and Civil Society in European Political Thought from the Twelfth Century to the Present* (London: Methuen, 1984) *passim* and especially pp. 32–43.

3   I am not concerned here with the question of how such values are inculcated, or whether citizens are subject either to the Marcusian conception of 'false consciousness' or Lukes's conception of interests in his 'three dimensional' approach to power.

4   This approach is close to that of A. Butenko (a Professor at Moscow State University) who sees civil society as a system external to the state apparatus that links independent citizens (Правда, 8 August 1989, p. 3). Perhaps the most important theoretical difference between Rigby's and Butenko's approaches is that the latter implies civil society is one system whereas Rigby's approach is that it is the aggregate of a multitude of sets of autonomous activity. I would see Rigby's approach as being a more accurate reflection of the reality of civil society in the contemporary USSR.

5   In the real world, of course, they are not so clearly incompatible. The present unrest in the USSR—to take just one example—appears to indicate that there is a transitional phase from one to the other; the very notion of transition implies, at the least, a degree of coexistence on a temporary basis.

6   Leslie Holmes, *Crisis, Collapse and Corruption in the Communist World* (Cambridge: Polity Press, 1991) *passim* and especially Chapter 1.

7   Many analysts—see for example Alexander Dallin and George Breslauer, *Terror In Communist Systems* (Stanford: Stanford University Press, 1970) at p. 1—argue that there is a third way in which power is exercised, namely *material* power; if coercion is the stick, material power is the carrot. I do not accept that material power is a discrete form of power. Rather, I see it as a sub-division either of coercive or of normative (legitimation-based) power, depending on the particular circumstances.

8   For an analysis of this policy see T.H. Rigby, 'The Soviet Leadership: Towards a Self-Stabilising Oligarchy?', *Soviet Studies*, vol.22, no.2, April 1970, pp. 167–191, especially p. 179.

9   'Мы ждали, мы спали'. These words—used by Aganbegian in conversation with the author in October 1987—were actually used in reference to the Chernenko era; they are, however, very apt here.

10   For analyses of Soviet agricultural reform under Gorbachev see for example Karl-Eugen Wädekin, 'Agriculture' in Martin McCauley (ed.), *Gorbachev and Perestroika* (London: Macmillan, 1990) pp. 70–95; Stephen White, *Gorbachev in Power* (Cambridge: Cambridge University Press, 1990) at pp. 94–97.

11   For Weber's views see for example. Max Weber, 'Legitimacy, Politics and the State' in William Connolly (ed.), *Legitimacy and the State* (Oxford: Blackwell, 1984) pp. 32–62, especially at p. 34. For Poggi's argument see Gianfranco Poggi, *The Development of the Modern State* (London: Hutchinson, 1978).

12   For the speech in which Gorbachev first used this term see Правда, 11 May 1988, p. 2.

13   By 'new traditionalism' I mean a form of legitimation which harks back to the early days of communist rule (that is, the Lenin era) and contrasts this with the distortions created by Stalin and Stalinism; for a fuller elaboration see Holmes, *Crisis, Collapse and Corruption in the Communist World*, Chapter 1.

14   See *Moscow News*, no.7, 1990, pp. 8–9 and no.28, 1990, pp. 8–9; Известия, 1 April 1990, p. 1. For an analysis of the emergence and nature of the 'informals' (неформалы) in Russia between 1988 and 1989 see Vladimir Brovkin, 'Revolution from Below: Informal Political Associations in Russia 1988–1989', *Soviet Studies*, vol.42, no.2, April 1990, pp. 233–257. For a more recent analysis of Soviet and Russian parties see E. Robson, 'Political Parties in the USSR', *Soviet Analyst*, vol. 19, no. 13, 4 July 1990, pp. 2–5.

15   See Известия, 31 May 1990, pp. 1 and 4.

16   *Moscow News*, no. 12, 1990, p. 10. For a Western analysis of the development of both individual and cooperative activity see Karin Plokker, 'The Development of Individual and Cooperative Labour Activity in the Soviet Union', *Soviet Studies*, vol.42, no.3, July 1990, pp. 403–428.

17   See Известия, 31 May 1990, p. 4.

18   On religious policy up to the mid-1980s see for example T.H. Rigby, 'Regime and Religion in the USSR', in R.F. Miller and T.H. Rigby (eds), *Religion and Politics in Communist States* (Canberra: Department of Political Science, Research School of Social Sciences, Australian National University, 1986) pp. 10–27; there is an extensive bibliography in footnote 35. For a more up-to-date overview that also explicitly considers the relationship between nationality and religious policies in the USSR see Bohdan Bociurkiw, 'Nationalities and Soviet Religious Policies', in L. Hajda and M. Bessinger (eds), *The Nationalities Factor in Soviet Politics and Society* (Boulder: Westview Press, 1990) pp. 148–174. For the new 'Law on the Freedom of Conscience and of Religious Organisations' adopted on 1 October 1990 see Ведомости Съезда

Народных Депутатов СССР и Верховного Совета СССР, no. 41, 1990, pp. 991–999; its promulgation is to be found on pp. 1000-1001.

19 On changes in the legal system and climate see for example John Löwenhardt, 'Political Reform under Gorbachev', unpublished paper presented at the State University of Gröningen, 2-4 December 1987, especially at pp. 21–25; Nicholas Lampert, 'The Socialist Legal State', in Martin McCauley (ed.), *Gorbachev and Perestroika* (London: Macmillan, 1990) pp. 116–134; and W.E. Butler, 'The Rule of Law and the Legal System', in Stephen White, Alex Pravda and Zvi Gitelman (eds), *Developments in Soviet Politics* (London: Macmillan, 1990) pp. 104–119.

20 For a recent analysis of inflation in the USSR see Boris Rumer, 'Soviet Estimates of the Rate of Inflation', *Soviet Studies*, vol.41, no.2, April 1989, pp. 298–317; on unemployment, see Itzchok Adirim, 'A Note on the Current Level, Pattern and Trends of Unemployment in the USSR', *Soviet Studies*, vol.41, no.3, July 1989, pp. 449–461.

21 Margot Jacobs, 'Civil Society and the Changing Soviet Citizen', *Sovset News*, vol.6, no.1, January 1990.

22 However, the logic of my argument leads unequivocally to the conclusion that the People's Republic of China *will* get into the same sort of crisis within a few years.

8

Soviet Bureaucracy
and Civil Society

STEPHEN FORTESCUE

I

I will deal in this essay with the *industrial* state bureaucracy, specifically the industrial ministries. This restriction in coverage of the Soviet bureaucracy determines that aspect of civil society on which we will concentrate. As Kukathas and Lovell suggest in chapter 2, the concept of civil society, ever since it took on independent meaning in the sixteenth and seventeenth centuries, has been rooted in the idea of human relations being mediated through the market, in both its commercial and legal aspects. Thus, while particularly in the early stages of the Gorbachev revolution the 'political' aspects of civil society might have seemed dominant, no less relevant to an examination of the concept in the context of change in communist systems are the 'economic' aspects. The question of the marketisation of the economy is quite clearly on the agenda in the Soviet Union, and the concept of civil society is therefore relevant to current considerations of economic reform.

II

Economic civil society is a vague and wide-ranging concept which nevertheless has become particularly important in Western political and economic debate in recent years with the rise of the neo-conservative or New Right critique of the Keynesian welfare state. That critique sees the welfare state as economically and socially inefficient. 'A selective withdrawal of state power from civil society and the gradual renewal of private competition and market ethics are envisaged. That state, in this view, should be biased more openly in favour of commodity production and exchange.'[1] That is, maximum efficiency is provided by guaranteeing the greatest possible autonomy of producer units and the minimum possible role for the state and its bureaucracy. However, it does not exclude the need for or legitimate role of the state and its bureaucracy altogether. Indeed it has been suggested that the neo-conservatives require a *strengthened* role for the state, in order to control sectional interests, albeit a role more limited in its scope.[2] There exist two alternative views of the role of the state bureaucracy. The first is that the state bureaucracy should operate strictly and only as the representative of the state. The state has legitimate interests—the interests of society as a whole—and it is the task of its bureaucracy to enforce those interests. Clearly this should not entail major encroachment on the autonomy of producers. The second view grants the state bureaucracy interests of its own. These interests are primarily the sorts of interests that most bureaucracies have: maintaining their own survival and security, maximising staff numbers, and so on. In such circumstances the bureaucracy can be made to be socially effective only if it takes on a role as a 'producer' in the economic civil society, that is, if it becomes subject to the laws and pressures of the market place.[3]

III

Which of these views of the role of the state bureaucracy is most applicable to the Soviet industrial bureaucracy? It is formally supposed to represent the state interest. The current General Statute for ministries states:[4]

> A ministry of the USSR is a central organ of state management (*upravlenie*), exercising leadership of the relevant branch of the economy.

The essence of an organ of state management is that it directly represents the state interest, and so must be kept free of sectional interests.[5] They are responsible for the direct enforcement of state policies among their subordinate producer units. This implies that the activities of the industrial bureaucracy are determined by the state and its interests, suggesting in turn that if the state changes its perception of its own interests to make them compatible with the economic civil society the bureaucracy would follow suit. That would entail a radical reduction in the economic functions of the state and therefore its bureaucracy, through the breakdown of the command economy. This would entail the removal of the ministries' operational control over producer enterprises, leaving them with only residual policy-making functions. Many of those operational-control functions would be replaced by 'economic levers' such as tax and credit manipulation.

This is all based on the assumption that the industrial bureaucracy faithfully reflects, or can be made to reflect, the state interest, whatever that interest might be. That is a proposition that many find dubious if applied to any state bureaucracy in the world. Certainly most observers would suggest that the Soviet industrial bureaucracy does not act as a faithful agent of the state and that indeed its behaviour is determined by its own narrow interests.[6] These interests are similar to those one would expect from any bureaucracy and can be summed up in the Russian word *vedomstvennost'* (variously translated as 'sectionalism' or 'departmentalism').[7] It involves primarily highly autarchic tendencies, the minimisation of plan tasks and the maximisation of resource bids. Most ominously for the economic civil society it entails a high degree of detailed control over every aspect of the operations of producer units (*melochnaia opeka*).

It is not easy to deny the existence of *vedomstvennost'*, even for those who retain their faith in the importance of maintaining the state bureaucracy as the representative of the state interest. They state that the bureaucracy has to be made to represent that interest, believing that any attempt to remove the 'state' status of the bureaucracy and legitimating its own independent interests will only make the problem of *vedomstvennost'* worse.[8] As a beginning this is to be guarantied through the stricter legal regulation and rationalisation of the bureaucracy—the establishment of what we could call, using the old Prussian terminology, a *Gesetzstaat*.[9] Of course the Prussian *Gesetzstaat* was essentially a conservative structure,[10] and this approach is correspondingly compatible with the demands of conservatives in the Soviet Union. Marxism, including the Soviet Leninist and Stalinist versions of it, has a very strong anti-bureaucratic strand. Those operating in that tradition find it easy to · demand that the bureaucrats be brought to account through more precise descriptions and prescriptions of their role and through tighter control by such control agencies as the Committees for Party and People's Control and ministerial party organisations.

It is thus not surprising that Soviet reformers see *Gesetzstaat* as inadequate. They want to go beyond administrative law by introducing the 'political' aspects of civil society, that is, to introduce a *Rechtsstaat* rather than a *Gesetzstaat*.[11] This requires making the bureaucracy truly answerable to a democratic legislature, it being that legislature which determines the state interest.[12] Reformers adopting this approach believe that the state bureaucracy does or can faithfully reflect the state interest.

There are others who find the inevitability of the existence of 'sectional' interests of the bureaucracy too great to allow adherence to the state interest view. This leads them to call for adoption of the second approach to the establishment of an economic civil society, the 'economisation' of the bureaucracy. The only way to make the bureaucracy efficient, it is believed, is to make it economically responsible. The bureaucracy, and individual bureaucrats, should be obliged to pay their own way through the profitable sale of their services. This would lead to a leaner and more responsive bureaucracy, and of course one which was less involved in the day-to-day activities of producer units.

IV

That which has already happened or is on the agenda for future changes is a confusing mix of policies, with some clearly appropriate to the first approach, some to the second.

What evidence is there that the aim is to retain the 'state interest' role of the industrial bureaucracy within a reformed economy? We will not be able say with certainty that the industrial bureaucracy will retain its formal 'governmental' (*pravitel'stvennyi*) or 'state' (*gosudarstvennyi*) status until the new General Statute for ministries eventually appears. It had been under consideration for many years even before Gorbachev came to power, and one can only imagine that the clearly difficult drafting job has been made vastly more difficult in current conditions. However there is good evidence that the authorities are concerned to maintain the state interest approach. The concern with the *Gesetzstaat* that was typical of the Brezhnev era is still with us. Although it appears to have been only moderately successful in removing the legislative loopholes that leave room for bureaucratic interpretation and therefore arbitrariness,[13] considerable progress has been made in drawing up and often even publishing procedural regulations, duty statements, and so on. More impressively and importantly for our current concern the foundations have recently been laid for legislative accountability. Senior bureaucratic officials have suddenly found themselves subject to rather undignified confirmation procedures by Supreme Soviet commissions, while one assumes that those commissions will establish more effective oversight of the industrial bureaucracy than was typical of the old Supreme Soviet commissions.[14]

The *Gesetzstaat* and legislative accountability only lay the foundation for a state bureaucracy's legitimate place in an economic civil society. The essential feature is that the bureaucracy give autonomy to producer units through a radical reduction in its operational-control powers. The industrial ministries have indeed had their operational powers very considerably cut, formally at least. The Law on the Socialist Enterprise guarantees producer units a considerable degree of operational autonomy. In a couple of well-publicised cases enterprises have taken their ministries to court for imposing on them unreasonable plan tasks. The *goszakaz* system is supposed to leave an increasing proportion of enterprises' production capacity free for autonomous operation, while the promised establishment of a wholesale trade network and a freer pricing system are designed to add to that autonomy. Many of the old operational-control functions of the ministries are being transformed into 'economic levers' such as credit and tax regimes, operated by various central organs and the banks.

In these conditions the industrial ministries are to be left with residual policy-making functions, primarily related to long-term forecasting and strategic planning, investment and management of scientific-technical progress. There has been a move to take even these functions away from the ministries and give them to higher-level bodies, primarily the Bureaus of the Council of Ministers, on the grounds that the closer a 'state' administrative organ is situated to the centre of state power the more likely it is actually to serve the interests of that state power. Some commentators have suggested that in these circumstances the ministries could be abolished altogether, with those residual functions which do not go to the Bureaus going to departments of Gosplan.[15] Others are looking for a more regional approach. There were calls for the establishment of *sovnarkhoz*-type regional management bodies in the final years of the Brezhnev era,[16] and such calls continue.[17] With increasing economic management powers being given to *sovety* some regionalisation of economic management is occurring. Indeed complaints are already being made of ministerial *opeka* being replaced by that of the *sovety*.[18]

Many of the problems involved in the decentralisation strategy are already well-known and well-documented. The Law on the Socialist Enterprise has been largely ignored. A recent survey of enterprise managers found that 93.9 per cent did not believe that the ministries observed the law that they could not set enterprises' normatives and indicators above limits set by the Council of Ministers; nearly 75 per cent that higher organs continued to give directives outside their competence; and 53 per cent that rules on planning were not being observed.[19] The *goszakaz* system was initially abused by ministries setting as a matter of course *goszakazy* that took close to 100 per cent of the production capacity of enterprises. Since then they have been subjected to severe pressure to keep *goszakazy* at lower levels, but have responded by transforming supposedly voluntary production contracts into what are in effect obligatory plan tasks. The Vladimir Tractor Factory has been freed from *goszakaz* altogether, but is unable to refuse the 'voluntary' contracts which the ministry imposes on it, despite the fact that they guarantee it will make a loss, because the factory depends entirely on the ministry for funds and resources.[20] Indeed the ministries use a whole range of administrative weapons against recalcitrant enterprises, including the threat of dismissal of managers and the withholding of resources, particularly imported technology.[21] The non-existence or ineffectiveness of the wholesale trade network has ensured that most enterprises are far from willing to fight for the autonomy they have supposedly been granted. The ministries have also very effectively hijacked the new 'organs of economic leverage', most particularly the banks. The ministries have set up their own banks and use them to exert enormous financial pressure on enterprises. One example involves a ministry's bank refusing an enterprise credit because the workforce insisted on putting forward for election as director someone the ministry did not approve of. The enterprise was driven to near bankruptcy by the financial policies of the ministry.[22] Finally and not surprisingly higher-level organs are no more prepared to grant enterprises autonomy than the ministries (the Ministry of Finance has always been particularly notorious for its *melochnaia opeka*), while they are also highly susceptible to branch-oriented *vedomstvennost'*.[23]

There appear to be good grounds for scepticism about current efforts to retain the ministries as representatives of the state interest at the same time as granting enterprises the degree of autonomy one would expect in an economic civil society.

V

This leads some to put their hope in transforming the ministries into economic units. An important element of this approach has in fact

been in place for a number of years through the widespread
subjection of the ministries to the discipline of branch *khozraschet*.
Under this system a ministry is expected to maintain accounts for its
branch as a whole and register a profit. It is generally accepted that
this approach has in fact increased the *vedomstvennost'* of ministries.
They become even more determined to maintain branch autarchy,
while the autonomy of enterprises is further reduced as it becomes
more important for ministries to shift the burden of loss-making
enterprises onto profitable enterprises.[24]

This has led some to adopt an approach which concentrates on
making the central apparatus of the ministries and the individual
bureaucrats within it economically responsible rather than the
branch as a whole. The crudest approach is to introduce a system in
which ministries would be liable to pay compensation to enterprises
who had suffered materially through the errors of ministerial
bureaucrats. Such an approach is written into the Law on the
Socialist Enterprise.[25] An appropriate clause was included in the
contract which was drawn up between the Ministry of Chemical
Machine Building and the Sumy Machine Tool Association.
However the association's new ministry, the Ministry of Heavy
Machine Building, refuses to honour the agreement.[26] The difficulty
here is that ministerial apparatuses and the bureaucrats simply do
not generate resources on a scale that would make significant
restitution for bureaucratic errors feasible.[27] The reason that the
Ministry of Heavy Industry reneged on the agreement with the
Sumy Association was that it simply did not have the money
required. It could only obtain it by taking it from other enterprises in
the branch. The problem is well illustrated in the rather ridiculous
suggestion of one commentator that central budgetary allocations
should be made to ministries to cover the cost of such restitutions.[28]

A more sophisticated although limited approach consists of having
a narrow apparatus *khozraschet*; that is, the central apparatus of the
ministry and individual bureaucrats have to run a profit through the
sale of their services. The opponents of such approaches point out the
impossibility of putting a market price on most of the activities,
particularly the most sensitive activities, of industrial
bureaucracies.[29]

VI

The next approach is that producer units be given the opportunity to rid themselves of subordination to the ministries altogether. Clearly this applies to the cooperatives that have been set up in recent years, although it should be noted that now about 80 per cent of cooperatives are in fact 'state cooperatives' set up within existing enterprises with subordination to a ministry.[30] The new Law on Property, by establishing the legal basis for private property, including the private ownership of the means of production and employment of hired labour, clearly greatly extends the theoretical possibilities for enterprises operating outside the ministerial structure. However, these are developments on the radical fringe which require broader analysis than will be undertaken in this paper. Of more immediate concern for the bulk of Soviet enterprises and producers have been the reorganisations of ministries that have abolished their 'middle links', increased the importance of production and science-production associations (POs and NPOs), and allowed the establishment of groupings of enterprises outside ministerial control.

The middle link has always been seen as crucial in ministry-enterprise relations, because it is here that the day-to-day operational control of the enterprises is located. The *glavk* has been one of the most enduring bodies in Soviet industrial management and one of the most abused. The original intention of the administrative reform of the late 1960s was that they, as administrative organs, be abolished and replaced by 'economic' *ob"edineniia*, so described because they would be on *khozraschet* and because they would be situated, without any extensive apparatus or staff, within the enterprises they served. As has been well documented the reform became a typical Brezhnev compromise with two levels of *ob"edineniia* being established—the POs and NPOs as producer units and closest to the original aim of the reform, and the VPOs (all-Union industrial associations) as administrative organs which in practice differed in no significant way from the *glavki* they replaced.[31] Under Gorbachev the question of the middle link has shifted once again to a central place on the agenda. Indeed after considerable shenanigans, including the reappearance of *glavki* and then the GPOs (*gosudarstvennye proizvodstvennye ob"edineniia*, state production associations), yet another version of the same thing,[32] most ministries have now formally moved to a two-link structure, that is, a direct ministry-producer unit relationship

without the middle link. It is considered that this structure will keep
to a minimum the opportunities of the ministries to indulge in
melochnaia opeka and thus maximise the autonomy of producer
units. There is however very strong evidence that the POs and NPOs
are now taking on a middle-link role, with indeed the establishment
of many new NPOs which are in fact no more than the old VPOs
with new names.[33] Thus while in the past it might have been just
possible to argue that the POs and NPOs shared and respected the
interests of their constituent units it is now becoming increasingly
difficult to do so.

In what might appear to be a more radical approach, enterprises
have been allowed to remove themselves altogether from ministerial
subordination and organise themselves in cooperative ventures
known originally as MGOs (*mezhotraslevye gosudarstvennye
ob"edineniia*, interbranch state associations), but with such names as
kontserny and *kontsortiumy* now also becoming common.[34] The
original intention was that these bodies would be formed on an
entirely voluntary basis by producer units and would operate
according to highly democratic procedures, including the right of
veto of any member unit over any decision of the central board. The
new bodies, as the representatives of autonomous producer units,
would deal directly with the highest level state organs and in doing
so would be subject to the same *goszakazy*, normatives, supply quotas,
and so on as still govern the traditionally-organised sectors.[35]
Anyone with a true commitment to the economic civil society
would have wondered, right from the beginning, why the MGOs
were needed, particularly when the enterprises involved tended to be
the biggest enterprises in the branches concerned. Such a person
certainly would not be surprised to discover strong evidence that the
MGOs are behaving rather like the ministries their members have
just escaped. The democratic procedures have proved unworkable and
more familiar Soviet hierarchical patterns are being introduced.[36]
The MGOs use their own banks and insurance funds to blackmail
constituent units and to engage in that classical ministerial
procedure of shifting the burden of loss-making enterprises onto
profitable ones.[37] The MGO 'Kvantemp' has an 'insurance fund'
which it uses to redistribute profits from successful enterprises to
loss-makers. It also has a 'joint-stock commercial bank' which buys
technical innovations from the MGO's institutes and then sells them
on to its enterprises. Enterprises which are unwilling to put the
innovations into production have their interest rates increased.[38] As
one commentator has put it, the new bodies were supposed to be
'complexes of independent enterprises'; instead they are 'independent

economic complexes'.[39] While they might have independence from ministries, that does not mean that producer units have autonomy.

However, even their independence from the ministries is open to question. The head of the major Leningrad MGO 'Tekhnokhim' has declared that while initially they were 'drunk with their freedom from the ministry', they now realise that some links have to be retained, particularly in the area of supplies.[40] Nor should one be surprised to learn that the ministries have quickly jumped in and started setting up *kontserny* of their own, which are nothing more than yet another variation on the *glavk* theme. In another variation the new *kontserny* are in fact old 'abolished' ministries under a new name. Thus it is somewhat suspicious that N.M. Ol'shanskii, the minister of the former Ministry of Mineral Fertilisers, is now the freely-elected chairman of the 'state association (*assotsiatsiia*)' Agrokhim (Agricultural Chemicals), operating under the auspices of the Ministry of Chemical Industry.[41] It is openly recognised that the new *kontsern* 'Gazprom' (Gas industry) is nothing more than the former Ministry of Gas Industry, set up two days after it was announced that the Ministry of Gas Industry was to be merged with the Ministry of Oil Industry.[42] Depending on one's point of view this step was either a cynical exercise by gas industry officials to frustrate the merger or their justifiable demonstration of dissatisfaction over lack of consultation.[43]

Thus plans, tried and proposed, to transform ministries into 'economic' units or to replace them with such units appear to promise little. Certainly the gains to producer units in terms of autonomy appear to be minimal.

VII

We have now examined both models of a ministerial bureaucracy within an economic civil society as applied to the current Soviet situation and in both cases we see a picture of ministries or quasi-ministries retaining their capacity to operate in the same old way, protecting themselves and their *vedomstvennost'* and frustrating any attempts to give autonomy to producer units. This might suggest that it is indeed the ministries who are, as many in the Soviet Union seem to believe, the greatest barrier to the establishment of an economic civil society. However before we accept this view we have to look more closely at the interests of the ministries, summed up in terms of the notorious *vedomstvennost'*, and in particular its relationship with the state interest.

It would be easy to explain *vedomstvennost'* in terms of traditional and universal bureaucratic behaviour which can be observed in any society in the world. Very simply, any bureaucracy wants as much control over its environment as possible and will oppose anything that threatens that control.[44] I am not certain however that this is an adequate explanation of the behaviour of the Soviet industrial bureaucracy (if indeed it is an adequate explanation of the behaviour of any bureaucracy). My first reason for doubt is a vague and uncertain one. The typical bureaucratic behaviour just described is usually made to sound very aggressive, with in fact 'empire building' being an important part of it. I am not sure that the behaviour of Soviet industrial ministries can be described in these terms. Clearly they are just as interested as any other bureaucracy in increasing staff numbers as much as possible. However I am less certain that Soviet ministries are aggressive in the sense of wanting to expand the boundaries of their operations, taking over new areas of activities, poaching the enterprises of their rivals, and so on.[45] This would suggest that the ministries are reactive or defensive in their behaviour; that is, their interests are not the self-determined interests of aggressive and ambitious bureaucrats, but rather defensive interests that have been forced on them by an outside force.[46]

That outside force is not difficult to identify. It is, of course, the plan. Virtually every aspect of the behaviour of the industrial ministries, certainly all aspects of their relationships with higher-level state organs and with subordinate enterprises, can be explained in terms of efforts to guarantee branch-level plan fulfilment. In their dealings with higher bodies they attempt to minimise plan targets and maximise resource allocations.[47] It could well be here that the explanation is to be found for any lack of aggressiveness on the part of industrial ministries. Once the plan has been set they try to guarantee fulfilment by keeping the closest possible control over all necessary inputs, by building up as autarchic a structure as possible and by maintaining the tightest possible control over subordinate enterprises. That control over enterprises includes being in a position to shift the burden of non-fulfilment in weak enterprises onto the strong enterprises.

Thus the behaviour of ministries can be convincingly explained in terms of plan fulfilment, rather than bureaucratic self-aggrandisement. The ministries see plan fulfilment as an externally imposed task, imposed on them by the state. Outside analysts put it more delicately by suggesting that ministry behaviour is determined by 'objective economic circumstances'.[48] It might be possible to argue that the state is in fact trying to set the ministries other tasks, such as output or efficiency maximisation or even the establishment of an economic civil society, but the ministries choose to see their task as plan fulfilment because that is the task which best justifies the maintenance of their positions of power and dominance within their branches. However I am prepared to accept the ministries' protestations that they are only doing what they have to do to meet the task set them by the state. That does not mean for a moment that I believe that the ministries are not engaging in some pretty cynical and self-interested obstruction of important elements of the current reform programme or that they are ardent supporters of the economic civil society. Since they have grown out of the 'command-administrative' economy it is not surprising that they feel comfortable within it and are interested in its maintenance. However they are not able to maintain it on their own. That leads to the perhaps unremarkable conclusion that the failure so far of economic reform, including reform which has been specifically directed against the industrial bureaucracy, is to be explained not by the obstruction of the ministries but by the weaknesses of the programme as put forward by the state. This is not the place for a detailed exposition of the difficulties facing economic reform in the Soviet Union. But the existence of a seriously deficit economy, plus a full range of ideological, political and 'cultural' restraints, suggest that the 'system' still demands the traditional approach. While one can have sympathy for Gorbachev in his efforts to face these difficulties, ultimately the existence or otherwise of the economic civil society depends not on the industrial bureaucracy but on the state.

Notes

1   John Keane, 'Introduction', in John Keane (ed.), *Civil Society and the State: New European perspectives*, (London and New York: Verso, 1988) pp. 1–31 at p. 10.

2   Ibid., p. 11.

3   The classic exposition of this approach is usually considered to be William A. Niskanen, *Bureaucracy and Representative Government* (Chicago: Aldine-Atherton, 1971). For commentary, see Jan-Erik Lane (ed.), *Bureaucracy and Public Choice* (London: Sage, 1987) especially pp. 13–16, 53–59.

4   *Собрание постановлений*, no.17, 1967, article 116, paragraph 1.

5   С.А. Авакьян, 'Министерство в новых условиях', *Советское государство и право*, no.3, March 1970, pp. 136–141 at p. 136.

6   И.С. Самощенко, 'Новый шаг в совершенствовании советского законодательства', *Советское государство и право*, no.2, February 1987, pp. 3–10. This is not a new debate in the Soviet literature. For an account of a burst of interest in the issues discussed in this paper, particularly the 'state' versus 'sectional' nature of the industrial ministries, in the early 1970s, see Stephen Fortescue, 'A Soviet Interest System', Work-in-Progress Seminar, Department of Political Science, Research School of Social Sciences, Australian National University, Canberra, April 1974, especially pp. 13–23.

7   Despite the fact that 'sectional' behaviour has long been one of the most documented phenomena in the Soviet system, in the past there was a reluctance to deal with it analytically or theoretically in the Soviet literature, presumably because of the 'new class' implications of any such analysis. Thus Zaslavskaia created a storm with her very rudimentary analysis in her famous 'Novosibirsk report' in 1983. Since then the theme has become a very popular one. See for example 'Дискуссия о проблемах бюрократизма', *Вопросы экономики,* no.12, December 1988, pp. 7–103.

8   В. Мерцалов, 'Блеск и нищета бюрократии', *Вопросы экономики,* no.12, December 1988, pp. 19–24 at p. 20.

9   Л.А. Сергиенко, 'Совершенствование законодательства о советской государственной службе', *советское государство и право*, no.5, May 1984, pp. 27-34 at p. 29; Г.Н. Манов, 'Социалистическое правовое государство: проблемы и перспективы', *Советское государство и право*, no.6, June 1989, pp. 3–10 at p. 8.

10 Hans-Ulrich Derlien, 'State and bureaucracy in Prussia and Germany', in Metin Heper (ed.), *The State and Public Bureaucracies: A comparative perspective* (Westport: Greenwood, 1987) pp. 89-105 at p. 92.

11 For an analysis of the origins of and differences between the two German words, see Derlien, 'State and bureaucracy in Prussia and Germany'. For a Soviet discussion of the difference, in terms of a distinction between a *gosudarstvo prava* and *gosudarstvo zakona*, see 'Советское правовое государство и юридическая наука', *Советское государство и право*, no.4, April 1989, pp. 58–70.

12 Ibid., p. 58.

13 Some question whether the need for such interpretation can ever be avoided. See John A. Rohr, *Ethics for Bureaucrats: An essay on law and value* (NY and Basel: Dekker, 1989) pp. 39–40,283.

14 On the first round of confirmation hearings, see Dawn Mann, 'Gorbachev's personnel policy: the USSR Council of Ministers', *Report on the USSR*, vol.1, no.46, 17 November 1989, pp. 8–13. The commissions of the old Supreme Soviet held occasional publicised hearings on the activities of ministries. No such hearings under the new order have yet been reported, perhaps because the commissions are so busy with new legislation.

15 For the most detailed account of how all the ministries' functions could be hived off, see В. Рапопорт, 'Принципы и направления перестройки организации отраслевого управления', *Вопросы экономики,* no.10, October 1989, pp. 14–25. See also *Известия,* 23 March 1989, p. 2.

16 For example, Р.А. Белоусов and Г.В. Хромушин (eds.), *Партийное руководство экономикой* (Moscow: Izdatel'stvo 'Ekonomika', 1981), p. 73.

17 Г. Горланов, 'Совершенствование организационной структуры управления как фактор ускорения', *Вопросы экономики,* no.1, January 1987, pp. 23–32 at p. 31.

18 *Социалистическая индустрия,* 12 May 1989, p. 2; *Известия,* 18 February 1990, p. 1.

19 Р.Ф. Каллистратова, 'Перестройка и будущее арбитража', *Советское государство и право,* no.5, May 1989, pp. 36–43. One half of those surveyed saw no need for ministries.

20 *Moscow News,* 26 March 1989, p. 13.

21 *Известия,* 22 October 1989, p. 2; Каллистратова, 'Перестройка и будущее арбитража', p. 39. V.M. Luk'ianenko has the advantage of experiencing the situation from both sides of the fence, having just returned to his former post as director of the Sumy Machine Tool Association, after a stint as Minister of Chemical Machine Building. He states that under the new conditions enterprises, particularly the big well-organised ones, have greatly increased freedom from their ministries, but at the same time he complains of directives coming from his ministerial superiors. *Известия,* 15 February 1990, p. 2.

22 *Известия,* 5 November 1989, p. 3. Some commentators have claimed that ministries deliberately put enterprises into impossible financial situations in order to increase their hold over them. See Д. Городецкий, 'Механизм торможения и его социально-экономическая основа', *Вопросы экономики,* no.12, December 1988, pp. 42–46 at p. 44.

23 The branch departments of Gosplan and the State Committee for Science and Technology are particularly notorious in this regard. Although reorganisations at this level have stressed the need to increase the role of 'functional' units, one cannot be overly optimistic that branch loyalties will disappear.

24 *Экономическаиа газета,* no.6, 1989, p. 8; 'XXVI съезд КПСС и организационно-правовые вопросы государственного управления', *Советское государство и право,* no.9, September 1981, pp. 3–12 at p. 5.

25 Article 9, paragraph 3. See *Правда,* 1 July 1987, p. 2.

26 *Известия,* 15 February 1990, p. 2.

27 Рапопорт, 'Принципы и направления перестройки организации отраслевого управления', pp. 16–7.

28 *Правительственный Вестник,* no.4, 1990.

29 See Рапопорт, 'Принципы и направления перестройки организации отраслевого управления', pp. 16–17, and В. Амелин, 'Смогут ли отраслевые министерства стать

субъектами инноваций?', *Вопросы экономики,* no.10, October 1989, p. 27.

30   *Moscow News,* 25 March 1990, p. 10.

31   On the reform proposals, see Leslie Holmes, *The Policy Process in Communist States: Politics and industrial administration* (London: Sage, 1981). On the implementation of the reorganisation, see W.J. Conyngham, *The Modernization of Soviet Industrial Management: Socio-economic development and the search for viability* (Cambridge: Cambridge University Press, 1982) especially Chapter 6.

32   For details on the GPOs, see Stephen Fortescue, 'Re-organization of the Industrial Ministries under Gorbachev', Paper presented to the Anniversary Conference of the Australasian Political Studies Association, University of New South Wales, Kensington, September 1989, pp. 8–11. There is no further news on the GPOs since that paper was written, that is, they are in a state of limbo while their future is considered, with one suspects no great sense of urgency, by the Council of Ministers.

33   Ю. Берлинер, 'Отраслевая наука в новых условиях хозяйствования', *Вопросы экономики,* no.6, June 1987,pp. 69–75 at p. 69; Л.М. Рутман, 'О некоторых пробелах в хозяйственном законодательстве', *Советское государство и право,* no.7, July 1989, pp. 57–64 at p. 59; and *Социалистическая индустрия,* 28 June 1988, p. 1; 6 July 1988, p. 2; 10 August 1988, p. 2. For earlier evidence, see Fortescue, 'Re-organization of the Industrial Ministries under Gorbachev', pp. 11–12.

34   For details on MGOs, see Fortescue, 'Re-organization of the Industrial Ministries under Gorbachev', pp. 15–18.

35   Б. Мильнер, 'Проблемы организационной интеграции на современном этапе', *Вопросы экономики,* no.10, October 1988, pp. 15–24 at p. 19.

36   *Известия,* 19 November 1989, p. 2.

37   *Социалистическая индустрия,* 27 September 1989, p. 2.

38   *Известия,* 22 October 1989, p. 2.

39   *Известия,* 19 November 1989, p. 2.

40   *Известия,* 22 October 1989, p. 2.

41   *Правда,*15 September 1989, p. 3.

42   *Известия,* 19 November 1989, p. 2. For another example, see the transformation of the Moldavian Ministry of Light Industry into the *kontsern* 'Moldlegprom'. *Правда,* 23 October 1989, p. 2.

43   *Социалистическая индустрия,* 27 September 1989, p. 2.

44   For a Soviet statement of this point, see Д. Кузин, 'Проблемы отраслевого управления в капиталистической экономике и практика перестройки', *Вопросы экономики,* no.10, October 1989, pp. 33–43 at p. 35.

45   This is no more than an impression, and I would be grateful for evidence, or clues as to what type of evidence should be sought, to decide the matter one way or another.

46   Of some relevance here might be what has been called the '*soglasovanie* economy', that is, an economic management system under which the

distribution of resources and indeed all decision making is based on long and all-encompassing negotiations between major institutional actors, with the nature of the process tending to lead to lowest-common-denominator decisions. One Soviet analyst has suggested that this system, which according to him was born after the death of Stalin and reached maturity under Brezhnev, introduced a type of market into the Soviet economy, but a market in which bureaucratic methods and values bring the best results: М.Н. Афанасьев, 'Бюрократия как социально-политический феномен', *Вестник Академии наук СССР*, no.7, July1989, pp. 62–70 at p. 68. Certainly it is not a market in which one would expect aggressive Western-style market behaviour. For more on *soglasovanie*, see Stephen Fortescue, 'Building consensus in the Japanese and Soviet bureaucracies', Work-in-Progress Seminar, Department of Politics, University College, University of New South Wales, Canberra, August 1988.

[47]   Рапопорт, 'Принципы и направления перестройки организации отраслевого управления', pp. 20–21.

[48]   Рапопорт, 'Принципы и направления перестройки организации отраслевого управления', p. 20.

9

The Implosion of the Collectivist Societies
and the Emergence of New Democratic Social Systems in Eastern Europe and the USSR

LÁSZLÓ CSAPÓ

I

The transformation processes under way in the former collectivist societies are comparable only to the tectonic forces, moving and shaping tectonic plates and changing the visible face of the earth. The forces operating and driving the transformation of the former collectivist societies are simultaneously changing and are coinciding with other processes observable in the non-collectivist societies of the West, South and East. One can safely conclude that these processes in the East-Central European societies and in the USSR, as well as in other collectivist societies, have induced and are part of a global change. They are changing the socio-economic environment of mankind on a global scale. It is not only the extent but the speed of the changes that is breathtaking.

The essence of the transformation processes of the collectivist societies is that since the mid-1950s a general crisis developed first in the peripheral countries (German Democratic Republic, 1953; Poland, 1953–1956; Hungary, 1953–1956) then penetrating into the centre (USSR), leading to implosions[1] of the system in East Europe, first in the late 1980s and now in the USSR.[2] Whilst the general crisis of the system goes into an implosion in the USSR, in East-Central Europe the emergence, the shaping, the 'birth pangs', of a new democratic social system are felt. Simultaneously in the West, the developed Corporate Enterprise Economies tend to form gigantic regional integrations. The EEC in Europe, the US-Canadian Free

Trade Agreement, and Japan organising its own economic integration with South-East Asia and the Pacific, represent this trend. The less developed poor countries of Africa, Asia and Latin-America are sliding further down relative to the more developed parts of the world with no clear direction or vision of the future. It is like the main features of a gigantic canvas, a background picture of the world, against which partial issues, processes, changes, ought to be investigated if one intends to draw realistic, workable, theoretical hypotheses.

One of the great scientists of the 20th century, John von Neumann, once remarked that what is extremely difficult to achieve in the social sciences is the clarity of the categories. One may add that therefore the confusion always originates from the conceptual area. Under such changes as I referred to above, it is even more difficult to form clear categories for investigating the phenomena at hand. Notwithstanding the difficulties, however, this precisely is the most interesting intellectual challenge.

I believe, after long hesitation and reflection on those processes, that the category of 'civil society' is neither 'a clear category' nor an optional category for the investigation of social changes in the current context in our time. Neither do I believe that the category of 'civil society' as it emerged from the 17th-19th century classical, political and social philosophies as a weapon against the absolutist monarchy and for the establishment of 'a fledgling democracy' instead of a mediaeval-feudal social order, is applicable to describe the new democratic societies of the 21st century, emerging on the ruins of the collectivist states. From classical political philosophy, John Locke's statement is the clearest to me:[3]

> Where-ever therefore any number of Men are so united into one Society, as to quit every one his Executive Power of the Law of Nature, and to resign it to the publick, there and there only is a *Political, or Civil Society.*

Obviously Locke identifies the 'political or civil' society with a majority rule, lawful 'true democracy' as opposed to the lawless 'Natural order'.

Therefore, I will propose new categories to investigate the processes we observe today in order to construct working hypotheses about possible future outcomes. This requires a purely theoretical, very abstract digression about what the society is today as a system, and a set of subsystems, the elements of modern systems and the 'modus operandi' of systems, the dichotomy of autonomy and interdependence in modern systems, the management and control of systems, and the role of information flows. These problems simply do not fit into the category of 'civil society'.

I intend to define the elements, structures and processes of a modern society first. Then I will introduce conjectures and refutations concerning the emerging new societies. Finally, I will try to formulate some working hypotheses about the possible future of the new democratic systems, emerging from the ruins of the collectivist states.

II

The society is a whole. The structure of wholes cannot be described in terms of relationships, and holistic connections cannot be resolved into relationships. There is another way, another logic, suitable to the logical treatment of wholes; that is, the concept of the system.[4] In order to make clear the difference between a relationship and a system let us consider the following demonstration.

Figure 1:

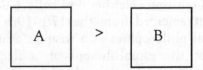

A > B is a relationship. Obviously a relationship is a simple logical form often used in scientific activity, comparing objects from the point of view of some of their immanent characteristics like shape, weight, and colour.

Figure 2:

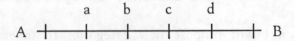

This is one of the simplest geometrical systems, the line segment A-B.

What are the differences between relations and systems? First, a relation requires two and only two members (relata) between which the relation is established. A complex relation can always be reduced into pairs of relata. The system cannot be analysed that way. A system—like ours, a simple linear system—may involve an unspecified number of elements. *A system is not a complex relation.* It is impossible to say what the relation between a and b, b and c, c and d, should be in order to constitute a linear system. When we are referring to a system, we abstract from its constituent 'elements' and we mean the organisation of those elements into a whole. Thus, a system is a holistic organisation.

Second, in a system, elements are not members of the system because of their immanent qualities but only by their position, arrangement, distribution, within the system. The element (member, object) does not participate in the system by its inherent quality but by its positional value in the system. In a linear system of the type described above, it is completely irrelevant what the shapes or inherent qualities of the objects representing elements are; whether dots, stars, people or any objects the members may be, what matters is that the members' positional value in the system, the arrangement of the members, remains the same. Similarly, in a social system, it does not matter what immanent characteristics the individuals have. Secondary connections can be established (and further deduced connections) in a system which are based on secondary positional values of its elements. For example, A is above B, or B depends on A, are such deduced connections. It is always assumed that elements have a positional value in the system.

Third, a system is always dimensional. A system is an arrangement (distribution) of its elements (members) in a dimensional domain. The separation of objects (whatever they may be) is presupposed in a system where connections are arranged between objects. Multiplicity of elements (objects) assumes some kind of dimensional domain (a manifold). We cannot speak of two or more objects unless they are in different points of time and space or unless they are distanced in some kind of a dimensional domain. Space and time are the most obvious dimensional domains, that is, *principia individuationis*: they are domains which 'create', 'makes possible', the multiplicity of objects. In systems, the dimensional domain participates in the formation of the system. In a relationship the role of the dimensional domain is to ensure the disjointedness of the relata.

Fourth, in relationships, the connection between relata is a direct one. The members of a system are related to each other through the system and not directly as a-b, b-c, d-e, et cetera. Consider the following as a good approximation of system connectedness:

Figure 3:

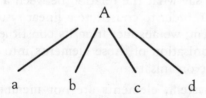

To state it explicitly: in a system, the members are, from the holistic point of view, not significantly connected with each other except with reference to the system as a whole.

Fifth, systems cannot be deduced from relations but the deduction of relationships (simple, complex, causal) from a system is a logical possibility. In this case, a relationship would be considered as a *subsystem*, reduced, simplified, appropriate, for the logical treatment of very simple constellations.

Sixth, the system cannot be derived from the parts; the system is an independent framework in which the parts are placed, arranged. Aggregation and system formation are completely different processes. In an aggregation, the parts are added; in systems, the parts are arranged in a dimensional domain. The whole is, to a large extent, independent of the individual parts. (Think about the human body as a system.)

Seventh, systems are always *unitas multiplex* and never undifferentiated wholes. (A simple element cannot be 'arranged'.) Wholes designate the concrete organised object, while the system is the way of arrangement of parts (pattern formation), the way of organisation itself.

Eighth, every system has one and only one construction (pattern-forming) principle. This is the '*unitas*' in the expression, '*unitas multiplex*'. There are 'perfect' or 'pure' systems in which all significant positions are occupied in accordance with the *unitas multiplex* but there are some where only a limited number of positions are in line with the *unitas multiplex* whilst 'others are out of position'.

The eight points above represent the most important characteristics of the logic of systems. We are going to utilise them in analysing the most complicated, the most intricate, the most difficult system of all—the human society.

III

The latest estimates concerning the existence of human society put its probable age at approximately five million years. For most of this time societies survived in some form or other of communal societies where the *unitas multiplex* or system-forming principle was kinship—family, extended family, clan, tribe. The community based on kinship was the system, the framework, within which every aspect of social and individual life was conducted. It was integrated, undifferentiated, in so far as every activity (economic, social, cultural, religious) was subordinated to the objective of the survival of the whole of the kinship unit. There was no such thing as an autonomous individual or family. The individual existed only (could survive only) as an integral part of the communal organisation and he did not exist separately as an individual either within or outside the community.

Slowly-developing specialisation of individual producers within the community and specialisation between communities led to the growth of productivity and social divisions and specialisation from hunting-gathering to animal husbandry and trade, and from there to agriculture and handicraft and foreign trade. As a result, individual families could become self-sufficient and survive as individual producers exchanging their produce first in barter and then in the markets. It is estimated that the market exchange economy on a fairly low level is about 16,000–20,000 years old. The fully developed market economy in which all basic goods produced became commodities produced and sold for money on the market is in the best case 300 years old. Applying somewhat stricter measures and assuming a modern labour market and other capitalist institutions as preconditions of a developed modern capitalist market economy, the market economy in its most developed form is about 150–200 years old.

The existence of a market economy in general has two preconditions, one necessary, one sufficient. The necessary condition is the division of labour, without which no exchange would be necessary or possible (everybody would produce everything for himself). Division of labour and specialisation, however, have existed since mankind existed at all. What did not exist was the separation of autonomous producers from each other, which was the result of changing property rights from communal to private (family) ownership and/or custodianship of the resources. The separation of producers is the sufficient condition of the existence of a market economy. If and only if these two conditions hold simultaneously is the economy a market economy. These are by definition, *ipso facto*, the conditions of the existence of a modern economy. This is the key to the understanding of the modern economy and the modern society. Under such conditions, the market, which is the organisational structure, pattern, of the exchange economy, fulfils three functions. First, it allocates and reallocates the available resources (capital, labour, land and its produce) between various activities (specialisation, division of labour) in different industries through the fluctuations of supply and demand and freely-moving prices which are the most important information flows. Second, it eliminates the less productive, weaker producers through various forms of competition. (Competition has been the most efficient selective mechanism.) Third, the constant threat of elimination in competition forces the individual (autonomous) producers to innovate, invent and invest in order to increase efficiency. Thereby the market organisational form proved to be the most dynamic, efficient system to increase productivity.

It is obvious that in such a modern economic system, the individual producers or their voluntary associations are separated from each other by private property rights; therefore, they are autonomous decision-making units. It is also obvious that the market integrates the autonomous units by creating institutions which best correspond to the functions the market has to fulfil. The most important among these is the modern state, with the separation of the legislative, the judiciary and the executive powers of the state. The history of the modern society can be described with a little exaggeration as a dynamically-changing relationship between the economy and the state. The dynamics may start with changing economic structures and processes, with changes in the state (internally or externally induced) or with changes in both. What the proponents and the opponents of the 'civil society' versus 'the state' or the *Gesellschaft* versus *Gemeinschaft* dichotomy never could understand was that a fully developed market economy separates and at the same time integrates the autonomous producers into a society which is becoming more and more the community as the democratic control of the social system as a whole develops and there is a gradual, slow but definite movement towards 'a true democracy' which emancipates the citizens into the state, and each individual into the community, represented by or 'almost' coinciding with the modern Welfare State. Integration, gradual and dynamic, of 'society' with 'the community', or the full emancipation of the individual into the modern Welfare State participating in the economic and political life simultaneously, is the late outcome of the dynamics between the economy and the state (from the mercantilist system to the modern 'consensus state' of tripartite power control by the employers, the trade unions and the state's executive arms, in the modern corporate enterprise system). Because of the integration of the natural-social (family) endowment, the economic, the political, the ideological (value) and the legal aspects of individual lives in the modern social and economic system, the category of 'civil society' does not explain anything; it is operationally empty in the modern context.

Since the 17th century, movements developed extending the progress towards a 'true democracy' in the highly developed Western Societies. General education, the labour movements and trade unions, the general suffrage, parties representing various segments of the population, human rights movements, environmentalist and consumer protection movements, legal services, international corporate enterprises, corporate enterprises with workers' representation in management, the emergence of the Welfare State, all kinds of government contracts—neither the proponents nor the opponents of the concept of 'civil society' could even dream about such development under modern capitalist conditions. One can conclude that the participation of the individual or the voluntary associations of individuals in the social and political decision-making is more or less assured.

IV

Our point of departure was the definition of the modern democratic society *as a system*. In order to establish the parameters, characteristics and *modus operandi* of the modern social system, one has to begin to identify the parts, elements of the system, their positional values in the dimensional domain (in real historical time and space). Then one has to establish the arrangement, the structures of the system in question. Finally one can establish how decisions are made under such structures.

Our starting definition requires clarification of the parts of the modern society as an organic whole, the relationships between them, and their connectedness to the whole, the society. We also have to define the ordering principle of a given society, which arranges the parts into a structure or pattern, which is recognisable, unique and exclusive to a given society.

Modern social and economic systems contain the following elements or parts (described as vectors):

i   Households [H1, H2, ... Hn] These may contain one or more individuals.

ii   Firms [F1, F2, ... Fn] A firm may contain one or one million persons.

iii   Government agencies [G1, G2, ... Gn] These are organisations of various types and can operate in production, distribution, exchange or consumption, or provide various services.

iv   Other organisations [O1, O2, ... On] These are organisations not belonging to any of the previous examples (for example, trade unions, churches, parties, and all kinds of non-profit or profit-seeking organisations). They may involve one or many individuals. They are the voluntary associations of autonomous individuals and are therefore autonomous themselves.

v   Activities [a1, a2, ... an] These are the result of the division of labour and specialisation.

vi   Messages [m1, m2, ... mn] These create an information flow network regulating the activity exchanges between and within units.

vii   Products [g1, g2, ... gn]

viii   Social and natural endowments [Ns1, Ns2, ... Nsn] As vectors, these include the family, materials found in nature, etc.

ix   The functions of the system are: production, distribution, exchange and consumption [P, D, E, C] These are the results of the information flows [m1, m2, ... mn] and real activities [a1, a2,...an] generating the economic spaces of [P, D, E, C] and their continuum in uni-directional real time which is the economic life of the society.

This is the most abstract way of defining the elements, parts, of a modern society without which it cannot function. The existence of these therefore can be considered as the necessary conditions of the existence of the modern societies, irrespective of the structure and characteristics of the existing pattern which arranges the elements, parts, in a specific way in the dimensional domain.

Any society which wants to survive has to produce a final bill of certain goods which ensure the physical survival of its members (consumption) and the repetition of production at least on the same level (if there is no population growth) or at a higher level (if there is a population expansion). The latter requires goods: machinery, tools, materials—investment goods—produced in appropriate quantities and assortment. So, the final bill of goods is $Y = C + I$, where $C =$ consumption goods and $I =$ investment goods. Depending on the given technology (which is always a given combination of (a) skills (labour), (b) raw materials, and (c) tools, machinery), the production of the final bill of goods requires a given quantity of inputs in given proportions depending on the technology as defined above. From a purely technical point of view the economic structure is given as input-output connections between the units given previously at a given moment in real time and space. This complicated network of inputs at given outputs and technology is described by the so-called Leontief Inverse $(1 - A)^{-1}$, which gives us in money terms the coefficients of necessary inputs to produce a final bill of goods. This is what I call the technical structure of the economic system.

In a market economy the flow of inputs and outputs cannot be achieved otherwise than through their exchange, with the help of money which acts as a medium of exchange and measure of value. The billions and billions of individual exchanges between two commodities create an organisational pattern or structure. If the elements or members of the system are autonomous individuals or their voluntary associations, this structure is the market (if the necessary and sufficient conditions of the exchange do exist as explained earlier). There are other organisational structures possible which are non-market structures (kinship-based distribution; no money no market no exchange; allocation by fiat in a war economy; a pure planning system where the exchange is by plan targets given from one centre to each participant as a compulsory order to allocate inputs and outputs). Depending on the organisational structure, the inputs and outputs are allocated and the whole process is controlled by the generation and dissemination of information. No allocation of real goods is possible without the appropriate flows of information; therefore the pattern of generating and disseminating information controls the operation of the system. The generation and dissemination of information, the billions and billions of information connections between the elements of the system constitute what I call the control structure. In a market economy the information is generated by the elements of the system described by vectors in the eight points above. It is price-money type information; it is spontaneous; it is uncertain; it is multicentric (every unit generates, disseminates and absorbs information); it is costly; it is imperfect. Still, it is the most efficient, the fastest, information system known. Finally, the economic system presupposes the existence of certain institutions among which the ownership and custodianship of the resources or the property rights are the most important. On the basis of a given property right environment develops a specific decision-making system. The property rights and the decision-making system determine the distribution of income and wealth between the members of the system. These elements together constitute the institutional structure. The institutional structure is the 'unitas multiplex' or it determines the 'differentia specifica' of the system. Therefore, this is the deepest hard core of a system. It is impossible to change a system without changing its institutional structure.

Taking these four systems (connections between the elements of the system) the IS (institutional structure), OS (organisational structure), TS (technical structure) and CS (control structure), and assuming the natural-social environment (NSE) as externally given, the modus operandi, the functioning, the outcome of the processes which the system generates, can be written as O (outcome) = f[IS, OS, CS, TS]. Each individual unit is system-bound, institutionally, organisationally, informationally (control) and technically. In a market economy each individual unit (household, firm, organisation, government organisation) can be autonomous but at the same time it is integrated into the system. Interdependence of relatively autonomous units integrates them more and more strongly into the chains of the system; the more developed the system, the stronger the integration and dependence of the units on each other. This can be summed up in the economic matrix, depicted on the next page.

To illustrate the point we have made, imagine the US economy with approximately 5 million firms, close to 100 million households and other organisations. Suppose electricity production stops for two days. The interdependence and integration of the units will be demonstrated very forcefully. Looking at the economic matrix, imagine going down the first column, in each square [TS, IS, OS, CS] billions and billions of connections developing between millions and millions of units, and those multibillion connections generate information influencing, directing, the decisions of millions of decision- makers. Nobody is capable of controlling the system. The system is controlling itself. It is self-regulating. This character ensures the relative autonomy of the units. Autonomy is relative, interdependence is absolute.

The Economic Matrix

TO: FROM:	Technical Structure $(1\text{-}A)^{-1}$ (TS)	Institutional Structure (IS)	Organisational Structure (OS)	Control Structure (C)	Natural Social Environment (NSE)
Technical Structure $(1\text{-}A)^{-1}$ (TS)	T → T	T → I	T → OS	T → C	T → NSE
Institutional Structure (IS)	I → T	I → I	I → OS	I → C	I → NSE
Organisational Structure (OS)	OS → T	OS → I	OS → OS	OS → C	OS → NSE
Control Structure (C)	C → T	C → I	C → OS	C → C	C → NSE
Natural Social Environment (NSE)	NSE → T	NSE → I	NSE → OS	NSE → C	NSE → NSE

From the point of view of the economic system, NSE is exogenously given. However, from the point of view of the society as a whole, the economic dimension is only an internal dimension of the multiplex social system connections. What we called earlier the Society as a whole, can be looked at from five different aspects or dimensions and these also can be summed up into a five by five social system matrix (see below).

The important characteristic of this matrix is that each member or unit of the system is bound by NSE, ES, PS, VS, and LS to the system and through the system to each other, and the relative autonomy of each unit can be achieved *if and only if* each unit or individual or their voluntary associations are actively involved in all five dimensions of social life. In a modern society one can disregard politics and not deal with it, but it does not ensure that the political system will not deal with the individual or unit in question.

The Social Matrix

TO: / FROM:	Natural-Social Endowment System (NSE)	Economic System (ES)	Political System (PS)	Value System (VS)	Legal System (LS)
Natural-Social Endowment System (NSE)	NSE → NSE	NSE → ES	NSE → PS	NSE → VS	NSE → LS
Economic System (ES)	ES → NSE	ES → ES	ES → PS	ES → VS	ES → LS
Political System (PS)	PS → NSE	PS → ES	PS → PS	PS → VS	PS → LS
Value System (VS)	VS → NSE	VS → ES	VS → PS	VS → VS	VS → LS
Legal System (LS)	LS → NSE	LS → ES	LS → PS	LS → VS	LS → LS

In the end, any social outcome Os = (f) [NSE,ES,PS,VS,LS]. The arrows indicate directions of inputs and messages.

The more developed and rich a modern society is, the more developed the division of labour and specialisation, and the stronger is the network which holds the relatively autonomous individual or unit integrated into the system. Therefore, the separation of the autonomous actions and associations of units or individuals out of the manifold, multiplex system connections known as 'civil society' makes no sense. The greatest difference between the 17-19th centuries' just-emerging capitalist market economies and corresponding social, legal and political structures and today's corporate enterprise capitalist economies and society is the information revolution which is changing the nature and speed of connections between the individuals. Television, in particular, drags people into the middle of every aspect of social and political life. Even in a passive way, they have to participate. Another consequence of the information and technological revolutions is the beginning of the decline of the nation state (at least in Western Europe) and the simultaneous increase of the importance of the smaller regional communities (the 'localised *Gemeinschaft*'). *Gemeinschaft* and *Gesellschaft* tend to coincide at the local and regional level. Finally, the 20th century brought with it two major changes: the transformation of the most developed economies into Corporate Enterprise Economies (further integration) and the emergence of the Welfare State. As a result the State is not simply 'the night watchman' as Adam Smith would have liked to keep it, but is itself a huge corporate conglomeration—it has been integrated into the economy and society as an organic part of it. As a result, neither the dichotomy between 'civil life' and 'political life' nor the dichotomy between the state and 'civil society' carries much weight. The stronger the progress is towards a 'true democracy' globally (as it is today), the more the category of 'civil society' loses its meaning.

V

The main question is: is it theoretically possible to build a 'true' democracy in a collectivist economy as we have known it, that is, of the Soviet type? My hypothesis is that the structure of the collectivist economy and society of the Soviet type is incompatible with and contrary to the existence of true democratic social order.[5] If this hypothesis is provable, the first conjecture is that a new democratic social order cannot be built without the destruction of the basic economic and social structures of the collectivist states. The second conjecture is that, without a revolutionary transformation, that is, without creating new fundamental economic and social structures, a democratic system cannot be built. The third conjecture follows from the first two—partial or overall reforms which modify but do not change fundamentally, qualitatively, the basic institutions of the society cannot solve the democratisation of the old system. Everybody who has studied the transformation of Eastern Europe and Russia would understand the far-reaching consequences of the above conjectures.

The fundamental, necessary condition of a 'true democratic' order is autonomy: the autonomy of the individual and of voluntary associations of individuals. Without autonomy the basic human rights cannot be exercised (free association, freedom of expression and conscious movement, life, liberty, security of the person, equality before the law, and so on). Without autonomy no free decision-making of the individual is possible. If the material foundation of social life, the economic system, is controlled by the state, and the right to property for the individual does not exist, the individual cannot be autonomous. Therefore the autonomy of the individuals (or their free associations) presupposes the transformation of collectivist property rights into private property rights, or the restoration of private property rights over basic resources. This is itself the revolution under way in Eastern Europe and Russia. The restoration of private property rights creates the necessary conditions for a new democratic order.

Autonomy itself is not enough to ensure the existence of a true democracy; it is a necessary but not sufficient condition of it. The Soviet Constitution of 1977 declared individual rights, and the USSR was party to the UN Charter and Declaration of Human Rights. In, spite of all these, the soviet model practically represented the most cruel, the most oppressive, modern form of 'Oriental Despotism'. There must be 'checks and balances', mechanisms of decision-making (particularly in the political system) which ensure the control of the autonomous individuals, units, over the state and the bureaucracy. The precondition of such controls is the separation of the legislative, the judiciary and the executive functions of the state. (This leads us back to Locke's definition of the political or civil society.) The independence of the judicial system ensures the defence of individuals against the state. Furthermore, the pluralistic information generation and dissemination, the multiparty system, and free political association create checks and balances which ensure the control of individuals over the state. These are the sufficient conditions without which no true democracy is possible.

In these days of the triumph of journalistic euphoria over subtle analysis, and political sloganeering over political understanding, it is particularly important to understand that it was not Lenin, or Trotsky, or Stalin, who personally 'made' the Soviet model. It is particularly important to understand the nature, the fundamental structures of the collectivist society which by its internal logic excludes the existence of a true democracy. It is also vital to understand that Mr Gorbachev's various statements about democracy mean nothing in themselves even if he thinks they do. The collectivist economy's basic characteristic is that it decries the autonomy of the individual, the household, the firm. It is built on the following assumptions:

i   The collectivisation of private property in the form of predominantly state ownership, or cooperative ownership controlled by the state, makes it necessary and possible to plan, manage, direct, the modern economy from one centre as if it were a single huge trust under one management in every detail.

ii   The centre has the necessary information to do so, which is costless, perfect, always available.

iii   There is no risk, no uncertainty. The future is known to the planner. (There is not even the possibility of planning error!)

iv   The interests of the individuals, the firms, and the society at large coincide. Therefore, interest conflicts (if any occur at all) will be solved by the planners or the state.

v   Since the state has the information, the state can decide, the individual cannot.

From the logic of this system follows the necessity of monocentric information generation and dissemination, controlled by the power centre, the State-Party. This monocentric control on the other hand necessarily transforms the society into a Party-State—where the party elite controls the state, and the state controls everybody else. Fiat, command, order through the hierarchy, is the fundamental method of system management. The basic characteristic is subordination to the centre. Subordination logically requires the elimination of the autonomy of the individuals which is the necessary condition of any true democracy. Subordination cannot allow the priority of individual objectives over the state's. Therefore the State-Party must control the legislature, the judiciary and the executive powers. The State-Party must have the absolute monopoly of power. This logically eliminates the checks and balances, the sufficient conditions of the true democracy cannot exist. The collectivist economy is incompatible with a democratic society. Therefore, the destruction of the State-Party, and the Party-State, is the necessary condition for the construction of a new democratic social order. Reforms are not sufficient. This conclusion is extremely important. It means a rather long and complicated historical process ahead, for the Eastern European societies and peoples of the USSR first to dismantle the State-Party and the Party-State, and construct a new economic and social matrix by changing every connection of those matrices.

VI

The collectivist model basically destroyed the foundations of any democratic society which either existed before it took over or could have developed during the last forty to seventy years. It is completely misleading to assume that these societies will simply return to the state they were in before the collectivist system took over. The simple restoration of the semifeudal backward capitalism is impossible. The collectivist society failed because it proved to be inadequate to modernise these backward societies—as did that peripheral semifeudal capitalism before it. This is why it is unacceptable to these people today. What they really want is the type of economy and society which exists in the highly developed Western Europe.

One of the consequences of the collectivist society was to provide a low-level security of life to the average citizens at a relatively low level of effort. The price paid, however, was too high: no modernisation, no democracy, no freedom. The existence of a low-level social security net (combined with fear and indoctrination and terror) ensured stability.

The transformation into a modern, privatised, market economy of the West European type takes away both the security at a low level and the stability of social life as well. This implies that the transformation of the social system into a true democracy has to take place under heightened expectations on the one hand and heightened inequalities and therefore tension on the other. The transformation of the economic matrix assumes a radical change in property rights towards various forms of private property and the creation of an owner-entrepreneurial middle class with relatively high incomes and crucial roles in decision-making. The hierarchical nature of the decision-making has to be reinforced for efficiency reasons. The inequality of income and wealth distribution must take place in order to be able to modernise. The property rights have to be internationalised in order to attract foreign capital and 'know how'. All these require deregulation, and the dramatic reduction of the state's role. As soon as the self-regulating mechanisms of the market take over, a freely-fluctuating price system comes into motion and a free labour market is required. Both tend to hit the working masses. This leads to resistance, and the fledgling organisations of democracy and parliament are in danger. There is a tendency to upheavals and anarchy. Democratically elected governments may have to use force against the masses which elected them. Therefore it will take a whole historical period before a competitive market economy and true democratic society can emerge.

There are other economic and social forces at work which will shape the concrete forms in which the new democracies will develop.

The demolition of the State-Party and the Party-State gave the large masses of population confidence against authority and state. That confidence will not disappear overnight and will be transmitted to the new state. The people of Eastern Europe and the USSR remain highly politicised. Strangely enough, this might be one of the checks and balances which may keep the fledgling democracies alive and protected. (Democracy cannot be 'truer' than in a mass revolution where the majority directly exercises power and control in accordance with their real or perceived economic interests.)

The other internal forces which influence the transformation are nationalism, religion and a strange mixture of old and new values and prejudices. Of these, the strongest and the most dangerous is nationalism.

Economists often and proudly claim that the 'rational economic man' and 'rational action' and 'collective choice' determine events. An observer of Eastern Europe and Russia may conclude that history and irrational sentiments play a more important role. Why? A rational transformation would require a decline of nationalist feelings, a weakening of the nation-state without which the East can never join the gigantic Western European integration. It would require an enlightened scientific approach, not religious bigotry. It would require inviting in the multinationals and letting local capital be internationalised and modernised. It would require a rather cosmopolitan approach. Precisely the opposite is happening. Prejudice is rampant, nationalism, antisemitism and anti-minority feelings all fly high. Politicians are opportunistically using the situation. Perhaps with the passing of time, rational considerations will play stronger and stronger roles. At this moment there is a strange mixture of very conservative and revolutionary views.

The structures emerging are not yet solid. It is safe to conjecture however that what is emerging is not a carbon copy of the Western European democracies. It is also not a continuity of the previous society with some modifications. What is emerging is a new democratic society; traditional institutions and organisations of western democracy bend and modify under large popular pressures. The reshaping of the world economy, the globalisation of the markets, the technological-informational revolution, the speeding up of technological change and integration of large economies into giant trading areas exert a pressure on the development of a specific form of East European parliamentary democracy. This East European form may give a greater role to the executive than the other forms.

What is emerging is neither the old nor the new 'civil society'; it is a new economic and social system, with its own conflicts and characteristics which did not exist before. All these immense transformations cannot be fitted into the theoretical procrustes-bed of the restoration of the civil society.

Notes

1   'Implosion' here means a collapse of the system from within. It is important to see that the collapse of the collectivist society is due to its own failure and not to the intervention of alien forces.

2   László Csapó, *The General Crisis of the Soviet Model of the Collectivist Society* (Melbourne: La Trobe University Research Paper Series. 1988). I first presented this idea of a general crisis of the Soviet Model to a conference in Canberra in 1987. This was the first and only presentation of general crisis of the system in the whole of the international literature. Today, there is no doubt that my hypothesis has been proved correct.

3   John Locke, 'The Second Treatise of Government', in John Locke, *Two Treatises of Government* (Cambridge: Cambridge University Press, 1988) pp. 265-428 at p. 325.

4   The Systems approach is mainly based on: A. Angyal: 'A logic of systems', 1946, and Ludwig von Bertalanffy: 'The theory of open systems in physics and biology', 1950. Both are available, among other interesting papers, in F.E. Emery (ed.), *Systems Thinking: Selected Readings* (Harmondsworth: Penguin 1969).

5   László Csapó, 'The End of Collectivism in Hungary', *Quadrant*, vol.34, no.6, June, 1990, pp. 31–35.

10

Ethnonationalism
and Civil Society
in the USSR

WILLIAM MALEY

I

The emergence of public politics in M.S. Gorbachev's Soviet Union
has been one of the great events of the late twentieth century. It
reminds one of nothing so much as the youthful Pushkin's tribute to
Chaadaev, prophesying that Russia would wake from her sleep, and
that on the fragments of autocracy would be written their two
names.[1] The difficulty faced by President Gorbachev, however, is
that it is not simply *Russia* which has awoken, but a whole range of
non-Russians who are broadly hostile to the pattern of rule which
has prevailed in the USSR for many years. The antagonisms
between different national groups which the policy of *glasnost'* has
allowed to surface have already led to bloody confrontations in
several parts of the Soviet Union, and in a number of dramatic cases
have prompted coercive intervention by the Soviet armed forces.
These breakdowns of order are more redolent of a Hobbesian state of
nature than of a society marked by rules which temper the war of all
against all. It therefore seems appropriate to consider the
contribution of ethnonationalism to the emergence and smooth
functioning of civil society. The recent experience of the Soviet
Union provides one with grounds for both hope and fear.

My aim in this essay is to demonstrate why this is so. I open by
discussing the nature of ethnonationalism, and the uneasy position
of national consciousness in both Marxist and Marxist-Leninist
theory. From there, I proceed to discuss certain political devices,
namely the use of coercion or threatened coercion, and the practice
of elite cooptation, which contributed to order amongst non-Russian

nationalities before 1985. This leads to a discussion of the
relationship of ethnonational consciousness to civil society, and
finally to a consideration of the lessons to be learned from recent
Soviet experience. The general conclusion which I seek to defend is
that while there are certain varieties of ethnonational assertiveness
within the Soviet Union which are symptomatic of, or can
contribute to, the flowering of a civil society, there are other
varieties which reflect the triumph of hatreds which in a deep sense
are anything but civil.

II

The notions of 'ethnicity' and 'nationality', which the broad label
'ethnonationalism' embraces, prove on closer inspection to be almost
as elusive as Lewis Carroll's Cheshire Cat. Nonetheless, with a little
care they can be deployed in a way which avoids both triviality and
over-simplification. Jon Elster has recently argued that while there
are 'no societies, only individuals who interact with each other', the
'structure of interaction allows us to identify clusters of individuals
who interact more strongly with each other than with people in
other clusters'.[2] This usefully drives home the fundamental point
that ethnicity and nationality in the senses with which we are
concerned are subjective notions related to the *dispositions* or
behaviour of individuals, rather than ascriptive characteristics with
which individuals are indelibly stamped. No one, in this sense of the
term, is 'ethnic' or 'national' from birth; rather, ethnic and national
identity are cultural characteristics, generated by the process of
socialisation. Nonetheless, while an individual's sense of ethnic
identity is not as a rule the product of an interest-driven calculation,
it may often be the case that ethnic differences in a broader sense
may be reinforced by the benefits which can be provided by
distinctiveness.[3]

Ethnic groups, an experienced student of ethnicity has reminded
us, 'share *clusters* of beliefs and values'.[4] But of what kind? Anthony
D. Smith's recent attempt to identify the various dimensions of an
ethnic group is here a helpful one. He points to six in particular: (a) a
collective name (b) a common myth of descent (c) a shared history
(d) a distinctive shared culture (e) an association with a specific
territory, and (f) a sense of solidarity.[5] It is the last three of these
which are on the whole the most politically potent. Distinctive
shared cultures often have strong roots in language and religion—
and as language skills and religious attachments are among the

earliest acquired during the socialisation process, they tend to be those which their possessors most resent being forced to abandon in favour of others. Association with a specific territory creates the potential for conflict whenever dominion within the territory is seen to be exercised by individuals outside the associated ethnic group, and has led to quite tragic conflicts where members of different ethnic groups all feel that a particular piece of territory is uniquely associated with them. And solidarity by definition implies obligations, which may dominate prudential calculations of interest which an individual might otherwise be disposed to make.

Shared ethnic background need not, of course, imply that the individuals concerned are either subordinated to a common political structure, or function as economic agents within the one spontaneous order. These further elements tend to be associated with the emergence of national, rather than simply ethnic, groups, and it is partly for this reason that many writers have associated nationalism distinctively with the extended orders which emerged in the wake of the Industrial Revolution rather than with the localised communities characteristic of conquest empires.[6] This common association in part explains why national sentiments have posed such an awkward problem for Marxist-Leninist ideology. Marx's theory of revolution was based on the consciousness of the proletariat as a class for itself, and allowed no real room for the effects of national solidarity, which could divert the proletariat from its role as a universal class. Large scale industry, claimed Marx and Engels in *The German Ideology*, 'created a class which in all nations has the same interest, and for which nationality is already dead'.[7] Marx's views over time shifted somewhat from this position, but largely on an *ad hoc* basis, rather than as a result of a fundamental recasting of his theoretical position.[8] As a result, those who seek to depict themselves as Marxists have always had difficulty in coming to terms with manifestations of national sentiment.[9]

This was particularly a problem for the Bolsheviks, because the Russia of which they moved to take control in 1917 was very much a multi-ethnic empire as a result of expansion under the *ancien régime*. As a distinguished historian has noted, in the one-and-a-half centuries between 1550 and 1700, the Russian state acquired on average every year 'an area equivalent to modern Holland'.[10] This brought under Russian sway a great number of non-Russians, and even non-Slavs. Lenin in some of his writings foresaw a process of 'coming together' (*sblizhenie*) and 'merging' (*sliianie*) as the long-term future of these different groups.[11] However, the tactical advantages flowing from offers of self-determination to these peoples were obvious to Lenin in the aftermath of the February Revolution, and a resolution adopted at the Seventh All-Russian Conference of the Russian Social Democratic Labour Party in May 1917 affirmed that every nation forming a part of Russia 'must be recognised as having the right to secede freely and form an independent state'.[12] While this benign attitude towards minority nationalism was undoubtedly useful at the time, it was rapidly adulterated by Stalin, who as Commissar for Nationalities redefined self-determination (*samoopredelenie*) as a right only for the working masses.[13] Indeed, except in the Baltic,[14] the years immediately after the revolution were marked not so much by exercises of national self-determination as by the re-incorporation within the Soviet Russian state of various territories whose residents had seized the opportunity presented by disorder within the Russian Empire to proclaim their independence. These included most notably the Transcaucasian Republics of Georgia, Armenia and Azerbaijan;[15] and the Protectorates of Khiva and Bokhara in Central Asia.[16] Opposition from Lenin was sufficient to derail Stalin's desire to incorporate these nationals within an expanded Russian Republic, and only days after Lenin's death in January 1924, the new Soviet Union, embodying a federal political structure, was brought into being. Nonetheless, Lenin's stroke in March 1923, on the eve of the Twelfth Party Congress, had permitted Stalin to secure a considerable weakening of the independence of the institutions of rule within the Union Republic of the Soviet Union, and in this respect, Richard Pipes is undoubtedly correct in arguing that the Congress ended 'in the complete triumph of Stalin'.[17]

III

The adoption of a federal constitutional structure was of some use in containing nationalist sentiments. Particularly amongst the Muslims of Central Asia, it took the form of a 'divide and rule' policy. At the individual level, this was reflected in the requirement instituted in 1932 that a person's 'nationality' be recorded on his identity card, which in the context of the emerging bureaucratic-administrative political system accorded to the 'nationality' a quasi-ascriptive character.[18] At a collective level, it occurred through the political and administrative separation of segments of the population which had previously tended towards cultural homogeneity. In 1924, the Uzbek and Turkmen republics were carved from within the

Russian Republic; in 1929 the Tajik autonomous republic was elevated to Union Republic status; and in 1936 the same happened to the Kirghiz and Kazakh autonomous republics. This was a somewhat different policy from that of 'Muslim National Communism' advocated by supporters of the Volga Tatar Mir-Said Sultan Galiev, who strongly opposed the division, largely on linguistic lines, of individuals thitherto united by a shared Islamic culture.[19] Nonetheless, it proved quite effective, especially in the context of the specific strategy of elite cooptation or 'indigenisation' (*korenizatsiia*),[20] which had been adopted at the Twelfth Party Congress, and which was subsequently put vigorously into practice. One casualty of this strategy was the *Basmachi* resistance movement, which, while not organisationally cohesive, had proved more resilient than similar conservative Islamic movements in Daghestan and Chechnia. Muslims often came to constitute a majority within local party and state institutions, and as a result, in the words of Alexandre Bennigsen, the Bolshevik takeover 'did not seem to the masses of Moslems to be a dramatic capture of power by an alien Russian government, but rather to be the formation of a kind of native government'.[21] This ultimately proved to be the way in which Islam, undoubtedly a key factor in the *Basmachi* movement,[22] was defused. The cooptation of elites was a psychological blow to the *Basmachis*, and lessened Islam as a 'driving force'.[23] *Korenizatsiia* was also used effectively in Kazakhstan, where tribal leaders and mullahs who secured entry to the Party were followed on occasion by substantial groups of loyal supporters.[24] The limitations of the policy became apparent, however, in the Ukraine, where the indigenous elite proved so Ukrainian that it lapsed into 'national deviations'.[25]

This muted policy changed once Stalin had consolidated his broader political position. The process of collectivisation of agriculture, and the associated liquidation of the kulaks (*raskulachivanie*), had enormous implications not simply for Russia, but for non-Russian ethnic minorities. The effects were most lethally felt in the Ukraine[26] and Kazakhstan,[27] both of which experienced horrendous famines as a result of regime policies. It is doubtful whether there will ever be a decisive answer to the question of whether what happened in the early 1930s in the Ukraine was a *class* genocide or an *ethnic* genocide. But a holocaust it proved to be. Its impact was most directly felt amongst non-elite Ukrainians, especially those engaged in sedentary agricultural activities. The *Ezhovshchina* of 1936–1938, however, wiped out large segments of the indigenous elite. This proved to be the case in Kazakhstan as well.

The first phase of *korenizatsiia* was well and truly over. Coercion had taken its place as the principal device for securing compliance from non-Russian subjects of the USSR. This was driven home during the Second World War when eight entire 'nationalities'—the Karachai, Kalmyks, Chechen, Ingush, Balkars, Volga Germans, Crimean Tatars and Meskhetians—were deported, basically on the pretext that they had collaborated with the enemy.[28] A clearer illustration of the Soviet regime's continuing suspicion of minority nationalism, and reliance on crude force to contain it, could hardly be imagined.

The period following Stalin's death in March 1953 brought considerable changes in the approach to the control of minority nationalities. The new oligarchical leadership placed far less emphasis on mass overt coercion, finding it more comfortable to rely on institutional structures the existence of which deterred the voicing of heterodox opinions.[29] Given the vivid memories which many individuals retained of life during the Great Terror, this deterrent proved quite effective,[30] although the KGB remained available to decapitate any organisations which attempted to provide a focus for ethnonational dissent.[31] A version of *korenizatsiia* was also given renewed emphasis—with a safety valve in the form of a special role for the Second Secretaries of republican Central Committees, usually ethnic Russians, who held office, by virtue of the *nomenklatura* system, at the discretion of the All-Union Politburo.[32] Once Brezhnev came to office, a curiously ambivalent approach to ethnic identity was taken. While *sliianie* was clearly identified as a goal for the distant future,[33] attempts were made to increase the use of the Russian language and to withdraw the constitutionally-protected status of the languages of the titular nationalities in the Transcaucasian republics, a move which was abandoned after mass demonstrations in Georgia in 1978.[34] On the other hand, a kind of perverted *korenizatsiia* became the norm. In return for guarantees of order and economic achievement within the union republics, the All-Union state and party apparatuses were prepared for the most part to turn a blind eye to even the most blatant irregularities on the part of republican leaderships. Occasionally, a republican leader would fall because of his inability to deliver order and progress: the replacement of V.P. Mzhavanadze, First Secretary of the Georgian Central Committee from 1953 to 1972 is a case in point.[35] However, against this one must set the cases of Sh.R. Rashidov, First Secretary of the Uzbek Central Committee from 1959 until his death in 1983, and D.A. Kunaev, First Secretary of the Kazakh Central Committee from 1960 to 1962, and again from 1964 to 1986. Both these individuals survived throughout the Brezhnev period, even though they ran political machines which were staggeringly corrupt.

Underlying this curious policy may have been the conviction that the route to *sblizhenie* lay through a process of modernisation which would restructure the dimensions of ethnic identity which I canvassed earlier. And if modernisation in turn could be fostered by *korenizatsiia*, even of the perverted variety, then a case for this kind of autonomy could perhaps be made out. However, both steps in this line of reasoning are suspect. First, the corruption which flourished at the Union Republic level was as likely to produce net costs as to generate benefits.[36] Second, and more importantly, a process of economic modernisation, while fostering *sblizhenie* in certain circumstances, might hinder it in others. All depends upon the context within which social mobilisation occurs, a point made many years ago by Karl W. Deutsch.[37] In the USSR, as Teresa Rakowska-Harmstone argued even before the events of the *glasnost'* period made it blatantly obvious, the effect of modernisation was simply 'to reintegrate traditional ethnic identity on a modern basis'.[38] This conclusion found powerful support from survey evidence, which left no room for doubt that ethnic identity was a major source of social distance between different segments of the Soviet population.[39]

IV

If the various nations of the USSR were not merging before 1985, at least their passions were being held reasonably in check. The deterrent effects of coercive institutions had proved sufficient to prevent mass political opposition from different ethnic groups, and one sober analyst, addressing the question of whether the non-Russians would rebel, came to the conclusion that this was improbable because the instrumentalities of coercion were unlikely to be rendered ineffective by subversion from below.[40] Ironically, his analysis paid little attention to the possibility of subversion from above. Yet this was precisely what occurred following the accession of Gorbachev, and it is by now a commonplace that one of the most dramatic consequences has been the recrudescence of national sentiment, both amongst Russians and non-Russians.[41] The rest of this chapter is devoted to an examination of this phenomenon, but from a particular perspective, namely that of civil society. It is therefore necessary to turn aside for one moment in order to consider what such a perspective entails.

In chapter 2, Kukathas and Lovell defined civil society as 'a complex of institutions and practices which make up "the market", as well as associations of individuals who join together to pursue all sorts of goals beyond narrowly economic ones'. Rigby's approach is slightly different: in chapter 6, he defines civil society as 'those structures and processes through which individuals and groups interact autonomously of the command structures of the state in pursuit of their particular concerns'. It is clear that any difference in focus here relates to the *content* of the institutions and practices, the structures and processes which are being included in the respective definitions. And here, the difference between the two definitions does not appear very sharp. Kukathas and Lovell refer specifically to the market, and Rigby, using the language of Tönnies, makes it clear that it is 'the contractual *Gesellschaft* dimension' of 'unofficial' social activity that is central to his analysis. Nonetheless, while one can readily accept that nationalism may foster autonomy from the command structures of the state, it is questionable whether nationalist associations pursuing goals beyond narrowly economic ones necessarily promote 'sustainable political freedoms and material well-being'. For in my view, it is necessary to recognise that there are two *different* ideal types of nationalism, which I label *communitarian* nationalism, and *extended-order* nationalism.

These bear some superficial similarity to what Plamenatz called western and eastern nationalism. However, there are differences between his usage and mine which are significant in practice. Plamenatz saw nationalism as 'a phenomenon peculiar to peoples who share a cosmopolitan and secular culture in which the belief in progress is strong'.[42] For reasons which will shortly become apparent, his emphasis on the secular character of culture is unduly restrictive when one's concern is ethnonationalism in the Soviet Union. Furthermore, his distinction was primarily between the nationalism of those whose aim was centrally 'to acquire national states of their own' (western nationalism), and the nationalism of those who, being drawn into an alien civilisation 'had to re-equip themselves culturally' (eastern nationalism).[43] The distinction which I wish to draw is related to two of the dimensions of an ethnic group which I mentioned earlier: namely a distinctive shared culture, and a sense of solidarity.

Communitarian nationalism is an attitudinal disposition characteristic of residents of integrated traditional societies, where custom remains an important mechanism of social coordination. The socialisation process within the unit emphasises the importance of rules defining reciprocal obligations between its members, and of the unit's practices and rituals as a source of meaning for the life of the individual. These practices or rituals are often religious in character, and may be a significant source of political legitimation. The sense of solidarity associated with this kind of sentiment is normative in character, and prone to override the temptation which an individual may feel to associate with members of other groups. The group's enemies are likely to be identified more in ethnonational than ideological terms. *Extended-order nationalism* displays few of these features. It is rather the disposition characteristic of residents of diversified societies with complex productive processes based on contract. Church and state are separate; the culture within these orders is individualistic and pluralist rather than collectivist, and while the residents may act cooperatively to defend the order from external attack, they do not collectively constitute a mutual-aid association. Individual acts of political dissent take place. The sense of solidarity which unites the residents does not normally preclude them from associating with members of other groups. The group's enemies are likely to be identified more in ideological than ethnonational terms.

V

These ideal types are not of course fully realised in any contemporary Soviet groups. The nationalisms which one encounters are admixtures of communitarian and extended-order nationalisms, and it is the balance between these elements which determines the specific form which particular nationalisms take. Years of centralised administrative control, with command playing a major role in social coordination,[44] have inevitably affected the rules, practices, rituals and *Weltanschauungen* of different groups. Furthermore, the political behaviour of individuals may reflect a whole complex of influences, of which national sentiment is but one. Yet it is remarkable to what extent the lessening of coercion has led to a resurfacing of patterns of behaviour which can be broadly associated with one or the other ideal type. And in my view, while those patterns broadly associated with extended-order nationalism may well promote sustainable political freedoms and material well-being, it is problematical whether those broadly associated with communitarian nationalism will have the same effect. To substantiate this point, I propose to focus first on nationalism in the Baltic States, which most closely approaches extended-order nationalism; second on nationalism in the Transcaucasian republics and Central Asia, which most closely approaches communitarian nationalism; and finally, on Russian nationalism.

The Baltic States of Latvia, Lithuania and Estonia are in one respect radically different from other seats of minority nationalism within the USSR.[45] They experienced twenty years of independence between 1920, when the Bolshevik regime concluded peace treaties with them in which 'Russian claims to sovereignty over their territories were renounced in perpetuity',[46] and 1939, when the Secret Protocols to the Nonaggression Pact between Nazi Germany and the Soviet Union triggered the process by which the Baltic States were finally incorporated in the USSR.[47] The effects of this experience can hardly be underestimated. 'In part because of ... pre-1940 achievements', wrote one observer in 1975, 'popular memories of the independence period have not only survived in the Baltic republics but also have been glamorized and romanticized, especially by a younger generation which never actually experienced that independence'.[48] The institutions of government in all three states were initially democratic in character but gave way in time to authoritarian political forms. Nonetheless, the economies in all three states continued to be based on agricultural production for both domestic consumption and export, carried out by independent farmers; and the influence of the church as a counterweight to the state remained important, both in Lithuania, which had been under the influence of Roman Catholicism since 1386, and in Latvia and Estonia, which had come under the sway of Lutheranism during the period of Swedish domination following the Livonian Wars.

Here, it is clear, lay the foundations for something approaching extended-order nationalism. Contract was the dominant mode of social organisation, the social separation of powers was considerable, and the solidarity which united the nationals of the various states was non-exclusive. Even before 1985, there were significant indicators of latent extended-order nationalism at work. Dissident activity was always strong, and in Lithuania went so far as to involve spectacular self-immolations.[49] The semi-autonomous religious infrastructure also assisted the preservation of a distinct sense of Lithuanian identity, and the *Chronicle of the Catholic Church of Lithuania* became an important *samizdat* publication. National assertion—which became manifest as coercion was loosened after 1985—proved remarkably free of crude anti-Russian dimensions, notwithstanding the well-documented sense of social distance between Balts and Russians. This was most striking in Latvia, a republic in which Latvians by the time of the 1989 census had been reduced to a mere 52.0 per cent of the population.[50] There, the Popular Front took pains to appeal to the political concerns of non-Latvian minorities, and even claimed that 14 per cent of its members were non-Latvian.[51] The moves towards secession of the Baltic states from the USSR, which became possible after the effectively free and contested elections to the Supreme Soviets of the three republics in early 1990 were won by the Popular Fronts, were again not accompanied by attacks on Russians; and even in the face of considerable provocation from the Soviet Army in the weeks following the Lithuanian declaration of independence on 11 March, the population remained resolutely committed to political pluralism, and avoided violence of the kind which could have provided the pretext for the imposition of coercive central rule. The increasingly autonomous associations of Baltic nationalism could claim a civic, as opposed to simply ethnonational, agenda, and as a consequence, their contribution to the flourishing of civil society was a positive one.

The situation in the Baltic contrasts starkly with that in Central Asia. The cultural context is radically different, not only in terms of social structure, but also in terms of rules, practices, and rituals. Traditional society tended towards communitarian nationalism, marked by intense and exclusive solidarity, and this in certain respects has been reinforced by Islamic values. It is important to note that our concern here is with religion as a dimension of culture, rather than of personal faith. As a consequence, it is not sufficient to speak *simply* of Islam. Rather, one must distinguish between the distinct forms of Islam which the intersection of religious doctrines and local cultures has produced.[52] That said, it is certainly the case that one of the effects of the destruction of traditional social structures in Central Asia was a reinforcement of traditional value systems, broadly clustered around Islam, which were less directly vulnerable to attack.

The case of Kazakhstan is instructive in this respect, especially as it was the site of the first ethnonational violence of the *glasnost'* period. In Kazakhstan, as was noted earlier, the famine of the early 1930s had a devastating effect on traditional lifestyles, which were centred upon the tending of flocks and herds by pastoral nomads organised in clans, and at a higher level into hordes. The Kazakh elite was largely obliterated. Amongst the nomadic and largely non-literate Kazakhs, Miller has argued, to 'destroy their élite was literally to decapitate society ... to destroy the cohesiveness and self-awareness of Kazakhs as a society. The survivors, in developing new authority patterns, will have been ideal candidates for assimilation into someone else's culture'.[53] Miller took this to explain, at least in part, the unusually high party saturation rate amongst Kazakhs. The events of December 1986, when student rioting broke out in the Kazakh capital of Alma-ata, may incline one to wonder, however, whether party membership may not have been taken up purely for reasons of expedience, with Islamic institutions filling the void created by the dissolution of traditional society. The trigger for the riots was the announcement that Party First Secretary Kunaev had been replaced by an ethnic Russian, G.V. Kolbin. While initial reports of the death toll appear to have been exaggerated, the psychological impact of the events was considerable. A remarkable article in *Literaturnaia gazeta* some months later claimed that the demonstrators 'were manipulated by Muslim fanatics—Sufis—who infiltrated the student environment'.[54]

Kazakhstan was almost certainly the Central Asian republic most direly affected by the events of the 1930s. However, it is by no means the only republic in which Islam has proved politically potent. Indeed, there is evidence of a re-emphasising of self-identification in terms of a community of believers (*ummah*), going beyond mere self-identification as a Muslim. This community is not, of course, an ascriptive group, but rather a collection of individuals united by 'adherence to a particular set of values, ideologies and practices'.[55] This communal self-identification is of the kind which one associates with communitarian nationalism, and even before the *glasnost'* period there were reasons to treat it seriously. Sketchy survey evidence cited by Bennigsen from Uzbekistan and Tajikistan suggested a considerable increase in Islamic adherence between 1973 and 1986. Islamic rituals were pervasive, 'parallel' Islam in the form of Sufi brotherhoods flourished, and Islam acquired increasingly political overtones.[56] The use of the adjective 'parallel' serves as an important reminder that the Soviet regime had attempted to institutionalise an Islamic clerical hierarchy, through the Board of Muslim Deputies of Soviet Central Asia and Kazakhstan. However, the attempt was probably doomed from the start, given that Islam has no clergy in the strict sense. In any case, the gap between official and non-official Islam grew wide over time, culminating in demonstrations in Tashkent in February 1989 which resulted in the replacement of the Grand Mufti—who according to Almaz Estekov, Chairman of the informal group 'Islam and Democracy', drank, womanised, and literally knew not one chapter of the Koran verbatim![57]

That Sufi brotherhoods may have been the organisational focus for oppositional behaviour is especially interesting. Sufism is not a worldly philosophy, and emphasises direct esoteric or intuitive revelation.[58] For this reason, its adherents have frequently been anathematised by Islamic radicals. Yet its distinctive pattern of organisation into networks often linked to a particular mentor may have rendered it a peculiarly comfortable retreat for those forcibly detached from the integrated units of traditional societies.

In the light of recent events in Uzbekistan, however, it is important to repeat the warning I voiced earlier about ascribing unity to the world of Islam. In June 1989, groups of Uzbeks embarked on the systematic slaughter of large numbers of Meskhetians in the Fergana Valley of Uzbekistan. Nearly a hundred Meskhetians were killed, many more were injured, and within a month between 35,000-40,000 of them had left Uzbekistan as internal refugees. The Meskhetians, of course, are Muslims, just as are the Uzbeks; but they originated from Georgia and Armenia, and found themselves in Uzbekistan only when deported by the Soviet authorities during the Second World War. As 1989 drew on, articles in the Soviet press began to attribute the massacres to the influence amongst young Uzbeks of the Saudi Arabian-based Wahhabi sect, which is notoriously puritanical and intolerant of any Islamic practices which it views as deviationist.[59] How seriously this claim can be taken is open to question;[60] but the events in the Fergana Valley demonstrate quite clearly the lethal consequences which can flow from the patterns of thinking which lead the adherents of communitarian nationalism to view their territorial neighbours not as individuals but as components of an alien collective.

Where these modes of thinking are linked to distinct territorial conflicts, the consequences can be horrific. The classic illustration of this has been the conflict over the Nagorno-Karabakh Autonomous *Oblast'* in the Republic of Azerbaijan. This region was founded on 7 July 1923, and in 1979 it had a population of 162,181. Of these, 37,264, or 23.0 per cent, were Azeris, while 123,076, or 75.9 per cent, were Armenians.[61] In 1987, 75,000 citizens petitioned for the return of the region to Armenia. The rebuffing of this request (by a low level party official) sparked disturbances which began in February 1988. Hostility between Azeris and Armenians escalated despite serious attempts by the central Soviet leadership to restructure both party and state instrumentalities in the two republics. Ultimately,

late on the night of 19 January 1990, Soviet tanks smashed their way
to the centre of Baku in order to put down groups which had been
staging anti-Armenian pogroms. It would be premature at the
moment to speculate on what precise role Islam may have played in
fostering a sense of identity amongst the Azeris. Nonetheless, it is
useful to recall that Azeris are predominantly Shi'ite Muslims, and
that knowledge of this fact should prompt us to bear certain things in
mind when interpreting their observable behaviour. By this I do not
mean to suggest that they are 'inherently revolutionary' in the
Iranian mould: indeed, the leading Shi'ite theologian of Iranian
Azerbaijan, Ayatollah Sayyid Qassem Shariatmadari, was a notable
opponent of the mixing of politics and religion.[62] Rather, I would
point to the doctrine of prudential dissimulation (taqiyya), which
Shia consider lawful 'where there is overwhelming danger of loss of
life or property and where no danger to religion would occur
thereby'.[63] The frequency of its practice was noted by Beliaev, who
depicted Azerbaijan as a republic 'where hundreds of "parallel"
mosques are functioning and where there are very active sectarians
declaring themselves atheists'.[64] A believer obliged to practise
prudential dissimulation is likely, over time, to become increasingly
alienated from the order which prompts such conduct, and implicitly
from those territorial neighbours who are not similarly obliged to
dissemble. Here, once again, one can find fertile ground for evolution
of the exclusivist Weltanschauung characteristically associated with
communitarian nationalism.

Russian nationalism is a phenomenon of enormous complexity,
and one cannot possibly do it justice in a few paragraphs. From the
moment when Chaadaev pronounced the Russians to be a people
without history,[65] the character of the Russian nation had been a
matter of considerable controversy within the pre-revolutionary
Russian intelligentsia. The nineteenth-century Slavophiles believed,
according to Walicki, that 'Old Russia' could preserve 'the pure form
of Gemeinschaft', because she was 'not encumbered by the heritage
of rationalistic Roman culture'.[66] Yet while Slavophilism as a
distinct philosophy disintegrated fairly rapidly, at least some of the
traditions and customs which it venerated managed to survive the
traumas of the next century, while the tradition of law to which
Slavophilism was especially antithetical developed only the
shallowest roots before the events of 1917 set the scene for the
development of the command-administrative system.[67] In addition,
Stalin's blatant exploitation of Russian nationalist symbols as a
regime-maintenance device in the face of external aggression—'We
will never rouse the people to war with Marxism-Leninism alone', he

reportedly remarked[68]—gave - Russian nationalism a degree of legitimacy which no minority nationalism could claim.[69] As a result, various forms of Russian nationalism managed to survive communist rule.

As well as allowing a voice for the familiar nationalism of such a distinguished writer as Aleksandr Solzhenitsyn, who has recently defended political pluralism, a market economy, and a retreat from empire,[70] the policy of *glasnost'* has permitted some of the nastier forms of Russian nationalism to take off with a vengeance. There are many Russian nationalists whose attitudes closely approach those associated with communitarian nationalism in its pure form. In intellectual circles there had long been evidence that Russian chauvinism, often allied with virulent anti-semitism, was far from dead, finding an outlet at different times in journals such as *Molodaia gvardiia*[71] and *Nash sovremennik.*[72] In recent years, these strands of thought have taken on organised forms. The most obvious manifestation of this is of course the *Pamiat'* group, headed by Dmitrii Vasil'ev, which demands the restoration of the monarchy and the reestablishment of the Russian Orthodox Church as a state church. Vasil'ev, a recent interviewer has concluded, is a fervent believer in the existence of a Zionist-Masonic conspiracy.[73] This could be dismissed as marginal, were it not for the undeniable intensification of anti-Semitism in the *glasnost'* period. In numerical terms, the active supporters of *Pamiat'* probably are insignificant— but they are active enough to cause a lot of suffering to a lot of people. The disintegration of the Eastern Bloc, together with the challenge to the integrity of the Soviet Union posed by economic crisis and the pluralisation of politics, has thrown the future role of Russian nationalism sharply into focus. A leadership committed to eschewing the use of coercive means of control, but no longer in a position realistically to legitimate its rule by reference to familiar tenets of Marxist-Leninist ideology, may be tempted to resort to the legitimating potential of Russian nationalism in much the same way as Stalin did in 1941.[74] Depending upon which individuals came to the fore as a result of such an exercise, this could be a development of profound concern.[75]

VI

Where does all this lead us? The answer, I would suggest, is towards a more nuanced view of the virtues of associational autonomy.

There is no doubt that in the aftermath of decades of command-administrative domination, the idea of the re-emergence of civil society based on autonomous associations of individuals pursuing conjoint private goals is an appealing one. In parts of the Soviet Union, the form which recrudescent civil society has taken is just as appealing. But if this chapter has a message, it is that there can be a dark side to recrudescent civil society as well. The events in places like the Fergana Valley demonstrate that communitarian nationalism can produce autonomous units which are integrated by value-systems in which respect for individual freedom does not figure prominently. This is not to say that from the point of view of individuals within those units, life is not infinitely improved by the autonomy of those groups. It is simply to note that for the neighbours of those groups, their increasing autonomy can be absolutely terrifying.

Notes

1 'К Чаадаеву', in А.С. Пушкин, *Стихотворения* (Moscow: Izdatel'stvo 'khudozhestvennaia literatura', 1966) pp. 36–37.

2 Jon Elster, *The cement of society: A study of social order* (Cambridge: Cambridge University Press, 1989) p. 248.

3 For a discussion which emphasises this point, see Joan Vincent, 'The Structuring of Ethnicity', *Human Organization*, vol.33, no.4, Winter 1974, pp. 375–379, at pp. 376–377.

4 Cynthia H. Enloe, *Ethnic Conflict and Political Development* (Boston: Little, Brown & Co., 1973) p. 17.

5 Anthony D. Smith, *The Ethnic Origins of Nations* (Oxford: Basil Blackwell, 1986) pp. 22–31.

6 See, for example, Ernest Gellner, *Nations and Nationalism* (Oxford: Basil Blackwell, 1983) p. 55.

7 Karl Marx and Friedrich Engels, *The German Ideology* (Moscow: Progress Publishers, 1976) p. 82.

8 For a discussion of these peregrinations, see David W. Lovell, *Marx's Proletariat: The Making of a Myth* (London: Routledge, 1988) p. 178.

9 For general discussions, see Ian Cummins, *Marx, Engels and National Movements* (New York: St Martin's Press, 1980), and Walker Connor, *The National Question in Marxist-Leninist Theory and Practice* (Princeton: Princeton University Press, 1984)

10 Richard Pipes, *Russia under the Old Regime* (Harmondsworth: Penguin, 1974) p. 83.

11 See Peter Duncan, 'Ideology and the National Question: Marxism-Leninism and the Nationality Policy of the Communist Party of the Soviet Union', in Stephen White and Alex Pravda (eds), *Ideology and Soviet Politics* (London: Macmillan, 1988) pp. 180–202, at p. 182.

12 'По национальному вопросу', *Коммунистическая Партия Советского Союза в резолюциях и решениях съездов, конференций и пленумов ЦК* (Moscow: Politizdat, 1970) Vol.I, pp. 448–449.

13 И.В. Сталин, 'Доклад по национальному вопросу', in И.В. Сталин, *Сочинения* (Moscow: Gospolitizdat, 1947) Vol.IV, pp. 30–32, at pp. 31–32.

14 See Georg Von Rauch, *The Baltic States: The Years of Independence. Estonia, Latvia, Lithuania 1917–1940* (Berkeley & Los Angeles: University of California Press, 1974).

15 For discussion of these cases, see Ronald Grigor Suny, *The Making of the Georgian Nation* (Bloomington: Indiana University Press, 1988) pp. 202–208; Richard G. Hovannisian, *The Republic of Armenia: The First Year, 1918–1919* (Berkeley & Los Angeles: University of California Press, 1971); and Tadeusz Swietochowski, *Russian Azerbaijan, 1905–1920: The Shaping of National Identity in a Muslim Community* (Cambridge: Cambridge University Press, 1985) pp. 129–190.

16 On these protectorates, see Seymour Becker, *Russia's Protectorates in Central Asia: Bukhara and Khiva, 1865–1924* (Cambridge: Harvard University Press, 1968).

17 Richard Pipes, *The Formation of the Soviet Union: Communism and Nationalism 1917–1923* (Cambridge: Harvard University Press, 1964) p. 293.

18 On this procedure, see Victor Zaslavsky, *The Neo-Stalinist State: Class, Ethnicity, and Consensus in Soviet Society* (New York: M.E. Sharpe, 1982) pp. 92–94. Soviet ethnographic research, it need hardly be added, is light years ahead of bureaucratic procedures in its appreciation of the complexity of ethnic categorisations. See Ernest Gellner, *State and Society in Soviet Thought* (Oxford: Basil Blackwell, 1988) pp. 115–136.

19 On this phenomenon, see Alexandre A. Bennigsen and S. Enders Wimbush, *Muslim National Communism in the Soviet Union: A Revolutionary Strategy for the Colonial World* (Chicago: University of Chicago Press, 1979); and Alexandre Bennigsen and Chantal Lemercier-Quelquejay, *Sultan Galiev, Le père de la révolution tiers-mondiste* (Paris: Fayard, 1986).

20 See Bernard V. Olivier, 'Korenizatsiia', *Central Asian Survey*, vol.9, no.3, 1990, pp. 77-98.

21 Alexandre Bennigsen, 'The Bolshevik Conquest of the Moslem Borderlands', in Thomas T. Hammond (ed.), *The Anatomy of Communist Takeovers* (New Haven: Yale University Press, 1975) pp. 61–70, at p. 69.

22 Martha Brill Olcott, 'The Basmachi or Freemen's Revolt in Turkestan 1918–1924', *Soviet Studies*, vol.33, no.3, July 1981, pp. 352–369, at p. 364.

23 See Eden Naby, 'The Concept of Jihad in Opposition to Communist Rule: Turkestan and Afghanistan', *Studies in Comparative Communism*, vol.19, nos.3-4, Autumn-Winter 1986, pp. 287–300.

24 Martha Brill Olcott, *The Kazakhs* (Stanford: Hoover Institution Press, 1987) p. 202.

25   James E. Mace, *Communism and the Dilemmas of National Liberation: National Communism in Soviet Ukraine, 1918–1933* (Cambridge: Harvard University Press, 1983).

26   On the Ukrainian famine, see James E. Mace, 'Famine and Nationalism in Soviet Ukraine', *Problems of Communism*, vol.33, no.3, May–June 1984, pp. 37–50; and Robert Conquest, *The Harvest of Sorrow: Soviet collectivization and the terror famine* (London: Hutchinson, 1986).

27   See Ж.Б. Абылхожин, М.К. Козыбаев, and М.Б. Татимов, 'Казахстанская трагедия', *Вопросы истории*, no.7, 1989, pp. 53–71.

28   For details, see Robert Conquest, *The Nation Killers: The Soviet Deportation of Nationalities* (London: Macmillan, 1970); Aleksandr Nekrich, *The Punished Peoples: The deportation and fate of Soviet minorities at the end of the Second World War* (New York: W.W. Norton & Co., 1978), and Isabelle Kreindler, 'The Soviet Deported Nationalities: A Summary and an Update', *Soviet Studies*, vol.38, no.3, July 1986, pp. 387–405.

29   See Rasma Karklins, 'The Dissent/Coercion Nexus in the USSR', *Studies in Comparative Communism*, vol.20, nos.3–4, Autumn-Winter 1987, pp. 321–341, at p. 338.

30   This view is supported by evidence from the Soviet Interview Project. See Donna Bahry and Brian D. Silver, 'Intimidation and the Symbolic Uses of Terror in the USSR', *American Political Science Review*, vol.81, no.4, December 1987, pp. 1065–1098, at p. 1090.

31   Amy W. Knight, *The KGB: Police and Politics in the Soviet Union* (London: Unwin Hyman, 1988) p. 207.

32   See T.H. Rigby, *Political Elites in the USSR: Central leaders and local cadres from Lenin to Gorbachev* (Aldershot: Edward Elgar, 1990) p. 283.

33   Gail Warshofsky Lapidus, 'Ethnonationalism and Political Stability: The Soviet Case', *World Politics*, vol.36, no.4, July 1984, pp. 555–580, at pp. 562–565.

34   Suny, *The Making of the Georgian Nation*, p. 309. See also Roman Solchanyk, 'Russian Language and Soviet Politics', *Soviet Studies*, vol.34, no.1, January 1982, pp. 23–42.

35   For a revealing discussion of the Mzhavanadze case, see Konstantin Simis, *USSR: Secrets of a Corrupt Society* (London: J.M. Dent, 1982) pp. 34–40.

36   On the costs and benefits of corruption, see J.S. Nye, 'Corruption and Political Development: A Cost-Benefit Analysis', *American Political Science Review*, vol.61. no.2, June 1967, pp. 417–427.

37   Karl W. Deutsch, 'Social Mobilization and Political Development', *American Political Science Review*, vol.55, no.3, September 1961, pp. 493–514, at p. 501.

38   Teresa Rakowska-Harmstone, 'Minority Nationalism Today: An Overview', in Robert Conquest (ed.), *The Last Empire: Nationality and the Soviet Future* (Stanford: Hoover Institution Press, 1986) pp. 235–264, at p. 240.

39   See Zvi Gitelman, 'Are Nations Merging in the USSR?', *Problems of Communism*, vol.32, no.5, September-October 1983, pp. 35–47; Rasma

Karklins, *Ethnic Relations in the USSR: The Perspective From Below* (Boston: Allen & Unwin, 1986) pp. 66–71; and Rasma Karklins, 'Nationality policy and ethnic relations in the USSR', in James R. Millar (ed.), *Politics, work, and daily life in the USSR: A survey of former Soviet citizens* (Cambridge: Cambridge University Press, 1987) pp. 301–331, at pp. 312–314.

40   Alexander J. Motyl, *Will the Non-Russians Rebel?: State, Ethnicity, and Stability in the USSR* (Ithaca: Cornel University Press, 1987) p. 170.

41   For various perspectives, see Patrick Cockburn, 'Dateline USSR; Ethnic Tremors', *Foreign Policy*, no.74, Spring 1989, pp. 168–184; Paul Goble, 'Soviet Ethnic Politics', *Problems of Communism*, vol.38, no.4, July-August 1989, pp. 1–14; Gail W. Lapidus, 'Gorbachev's Nationalities Problem', *Foreign Affairs*, vol.68, no.4, Spring 1989, pp. 92–108; Zbigniew Brzezinski, 'Post-Communist Nationalism', *Foreign Affairs*, vol.68, no.5, Winter 1989–90, pp. 1–25; Ronald G. Suny, 'Nationalities and Nationalism', in Abraham Brumberg (ed.), *Chronicle of a Revolution: A Western-Soviet Inquiry into Perestroika* (New York: Pantheon, 1990) pp. 108-128; and Bohdan Nahaylo and Victor Swoboda, *Soviet Disunion: A History of the Nationalities Problem in the USSR* (New York: The Free Press, 1990) pp. 231–359.

42   John Plamenatz, 'Two Types of Nationalism', in Eugene Kamenka (ed.), *Nationalism: The nature and evolution of an idea* (Canberra: Australian National University Press, 1975) pp. 23–36, at p. 23.

43   Ibid., p. 30.

44   For the typology of custom, contract, and command, see T.H. Rigby, 'Traditional, Market and Organizational Societies and the USSR', *World Politics*, vol.16, no.4, July 1964, pp. 539–557, at pp. 539–540; and for some modification to the argument, see T.H. Rigby, 'Politics in the Mono-organizational Society', in Andrew C. Janos (ed.), *Authoritarian Politics in Communist Europe: Uniformity and Diversity in One-Party States* (Berkeley: Institute of International Studies, University of California, 1976) pp. 31–80, at pp. 33–34.

45   For a more detailed discussion of these examples, see William Maley, *The Politics of Baltic Nationalisms* (Canberra: Working Paper no.6, Department of International Relations, Research School of Pacific Studies, Australian National University, August 1990).

46   Romuald J. Misiunas and Rein Taagepera, *The Baltic States: Years of Dependence 1940–1980* (London: Hurst, 1983) p. 9.

47   For the texts of these protocols, see R.J. Sontag and J.S. Beddie, *Nazi-Soviet Relations 1939–1941: Documents from the Archives of the German Foreign Office* (Westport: Greenwood Press, 1976) pp. 78, 107.

48   V. Stanley Vardys, 'Modernization and Baltic Nationalism', *Problems of Communism*, vol.24, no.5, September-October 1975, pp. 32–48, at p. 36.

49   V. Stanley Vardys, *The Catholic Church, Nationality and Dissent in Soviet Lithuania* (Boulder: East European Quarterly, 1978) pp. 173–177.

50   Ann Sheehy, 'Latvians Remain Majority in Latvia', *Report on the USSR*, vol.1, no.46, 17 November 1989, pp. 20–21.

51   Nils R. Muiznieks, 'The Latvian Popular Front and Ethnic Relations', *Report on the USSR*, vol.1, no.42, 20 October 1989, pp. 20–22, at p. 20.

52   For an excellent recent discussion, see Yaacov Ro'i, 'The Islamic Influence on Nationalism in Soviet Central Asia', *Problems of Communism*, vol.39, no.4, July-August 1990, pp. 49–64.

53   John Miller, 'Political Culture: Some Perennial Questions Reopened', in Archie Brown (ed.), *Political Culture and Communist Studies* (London: Macmillan, 1984) pp. 40–61, at p. 57.

54   Игорь Беляев, 'Ислам и политика', *Литературная газета*, 20 May 1987, p. 12.

55   M. Nazif Shahrani, '"From Tribe to Umma": Comments on the Dynamics of Identity in Muslim Soviet Central Asia', *Central Asian Survey*, vol.3, no.3, 1985, pp. 27–38, at p. 29.

56   Alexandre Bennigsen, 'Unrest in the World of Soviet Islam', *Third World Quarterly*, vol.10, no.2, April 1988, pp. 770–786.

57   Quoted in Annette Bohr, 'Background to Demonstration of Soviet Muslims in Tashkent', *Report on the USSR*, vol.1, no.11, 17 March 1989, pp. 18–19, at p. 19.

58   See Julian Baldick, *Mystical Islam: An Introduction to Sufism* (London: I.B. Tauris, 1989). On Sufism in the Soviet Union, see Alexandre Bennigsen and Chantal Lemercier-Quelquejay, *Le soufi et le commissaire: Les confréries musulmanes en URSS* (Paris: Éditions du Seuil, 1986).

59   See Ira M. Lapidus, *A History of Islamic Societies* (Cambridge: Cambridge University Press, 1988) pp. 673–675.

60   On this, see Ann Sheehy, 'Social and Economic Background to Recent Events in Fergana Valley', *Report on the USSR*, vol.1, no.27, 7 July 1989, pp. 21–23.

61   Alexandre Bennigsen and S. Enders Wimbush, *Muslims of the Soviet Empire: A Guide* (Bloomington: Indiana University Press, 1986) p. 136.

62   Cheryl Benard and Zalmay Khalilzad, *"The Government of God": Iran's Islamic Republic* (New York: Columbia University Press, 1984) p. 137.

63   Moojan Momen, *An Introduction to Shi'i Islam* (New Haven: Yale University Press, 1985) p. 183.

64   Беляев, 'Ислам и политика', p. 12.

65   See П. Я. Чаадаев, *Философические письма и Апология сумашедшего* (Ann Arbor: Ardis, 1978) pp. 6–26.

66   Andrzej Walicki, *A History of Russian Thought from the Enlightenment to Marxism* (Oxford: Oxford University Press, 1980) p. 109.

67   See Leonard Schapiro, *Russian Studies* (London: Collins Harvill, 1986) p. 41.

68   Roy Medvedev, *On Stalin and Stalinism* (Oxford: Oxford University Press, 1979) p. 124.

69   For a detailed discussion of the doctrine of 'Russian leadership', see Frederick C. Barghoorn, *Soviet Russian Nationalism* (New York: Oxford University Press, 1956) pp. 26–66.

70   А.И. Солженицын, 'Как нам обустроить Россию: Посильные соображения', *Комсомольская правда*, 18 September 1990.

71   See Alexander Yanov, *The Russian New Right: Right-Wing Ideologies in the Contemporary USSR* (Berkeley: Institute of International Studies, University of California, 1978) pp. 39–61.

72   John B. Dunlop, *The New Russian Nationalism* (New York: Praeger, 1985) pp. 19–25.

73   John B. Dunlop, 'A Conversation with Dmitrii Vasil'ev, the Leader of "Pamyat"', *Report on the USSR*, vol.1, no.50, 15 December 1989, pp. 12–16, at p. 14.

74   A resolution adopted in July 1990 by the 28th Congress of the Communist Party of the Soviet Union condemned 'chauvinism' and 'anti-semitism', but stopped short of directly criticising the more extreme variants of Russian nationalism: see 'Резолюция XXVIII съезда Коммунистической партии Советского союза: Демократическая национальная политика - путь к добровольному союзу, миру и согласию между народами', *Правда*, 15 July 1990, p. 4.

75   For differing perspectives on Russian nationalism, see John B. Dunlop, *The Faces of Contemporary Russian Nationalism* (Princeton: Princeton University Press, 1983), and Alexander Yanov, *The Russian Challenge and the Year 2000* (Oxford: Basil Blackwell, 1987). The most detailed recent appraisal of different Russian nationalist groups is Roman Szporluk, 'Dilemmas of Russian Nationalism', *Problems of Communism*, vol.38, no.4, July-August 1989, pp. 15–35.

11

Civil Society and the Soviet-Vietnamese Alliance

CARLYLE A. THAYER

I

The recrudescence of civil society in the Soviet Union is a process that has been underway for some time and pre-dates the Gorbachev period. Undoubtedly this process has been accelerated by Gorbachev's advocacy of *glasnost'* (candour), *perestroika* (restructuring), and *novoe politicheskoe myshlenie* (new political thinking). Previous chapters have documented the massive changes brought about in domestic Soviet society. Major changes have also occurred in the conduct of Soviet foreign policy in general, and in Soviet Union's relations with members of the 'socialist community' in particular. This chapter will address the impact of the emergence of civil society on Soviet alliance relations, with special reference to Vietnam.

According to S. Frederick Starr, the 'profound changes [that] have taken place in Soviet society ... will exert an influence upon both the traditional institutions of government and what George Kennan ... called "the mental world of the Soviet leaders"'[1] and these in turn will affect the conduct of Soviet foreign policy. Starr argued as follows:[2]

> Gorbachev's stated desire to turn inward has nothing to do with the rise of civil society as such. Many of the last century's great colonial powers were among the most developed civil societies of their time.
>
> Gorbachev frequently has asserted his belief in the priority of domestic over foreign affairs. This may be a convenient way to present the rival claims of guns and butter, but it oversimplifies the nature of foreign policy under civil societies. The academician Yevgeny Primakov's reference to the 'organic link' between domestic

and foreign affairs, cited in the July 9, 1987 issue of *Pravda*, states the relationship more accurately. He might have added that, as Karl Marx predicted of bourgeois states, the relevant domestic issues are the country's economic interests.

To succeed politically within the new social context, the Kremlin's foreign policy must be seen by the Soviet public as serving its interests and not just those of the Communist Party. Foreign-policy initiatives must pass muster with domestic public opinion, including the opinions held by both the cosmopolitan and the more chauvinistic sectors of society. And while Kremlin leaders will feel the impact of public opinion on their foreign policy, they will have fewer ways of influencing such opinion than in the past.

Starr's views were later echoed by Soviet Foreign Minister Eduard Shevardnadze. Shevardnadze wrote in the introduction to a survey of Soviet foreign policy, prepared by his Ministry for presentation to the People's Deputies of the Supreme Soviet, that[3]

(i)t [the survey] is a break with the tradition under which foreign-policy decisions were taken in a narrow circle, so that now and again even the members of the political leadership were left uninformed of the most important decisions affecting the vital interests of the state... Foreign policy is no longer a zone outside the ambit of *glasnost* ... We want Soviet citizens to have a fuller understanding that our foreign policy serves *perestroika* and is one of its motive forces and reserves. A bad foreign policy means wasteful expenditures, a tightening of belts, fear, and restricted democracy.

How then does the emergence of Soviet civil society relate to the Soviet Union's alliance relations? Here it is necessary to discuss the concept of 'new political thinking' and the changes which it has engendered in Soviet foreign policy.

II

'New political thinking', as Margot Light notes,[4] is a shorthand term used to refer 'to the reform of Soviet foreign policy'. Like the term 'civil society', it predates the Gorbachev period. Light identifies four main elements in Gorbachev's new political thinking: 'a thorough overhaul of personnel; the adoption of a more flexible and sophisticated diplomatic style; the promotion of more pragmatic policies; and the espousal of new theoretical principles together with an agenda for their future elaboration.' It is this last point which will be developed below.

In Shevardnadze's above-mentioned review of Soviet foreign policy,[5] the following five factors were held to influence the evolving concept of new political thinking:

(1) the rapid development of science and technology, especially in the areas of electronics and information;

(2) the mounting trend towards an interpenetration of economic mechanisms at regional and global level;

(3) changes in the political sphere where ideas of freedom and democracy, the supremacy of law and order, and freedom of choice are increasingly taking hold of people's thinking;

(4) change in the very concept of national security, with the stress less on military factors than economic, technological and monetary factors; and

(5) unity and interdependence of the world ... and the supremacy of universal interests.

Shevardnadze then concluded:

New political thinking presupposes renunciation of the concept of confrontation as a principle of foreign policy; it is aimed at ending the domination of ideological standards and at *deideologising state-to-state relations*. All the countries of the world are expected to learn to cooperate, to respect each other regardless of distinctions in ideology and to search for common ground in the interests of all rather than subordinate their foreign policy to the ideological principles of a large or small section of humanity, principles that are often antithetical in content. Needless to say, this conception of the problem does not annul our own convictions prompted by our worldview.

Robert Miller has noted that there were two main implications of Soviet new political thinking for Eastern Europe: 'First of all, Gorbachev has stated explicitly that refurbishing the reputation of socialism in the world is the collective responsibility of all the socialist countries. Thus, the various reforms designed to achieve this in the Soviet Union—*perestroika, glasnost', demokratizatsiia*, etc.— are incumbent on the leadership of the East European (and other) regimes as well.' Secondly, 'Another of the basic assumptions behind the "new political thinking" as applied to Eastern Europe is that the respective regimes have the will and the means to retain power.'[6]

According to Margot Light, the theoretical principles of Gorbachev's new political thinking related mainly to Soviet-American relations, especially in the area of strategic and conventional arms control. Here, as is well known, the Soviet Union has advanced the notion of comprehensive security and pursued arms control agreements with the United States. To a lesser extent, Light argued, Soviet new political thinking was also applied to Soviet relations with the Third World and did 'not relate directly to relations among socialist states, other members of the socialist commonwealth have been encouraged to adopt reform programmes of their own, while participating in a new plan for integrating their technologies'.[7]

Thus, until 1988, Soviet 'new political thinking' was relatively underdeveloped with respect to Soviet relations with other socialist states and was in the process of reformulation. In October 1989, on the eve of momentous changes in Eastern Europe, the Soviet Foreign Ministry observed that relations among socialist states would no longer be based on shared ideology but on more pragmatic factors:

> The foreign policy principles of new thinking must operate without fail in relations between socialist countries. There is not and cannot be two systems of values, that is, one for 'us' and the other for the rest. Our country has resolutely discarded various approaches (often called 'doctrines' in the West) implying that relations between sovereign socialist countries must be based on principles different from those universally accepted and that they are above international law. These relations should be characterised by fuller creative use of the opportunities offered by universally recognised standards of state-to-state relations.

The emergence of civil society in the Soviet Union was paralleled at the end of 1989 and during 1990 by similar transformations in Poland, East Germany, Hungary, Czechoslovakia and Rumania. In all cases, the organic link between domestic and foreign policy was the economic factor and the necessity in each case to restructure the domestic economy, carry out political reforms, and to integrate as rapidly as possible with the world economy. In the case of the Soviet Union this process was made all the more urgent by the emergence of centrifugal forces threatening the very Union of Soviet Socialist Republics.

The political and economic reform process now underway in the Soviet Union has resulted in the reshaping of party-state relations at the national level and the restructuring of the Soviet governmental apparatus. At the same time, as the constitutional powers of the Soviet President have been increased, the President is increasingly constrained by the power of the USSR's constituent republics. Soviet foreign policy makers must now take into account these new political realities.

Eastern Europe is no longer a Soviet preserve. Party-to-party ties, which once bound the socialist community, have atrophied with the emergence of non-Communist governments in Eastern Europe. Most dramatically, the Soviet Union acquiesced to the unification of Germany within NATO. The Warsaw Treaty Organisation is rent by internal divisions and has all but ceased to function. Several of its members will no longer accept Soviet command of their armed forces, and have declared their intention to withdraw completely.[8] Economic relations among the members of the Council for Mutual Economic Assistance (CMEA) are being refashioned along more pragmatic lines. In July 1990, for example, President Gorbachev issued a decree to the Soviet government requiring that CMEA partners pay for Soviet exports with hard currency as from 1 January 1991.[9]

The emergence of civil society in the Soviet Union has brought to the fore a number of groups and organisations concerned with issues such as economic reform and ethnic rights. Increasingly Soviet aid (economic and military) and trade policies are being scrutinised critically, thus establishing an organic link between domestic and foreign policy. According to The Guardian's Moscow correspondent:[10]

> President Gorbachev has given formal notice to countries dependent on Soviet aid that in the future it will be based on 'our country's real resources'.
>
> The warning... came in a presidential decree... on 'changes in external economic practice'.
>
> But it has never been issued with such a clear implication that aid will no longer be governed primarily by some political or strategic advantage.
>
> Bitter complaints have been voiced in the Soviet Parliament as well as at the recent Communist Party Congress, against the cost of foreign aid to Third World countries. The Soviet Union can ill afford such expense.
>
> The complaints reflect the mood of ordinary citizens who do not see why they should pay to prop up governments which, they believe, refuse to take painful corrective measures.

At the same time as Soviet officialdom has attempted to refashion its long standing relations with Third World socialist states along the lines dictated by 'new political thinking', it has come under domestic pressure to reduce its economic and military programs to these countries and to put trade relations on a more business-like basis. The next section will discuss the impact of these developments on Soviet-Vietnamese relations.

III

The current basis for Soviet-Vietnamese relations is the Treaty of Friendship and Cooperation signed in November 1978.[11] This treaty provided for cooperation between the two signatories in a wide variety of fields including politics, economics, science and technology

(Articles 1 and 2). Under the terms of Article 6, the two parties agreed, 'In case either Party is attacked or threatened with attack, the two parties signatory to the Treaty shall immediately consult each other with a view to eliminating that threat and taking appropriate and effective measures to ensure the peace and security of the two countries.' At that time the Brezhnev government was pursuing a 'containment' strategy towards China; it was also a period of heightened tensions in Indochina. The treaty thus served the security interests of both Moscow and Hanoi.

Since signing the treaty, the Vietnamese have termed their 'all round relationship' with the Soviet Union the 'corner stone' of Vietnam's foreign policy. Some Vietnamese military leaders have gone so far as to assert that Vietnam, as an outpost of socialism in Southeast Asia, was a part of the alliance network of the socialist states' system.[12] In the period since 1978, Vietnamese dependency on the USSR has grown in all fields. Vietnam has no modern armaments industry, for example, and relies overwhelmingly on the Soviet Union for weapons and equipment. Vietnam's Cambodia venture would not have been possible without Soviet assistance and support.

Dependency also prevails in the economic sphere. Approximately sixty-four per cent of Vietnamese trade is conducted with the Soviet Union. The Soviet Union is the source of virtually all Vietnamese development aid. Vietnam also relies on the Soviet Union for the supply of various strategic goods such as petroleum, oil and lubricants. Recent estimates suggest that Soviet combined aid accounts for one fourth of the Soviet Union's worldwide assistance program and that Vietnam ranks second only to Cuba as a recipient.[13]

Vietnamese dependency has entailed a price. Tens of thousands of Vietnamese 'guest workers' have been sent to the Soviet Union to fill labour shortages. A portion of their wages is retained to pay off state debts.[14] Large amounts of Vietnamese raw materials and agricultural produce are shipped to the Soviet Far East as payment for Soviet imports. Vietnam is not free to sell these commodities on the world market for hard currency. More importantly, Vietnam has had to make political concessions. Under Soviet pressure it joined the CMEA, and after 1978, acquiesced in hosting Soviet naval and air forces at Cam Ranh Bay.

In the decade since 1978, Soviet-Vietnamese relations have developed both extensively and intensively. There has been frequent and regular contact and consultation at all levels by the party, state, and military bureaucracies and mass organisations of each country. On the political level, for example, frequent high-level summits have been held between the General Secretary of the CPSU and the Secretary General of the Vietnam Communist Party (VCP).[15] There are also frequent exchanges between delegations representing the various Central Committee departments. Field-grade Vietnamese military leaders attend higher level military academies in the Soviet Union, while the vast majority of Vietnam's science and technology elite has been either trained or educated at Soviet educational institutes.[16] The main symbol of cooperation in this sphere was the participation of a Vietnamese cosmonaut in the Soviet space program.

Despite whatever underlying tensions existed in the Soviet-Vietnamese relationship, involving as it did two starkly different cultural traditions, it would appear that adherence to Marxist-Leninist ideology created a genuine bond between the political elites of both countries. This was reinforced by the long-standing historical nature of the relationship as well as the weight of cross-cutting personal and institutional linkages.[17] In addition, both shared a strategic antipathy towards China. Soviet-Vietnamese relations changed markedly after the advent of Gorbachev to power.

Initially, Gorbachev's foreign policy initiatives in the area of arms control and regional security in the Asia-Pacific region were generally well received by Vietnamese leaders.[18] During the course of a visit to Hanoi in October 1987, for example, the author held a discussion on Gorbachev's foreign policy initiatives with a Vietnamese professor just back from a colloquium with his Soviet colleagues.[19] The professor enthusiastically supported the 'new political thinking' in Soviet foreign policy which gave priority to the economic development of the Soviet Union. In his view, the USSR would need to end the arms race and reach out and develop trade relations with the free market economies. This would create interdependence among mixed economies and enable them to live in 'a world environment of coexistence.' He concluded:

> The Soviet Union does not want to break existing alliances. The old theory of war, as long as there is imperialism war will result, is not right any more. Because if there is war between imperialist countries in the nuclear era it will result in the complete destruction of the world ... We must spare no effort for common confidence between nations ... Our party admits it is weak in theory in understanding world affairs, and economic development...

Vietnam also applauded Gorbachev's policies of *glasnost'* and *perestroika*. Gorbachev's domestic policies were latched onto by

Vietnam's own reformers who succeeded in 1986 in having a Vietnamese variant—*dôi môi*, or renovation—adopted as party policy. However, as the events of 1989 unfolded, Vietnam's leaders stepped back aghast at developments unleashed by this process. They remain firm in the belief that the leading role of the VCP should not be challenged, and that the tides of pluralism and multi-party democracy sweeping the socialist community should not impact on Vietnam's shores.

Quite clearly the bonds between Vietnam and the Soviet Union are being eroded by differences in how to interpret and apply what was once a shared ideology. In public, Vietnam's leaders blame the machinations of 'imperialism and international reactionaries' as well as the failure of fraternal parties to adhere to the tenets of genuine Marxism-Leninism for these developments. In private, Vietnam's leaders are highly critical of Gorbachev for not exerting firm control over domestic affairs.

The emergence of civil society in the Soviet Union has brought domestic economic issues, including the need for radical reform, to the fore. The formulation of foreign policy goals, as well as a reassessment of past commitments, including Soviet-Vietnamese relations, has had to take these new priorities into account.

IV

In the late 1950s the Soviet Union became Vietnam's largest provider of economic aid and assistance, overtaking China. In 1973, with the signing of the Paris peace agreements, the USSR, along with other members of the socialist camp, cancelled all of Vietnam's outstanding debts. After the unification of the country, the USSR substantially increased its funding of Vietnam's economic development program, doubling its financial contributions to each successive five year plan (1976–80, 1981–85, 1986–90).

This funding has gone towards the construction of nearly 300 projects, including 100 major ones, in all areas of the Vietnamese economy.[20] An estimated thirty per cent of this aid has been earmarked for industrial development. Soviet assistance in this area has been mainly in large show-piece projects in the energy sector such as the Hoa Binh, Tri An and Pha Lai electricity generating complexes. The USSR has also played a major role in the development of Vietnam's off shore oil and gas industry.

Vietnam has come under Soviet pressure to take part in the socialist international division of labour within the CMEA context. The USSR has pressured the European members of the CMEA to share the burden of 'lifting up' Vietnam's economy (along with Cuba and Mongolia).[21] In October 1987, the CMEA announced a special long-term program of multi-lateral assistance to Vietnam to cover the period 1991–2005. This program would downplay the importance of foreign aid and stress instead a 'more effective mechanism for managing [Vietnam's] foreign and economic relations and of a structural policy of a new type.'[22] However, in March 1990 the CMEA decided to end multilateral cooperation and coordination of plans.[23] The CMEA has also set in train plans to abolish its present barter arrangements and shift to trade based on world prices and using hard currency. In these changed circumstances, it is unlikely the 1987 multilateral aid program to Vietnam will be carried out.

Initially, Soviet criticism of Vietnam's performance was muted and generally confined to private discussions. One of the first exceptions came in 1982 when Mikhail Gorbachev, then a relatively junior member of the CPSU Politburo, was dispatched to attend the 5th national congress of the VCP held in March. At that time the Vietnamese were berated for their inefficiency and threatened with decreased Soviet support.[24] Indeed, the Soviet Union withheld long-term support for Vietnam's 3rd FYP (1981–85) until it was well underway.

Since Gorbachev's rise to power, Soviet concerns to improve the efficiency of its economic aid program to Vietnam intensified. Soviet concerns focused on the problem of Vietnamese mismanagement, the appropriateness of Soviet aid projects, and the ability of the Vietnamese to absorb large-scale assistance. The Vietnamese leadership has been put on notice that they must undertake strenuous efforts to improve the efficiency of Soviet aid.

Soviet officials have become increasingly critical of Vietnamese ineptitude. Gorbachev's new team of economic specialists and advisers are hesitant, in Vietnam's case, to continue to throw good money after bad.[25] They see their prime task as the successful restructuring of the Soviet economy, including its external economic relations. Towards this end they have endeavoured to put their economic relationship with the Vietnamese on a more business-like footing.[26]

Vietnam's leaders are aware of this change of attitude and have responded with public admissions of their faults. In July 1986 Truong

Chinh, Vietnam's new party secretary general, was reportedly berated by Gorbachev himself.[27] On return to Hanoi Truong Chinh stated publicly that Vietnam had squandered Soviet aid.[28] Both the Central Committee of the CPSU and the Politburo of the VCP held special meetings to consider what steps to take to rectify the situation.[29] In May 1987, during the course of a visit to Moscow, Vietnam's present secretary general, Nguyên Vân Linh, was pressed by his Soviet counterpart to accept 'new forms of cooperation' such as joint enterprises and direct links between enterprises to ensure greater cost-accounting.[30]

Friction over Soviet aid surfaced in mid-1988 when the Tri An project shut down within days of opening due to a malfunction. Soviet commentary blamed the problem on hasty construction and lack of coordination among the Vietnamese ministries responsible.[31] The Vietnamese said it was due to the flawed design drawn up by Soviet engineers.

Complaints have also arisen over Soviet pricing policies. In 1988, for example, the Soviets reportedly doubled the price of goods delivered to Vietnam which the USSR had purchased in third countries. The Vietnamese also grumbled to visitors that they were frequently over-charged by the Soviets for outmoded technology, while receiving below-market prices for their exports of fruit and vegetables, seafood and industrial crops. Soviet economic managers, who demand prompt fulfilment of commercial contracts by the Vietnamese, have begun writing penalty clauses into such contracts.

Increasingly Soviet commentators have become openly critical of their aid program to Vietnam, admitting their failings.[32] Such views surfaced on the tenth anniversary of USSR-SRV Treaty of Friendship and Cooperation. One Soviet economist, after noting that several long-term construction projects were standing idle while others worked at half capacity, stated 'But instead [of advocating a Leninist NEP] we gave them chemical plants, large hydroelectric plants. They were attracted by the Chinese Great Leap Forward and had studied our Stalinist model of industrialisation.'[33]

As a result of questioning by the press and People's Deputies, a Soviet Deputy Finance Minister revealed that Vietnam's debts to the USSR totalled 9.13 billion rubles as of November 1989.[34] Vietnam is scheduled to start making repayments on 8.856 billion rubles of this amount in 1991 over a five year period. It is recognised that this probably will not be possible.[35] There is also a marked trade imbalance between Vietnam and the Soviet Union, with Vietnam importing far more than it can afford to pay via exports. This state of affairs has prompted a review, and in the next five-year planning cycle (1991–95) Vietnam will be expected to make payment in hard currency.

Changes in Soviet domestic and external economic policy have altered the nature of the Soviet-Vietnamese relationship. Hanoi can no longer count on the USSR—or its fraternal allies in Europe for that matter—for continued large amounts of economic largess. Recent reports suggest that the USSR is unable to meet its commitments to the final year of Vietnam's current Five-Year Plan and that Soviet support for the 1991–95 FYP will decrease.

A Soviet Foreign Ministry survey of relations with the 'other socialist countries' (which included Vietnam, Laos and Cambodia) stated:[36]

> Cooperation in the economic sphere is of key importance at the current stage. Over the past few years the CPSU Central Committee and the USSR Council of Ministers have adopted a number of decisions to overhaul economic ties with Vietnam, Laos and Cambodia and ensure the effectiveness of bilateral cooperation.
>
> The efforts taken by both sides to improve economic ties have yielded certain results. Soviet credits were reorientated in part to cooperation in implementing the priority economic programmes of Vietnam, Laos and Cambodia. Utilisation of the production potential created with Soviet assistance improved somewhat. Exports from the Indochinese countries to the USSR, including foods and some industrial consumer goods, began to increase ...
>
> However, we have failed thus far to attain the main goal, that of creating a thrift model of economic cooperation. The present practice of financing cooperation from the state budget prevents input-maximizing methods of interconnections from being broken down, allows crediting of excessively protracted construction projects, hampers reductions in the size of Soviet personnel at sites, etc. Both sides are focusing on efforts to resolve these problems without delay.

V

Initially, Vietnam also welcomed the process of glasnost' and perestroika in the Soviet Union and endorsed the domestic economic reform program of the CPSU's 27th Congress (February 1986). In December 1986 the 6th Congress of the Vietnam Communist Party formally adopted dôi mói, or renovation. In the political sphere this meant a gradual process of political change in three main areas: more 'openness' and honesty in press reporting; separation of party-state relations to end party interference in day-to-day affairs; and enhancing the role of law through reform of the National Assembly, its electoral procedures and committee structures.

Political reform in Vietnam has not embraced political pluralism or multi-party democracy. The leading role of the VCP, as enshrined in the state constitution, is sacrosanct. Quite simply political renovation was not intended radically to alter the structure, functions or policies of the Vietnam Communist Party. In the era of *đổi mới* the public was asked to assist the party in combating corruption, bureaucratism and other so-called 'negative phenomena'. But the party itself would take charge of its own reform.

The VCP reacted negatively to the pro-democracy (and anti-socialist) movements in Poland and Hungary. Developments in Poland were termed a 'counter-revolutionary coup d'etat.'[37] Demonstrations protesting these developments were organised in Hanoi and petitions delivered to the Polish Embassy. When the Polish government reacted sharply to what it considered interference in its internal affairs, Vietnamese authorities quickly retreated.[38]

The events in Hungary and Poland, as well as the emergence of pluralist tendencies in the Soviet Union, eventually attracted attention and some support within the VCP. Soon there were calls for a modification of the state constitution's clause on the leading role of the party and the direct election of the chairman of the National Assembly (in effect, Vietnam's president).

At the same time as the VCP's leadership resisted these demands, Gorbachev led the Soviet Union down the path of political reform, and the other fraternal states embraced multi-party democracy, political pluralism and free elections. The emergence of a pro-democracy movement in China and the swift collapse of the Ceausescu government in Romania startled the VCP. It now faced growing pressures to speed up the process of political reform in Vietnam.

It was in these circumstances that the VCP convened the 8th plenary session (6th Congress) of the Central Committee in March 1990. In an unprecedented move a draft program was circulated in public in an effort to solicit comment from the population at large.[39] The Central Committee then met in secret for several weeks. At the end of these deliberations economic renovation was re-endorsed but not political reform.[40] Trân Xuân Bách, a member of the Politburo, Secretary of the Central Committee, and a leading advocate of political reform, was dismissed from all his posts in a clear negative signal to advocates of change.[41]

In brief, the VCP has fallen back on orthodox ideological tenets to argue that they are the upholders of 'true socialism' as opposed to 'deformed socialism' elsewhere.[42] Over and over the party-controlled media has stressed the primacy of the party and the objective of building socialism in Vietnam.

Strains in Soviet-Vietnamese relations have now appeared on the political plane, especially in the area of socialist ideology.[43] The Vietnam Communist Party endorses economic renovation at home, but adamantly eschews political reform of the type which is unfolding in the USSR and elsewhere in the socialist community. Adherence to outmoded ideological conceptions leaves open the possibility that Vietnam may be left politically isolated from its economic benefactors.

Changes in Europe and the USSR—the end of the Cold War, the disintegration of the Warsaw Pact, the overthrow of communist regimes by more or less peaceful means, and the threat of secession in the Soviet Union—have posed severe ideological challenges to the Vietnamese leadership. Past declarations that they are part of the 'socialist community headed by the Soviet Union' ring hollow in the face of the momentous changes now unfolding. The ideological glue which has bound the Vietnamese to the Soviet Union has dried up and no longer appears to be serving its purpose.

VI

'New political thinking' has brought about dramatic shifts in the Soviet Union's foreign policy. The Vietnamese easily adjusted to Soviet initiatives in the area of arms control and improving relations with the United States. However, Soviet efforts to normalise relations with China in the 1985–89 period posed particular problems for the Vietnamese. Vietnam is a regional power with regional interests. The Soviet Union is a global power with global interests. Put simply, the utility to Moscow of Vietnam as an ally has faded in the face of Sino-Soviet normalisation.

Soviet efforts to improve relations with the People's Republic of China may be traced back to the last years of the Brezhnev government. They were intensified under Andropov, much to the discomfort of Hanoi. A swing back during the Chernenko period gave Vietnam momentary respite. Efforts to normalise Sino-Soviet relations were revived by Gorbachev and were highlighted in his landmark speech at Vladivostok in July 1986.[44] Quite clearly, considerable economic as well as political considerations lay behind this initiative.

As a result of the Sino-Soviet normalisation process, which culminated in a summit in May 1989, Vietnam came under sustained Soviet pressure to make concessions over Cambodia. In September of that year, Vietnam withdrew all its regular military units from Cambodia without precondition. The following year Vietnam agreed to accept the participation of elements of the Khmer Rouge in a Cambodian Supreme National Council. As a result, Sino-Vietnamese relations have improved, reaching a high point in early September 1990 when three top party officials made what was then a secret visit to southern China to offer further concessions.

VII

During the pre-Gorbachev period it was common among Western analysts of Soviet behaviour in the Third World to highlight the saliency of military aid as an instrument of Soviet influence.[45] Quite clearly the military dimension of the Soviet-Vietnamese relationship was of great importance. Vietnam served the USSR's strategy to contain China and it offered a base from which Soviet power could be projected in to the South and Southeast Asian regions. To the Vietnamese, Soviet military assistance was vital, as Vietnam possesses no armaments industry. All major items of military equipment from jet aircraft and air defence missiles to field guns and tanks must be imported from abroad.

The Brezhnev years were a period of military over-extension. For example, Vietnam could not have invaded and occupied Cambodia without prior Soviet approval and support. The Soviet invasion of Afghanistan followed a year later. During this period Soviet Defence Minister Ustinov was quoted as calling for the integration of Vietnam's military into the armed forces of the socialist community.[46] Vietnamese officials made similar statements. Some analaysts even speculated that Hanoi had accepted integrated war planning and the Vietnam People's Army would open a second front against China in the event of a Sino-Soviet war.[47]

The Gorbachev period brought about a marked alteration in its relationship with Vietnam in the military sphere. The Soviet Union adopted a doctrine of 'defence self-sufficiency' and extricated itself from the 'bleeding wound' of Afghanistan. The Soviet Union has also moved to assist in resolving regional conflicts, such as that in

Cambodia. It has also begun to scale down its naval presence in the Indian Ocean. In January 1990, Foreign Minister Shevardnadze told visiting US Senators that the USSR would withdraw all its military forces in Asia behind Soviet borders.[48]

In 1979, when the Sino-Vietnamese border war broke out, the Soviet Union signalled its support for Vietnam by dispatching a naval flotilla to the South China Sea. It later called in at Cam Ranh Bay. Cam Ranh then became an important Soviet staging point for operations in the region. Nine years later, when Chinese and Vietnamese naval forces fought an engagement in the Spratly Islands (March 1988), the Soviet response was quite different. In a clear signal of the changing relationship, the USSR adopted a more or less even-handed approach, calling on both parties to refrain from the use of force. This was quite remarkable, given that the naval clash appeared to have been provoked by China. Vietnam's leaders were reportedly shocked at the Soviet attitude.[49]

The Soviet Union's military presence in Vietnam has also decreased. In July 1986, in his speech at Vladivostok, Secretary General Gorbachev stated that a US withdrawal from its military bases in the Philippines would not go unanswered.[50] Later, in a speech given in Krasnoyarsk in September 1988, Gorbachev offered an explicit trade.[51] This statement clearly angered the Vietnamese,[52] and later the next year they staged several incidents at Cam Ranh in a symbolic assertion of their sovereignty.[53]

As a result of changes in Soviet strategic doctrine mentioned above, the utility of a base at Cam Ranh diminished. In late 1989 the Soviets unilaterally withdrew most of their planes and warships from the base,[54] and have stated they would withdraw all their military forces by 1992.[55] Thus the Vietnamese have lost an important lever in their relationship with Moscow.

In the aftermath of its military withdrawal from Cambodia, Vietnam announced long-term plans to demobilise its Vietnam People's Army. Although no specific target has been announced publicly, Vietnamese sources indicate the cuts could go as deep as 700,000 out of a regular force of 1.1 million.[56] This process is now underway. At the same time, the Soviet Union has indicated that its military assistance will decline by one-third starting in 1991,[57] and that Vietnam will be expected to pay for military equipment.[58] Given the parlous state of the Vietnamese economy, Vietnam will be hard pressed to pay for major equipment purchases and to modernise its armed forces to keep up with regional developments. Vietnam thus faces a future of declining military influence in the region which will make it more vulnerable to Chinese pressures.

VIII

Soviet-Vietnamese relations are undergoing a fundamental transformation as a result of the emergence of civil society in the USSR and 'new political thinking' in Soviet domestic and foreign policy. The saliency of ideology as a factor uniting these dissimilar states is fast eroding. The Vietnam Communist Party, which has always seen itself as a member of the socialist community headed by the Soviet Union, now appears to have more in common in ideological terms with neighbouring China and hardline socialist states such as North Korea and Cuba than with its Soviet and European allies. A recent *Izvestiia* interview by Secretary General Nguyên Vân Linh highlighted this point.[59] Linh once again stressed the 'three nos'—no pluralism, no multi-party system, and no opposition party. In discussing relations with the USSR, Linh only stressed Vietnamese gratitude for Soviet aid.

The closeness of Soviet-Vietnamese economic, political and military ties can be expected to weaken as the Soviet Union turns inward to solve its mounting domestic problems. Quite simply, the Soviet Union can no longer afford to dish out lavish amounts of economic and military credits to Vietnam.[60] As a global power, the Soviet Union has a greater stake in improving its relations with Beijing and Washington than in maintaining the historically close and costly relations with Vietnam. Soviet pressures on Hanoi for a political settlement of the Cambodian conflict can be expected to continue.

Vietnam has reacted to the changing nature of its relations with Moscow by trying to hold firm on the domestic front in order to ensure political stability and to forestall internal challenges to the legitimacy of one-party rule. The March 1990 eighth plenum of the VCP Central Committee marked a watershed in this development. The VCP clearly intends to attempt to insulate Vietnam from the political changes sweeping the socialist community. Following this plenum, Vietnamese police arrested scores of individuals on charges of undertaking activities threatening public security.

The pace of change both within the Soviet Union and in Eastern Europe has served to undermine the ideological dimension of relations among members of the socialist community. For the present it would appear meaningless to talk of relations among these states as being based on the ideological principles of 'socialist internationalism'. At least three of the five European members of the Warsaw Pact (Hungary, Poland, and Czechoslovakia) are now led by non-socialist governments. That is, the incumbent communist parties have been turned out of office by democratic means. At the June 1990 meeting of the Warsaw Treaty Organisation, delegations from these states and from the German Democratic Republic were no longer represented by their party chiefs but by representatives of the new democratic order—former political dissidents and anti-nuclear campaigners.

The emergence of civil society in the Soviet Union and Eastern Europe has had the effect of devaluing ideology as an important element in the relationship. This in turn has led to the erosion of socialist community cohesion. This has been recognised by the leaders of the Warsaw Pact who declared that the treaty organisation no longer reflects the spirit of the times and must be transformed into a new system embracing equal sovereign states and based on democratic principles.[61]

Not all changes in Soviet domestic and foreign policy can be attributed to the recrudescence of civil society. The latter was well developed before Mikhail Gorbachev began pushing for *glasnost'*, *perestroika* and 'new political thinking.' Together, however, these processes have led to an avalanche of change both at home and abroad from which there appears to be no turning back.

The Soviet Union is now facing a grave crisis which may well lead to the dismemberment of the Union of Soviet Socialist Republics. In this mix of events, militarism and foreign adventurism are policy options which the Soviet Union can no longer contemplate. This has led to a revolutionary change in the USSR's traditional alliance relationships. The German Democratic Republic, the centre piece of the Warsaw Pact, has been lost to the multitudinal forces comprising civil society, while the Warsaw Treaty Organisation has fractured beyond recognition. Elsewhere, the Soviet Union's alliance relationships with far flung outposts of the socialist community like Vietnam have withered on the economic vine.

Notes

1   S. Frederick Starr, 'Soviet Union: A Civil Society', *Foreign Policy*, no. 70, Spring 1988, pp. 26–41 at p. 39.

2   Ibid., p. 40

3   Eduard Shevardnadze, 'To "International Affairs" Readers', *International Affairs* (Moscow), January 1990, introduction.

4   Margot Light, *The Soviet Theory of International Relations* (Brighton: Wheatsheaf, 1988) p. 294.

5   'The Foreign Policy and Diplomatic Activity of the USSR (April 1985–October 1989). A Survey Prepared by the USSR Ministry of Foreign Affairs', *International Affairs* (Moscow), January 1990.

6   Robert F. Miller, 'Gorbachev's "New Thinking": The Diplomatic and Military Implications', *Quadrant*, vol.32, no.7, July 1988, pp. 15–19, at pp. 17–18.

7   Light, *The Soviet Theory of International Relations*, p. 295.

8   Dispatch from Budapest, *The Washington Times*, May 23, 1990, citing Hungary's new premier Jozsef Antall.

9   *Australian Financial Review*, July 27, 1990 citing wire services.

10   John Rettie dispatch from Moscow reprinted in *The Age*, July 27, 1990.

11   'Treaty of Friendship and Cooperation Between the Socialist Republic of Vietnam and the Union of Soviet Socialist Republics,' *Vietnam Courier*, no. 79, December 1978, pp. 4–5.

12   General Hoang Van Thai, 'Ve Quan He Hop Tac Dac Biet Giua Ba Dan Toc Dong Duong,' *Tap Chi Cong San*, no.1, January 1982, pp. 17-24.

13   Thai Quang Trung, 'When the Cornerstone is Crumbling: Soviet-Vietnamese Military Cooperation Reassessed', *Vietnam Commentary*, no. 13, January-February 1990, pp. 2–5, at p. 2.

14   Nayan Chanda, 'Now, the "flot" people,' *Far Eastern Economic Review*, May 14, 1982, pp. 28–29; Arch Puddington, 'The Plight of Vietnamese Migrant Workers,' *Workers Under Communism*, no. 4, Fall 1983, pp. 4–7.

15   There have been at least nine such meetings since March 1985: June-July 1985 Gorbachev-Le Duan; February-March 1986 Gorbachev-Le Duan; July-August 1986 Gorbachev-Truong Chinh; November 1986 Gorbachev-Truong Chinh; May 1987 Gorbachev-Nguyen Van Linh; October 1987 Gorbachev-Nguyen Van Linh; July-August 1988 Gorbachev-Nguyen Van Linh; April 1989 Gorbachev-Nguyen Van Linh; and October 1989 Gorbachev-Nguyen Van Linh (in Berlin).

16   Carlyle A. Thayer, 'Soviet Studies in Vietnam', in Charles E. Morrison and Pushpa Thambipillai (eds), *Soviet Studies in the Asia-Pacific Region* (Honolulu: Resource Systems Institute, East-West Center, 1986) pp. 101–122.

17   Carlyle A. Thayer, 'Vietnam and the Soviet Union: Perceptions and Policies', in Pushpa Thambipillai and Daniel C. Matuszewski (eds), *The Soviet Union and the Asia-Pacific Region: Views from the Region* (New York: Praeger Publishers, 1989) pp. 134–153.

18   Carlyle A. Thayer, 'Kampuchea: Soviet Initiatives and Regional Responses', in Ramesh Thakur and Carlyle A. Thayer (eds), *The Soviet Union as an Asian Pacific Power: Implications of Gorbachev's 1986 Vladivostok Initiative* (Boulder: Westview Press, 1987) pp. 171–200.

19   Interview with Professor Long, Institute of Southeast Asian Studies, Hanoi, October 31, 1987.

20   Hanoi International Service in English, September 21, 1989.

21   Communique of the VCP Politburo, Hanoi Home Service, November 13, 1986.

22   M. Trigubenko, 'Co-operation between CMEA and Vietnam: Checking the Slowdown', *Far Eastern Affairs* (Moscow), no.4, 1988, p. 24; see also Vietnam News Agency in English, October 15, 1987 and address by Vo Van Kiet to the 43rd special CEMA session held in Hanoi; Hanoi Domestic Service in Vietnamese, October 15, 1987.

23   Dispatch from Prague to *The Financial Times* reprinted in *The Sydney Morning Herald*, March 29, 1990.

24   Hoang Huu Quynh, 'Gorbachev and the Vietnamese Stake: Deflating an Inflated Value', *Vietnam Commentary*, no.13, January-February 1990, pp. 9–12, at p. 10; and Nayan Chanda, 'As Moscow's Ardour Cools, Hanoi Looks Elsewhere,' *Far Eastern Economic Review*, April 16, 1982, p. 18.

25   This is based in part on discussions with Soviet specialists in May 1988 and January 1989.

26   Soviet writers are also critical of Vietnam's 'open door' policy by which Vietnam has turned to the West for investment in joint ventures at the expense of the Soviet Union; see Ye. Bogatova and E. Kovalev, 'A New Dimension in Vietnam's Foreign Policy', *Far Eastern Affairs* (Moscow) no.1, 1990, pp. 37–51, at pp. 47–51.

27   Hoang Huu Quynh, 'Gorbachev and the Vietnamese Stake: Deflating an Inflated Value', p. 9.

28   AP dispatch from Moscow, citing TASS, *The Bangkok Post*, July 28, 1987; and UPI dispatch from Bangkok, *The Straits Times*, October 23, 1986.

29   Moscow Home Service, January 5, 1987; and Communique of the VCP Central Committee Politburo meeting, May 7, 1987 broadcast by Hanoi Home Service, May 7, 1987.

30   Full Text of Soviet-Vietnamese Joint Communique as carried by TASS in Russian for abroad, May 21, 1987.

31   S. Blagov, V. Burbulis and M. Kalmykov, 'Taking Account of Mistakes for the Future', *Sotsialisticheskaia Industriia*, March 23, 1988 translated in BBC *Summary of World Broadcasts*, FE/0110/A2/1, March 26, 1988.

32   Soviet Television, January 7, 1988 cited by BBC *Summary of World Broadcasts*, FE/0054 A/14, January 20, 1988.

33   Sophie Quinn Judge and Murray Hiebert, 'Ten Year Itch', *Far Eastern Economic Review*, November 10, 1988, p. 23.

34   *Chas Pik* (Rush Hour), newspaper of the Leningrad Division of the USSR Journalists' Union, February 26, 1990, no. 1 reprinted in 'To Whom We Have "Loaned" 85.8 Billion Rubles,' *Izvestiia*, March 1, 1990, p. 3 and translated in *The Current Digest of the Soviet Press*, vol.42,

no.9, 1990, p. 9. According to this report, prepared by V. G. Panskov, USSR Deputy Minister of Finance, 406.4 million roubles was written off in November 1989. See also Michael Byrnes, *The Australian Financial Review*, April 12, 1990 who provides a slightly higher figure of 9.5 billion roubles.

35   Cf. B. Vinogradov, 'Toward a Restructuring of Soviet-Vietnamese Economic Ties', *Izvestiia*, February 4, 1990 translated in *The Current Digest of the Soviet Press*, vol.42, no.5, 1990, pp. 20–21.

36   'The Foreign Policy and Diplomatic Activity of the USSR', p. 74.

37   Commentary, 'Political Crisis in Poland', *Nhan Dan*, August 25, 1989; Hanoi home service, August 25, 1989; and Vietnam News Agency, August 26, 1989. Solidarity was termed a 'reactionary organisation.'

38   Based on conversations in Hanoi with Western diplomats during the course of a visit in October 1989.

39   Broadcast by Hanoi Domestic Service in Vietnamese in three instalments, February 5, 1990.

40   See: Text of the communique of the Eighth Plenum of the Sixth Communist Party of Vietnam Central Committee, Hanoi Domestic Service in Vietnamese, March 28, 1990.

41   Carlyle A. Thayer, 'Vietnam: After Five Years on the Reformist Path, a Crisis of Doubt,' *The International Herald Tribune*, September 6, 1990.

42   See the perceptive analysis by Tony Hill, based on interviews with Vietnamese officials; Australian Broadcasting Corporation Radio, 'Correspondent's Report', January 21, 1990.

43   For analysis of similar problems in a different period consult, Gareth Porter, 'Vietnam and the Socialist Camp: Center or Periphery?' in William S. Turley (ed.), *Vietnamese Communism in Comparative Perspective* (Boulder: Westview Press, 1980) pp. 199–223.

44   Gary Klintworth, 'Gorbachev's China Diplomacy', in Ramesh Thakur and Carlyle A. Thayer (eds), *The Soviet Union as an Asian Pacific Power: Implications of Gorbachev's 1986 Vladivostok Initiative* (Boulder: Westview Press, 1987) pp. 39–57.

45   Daniel S. Papp, *Soviet Policies Toward the Developing World During the 1980s: The Dilemmas of Power and Presence* (Maxwell Air Force Base, Alabama: Air University Press, 1986) pp. 119–152.

46   Thai Quang Trung, 'When the Cornerstone is Crumbling: Soviet-Vietnamese Military Cooperation Reassessed'.

47   Douglas Pike, 'Vietnam, A Modern Sparta', *Pacific Defence Reporter*, April 1983, p. 38.

48   UPI dispatch from Moscow, *The Australian*, January 19, 1990.

49   Nayan Chanda, 'A Troubled Friendship', *Far Eastern Economic Review*, June 9, 1988, p. 17.

50   Gorbachev's actual words were: 'And in general I should like to say that if the USA were to renounce a military presence, say in the Phillipines, we should not be found wanting in a response.' Text of Speech by Mikhail Gorbachev in Vladivostok, 28 July 1986, in Ramesh Thakur and Carlyle A. Thayer (eds), *The Soviet Union as an Asian Pacific Power: Implications of Gorbachev's 1986 Vladivostok Initiative* (Boulder: Westview Press, 1987) p. 224.

51 'If the USA eliminates its military bases in the Philippines, the USSR will be prepared, by agreement with the government of Vietnam, to give up the naval material and technical support point in Cam Ranh Bay.' Text of broadcast of Gorbachev's speech at a meeting with people from Krasnoyarsk Kray, Moscow Home Service, and Soviet Television, September 16, 1988.

52 See Kyodo dispatch from Ho Chi Minh City, September 17, 1988 citing the reactions of Vietnam's Foreign Minister Nguyên Co Thach; and Murray Hiebert, 'Carping about Cam Ranh', *Far Eastern Economic Review*, October 27, 1988, p. 27.

53 Based on information provided by Western intelligence analysts, August 3, and December 5th and 18th, 1989.

54 These included a squadron of MiG-23 jets, a squadron of TU-16 bombers, and all submarines and large warships.

55 AP dispatch from Washington, citing a senior member of the House Armed Services Committee, *The Australian*, April 23, 1990.

56 Kyodo dispatch from Hanoi, April 12, 1989. Other Vietnamese sources state that the ideal size of a standing army would be around 500,000; see remarks by Lt. Gen. Le Kha Phieu cited by Michael Williams on 'Newsreel', BBC World Service, April 17, 1989.

57 Louise Williams dispatch from Bangkok, *The Sydney Morning Herald*, January 31, 1990 citing Western diplomatic sources. The decision was conveyed to the Vietnamese government late in 1989.

58 Soviet sales of military equipment to Vietnam are likewise being converted to a market cash-based system for implementation next year', see: Michael Byrnes, *The Australian Financial Review*, April 12, 1990.

59 Excerpts of which were broadcast by Voice of Vietnam, May 9, 1990.

60 Murray Hiebert, 'Straitened Superpowers', *Far Eastern Economic Review*, January 4, 1990, pp. 6–7.

61 BBC, 'World Roundup', carried by ABC Radio National, June 8, 1988.

NOTES ON
CONTRIBUTORS

László Csapó is Reader in Economics at La Trobe University. He was previously an economist in the Hungarian National Bank, and Rockefeller Professor of Economics at the Makarere University of Uganda. He has published extensively on the economics of socialism and central planning.

Stephen Fortescue is Senior Lecturer in Political Science at the University of New South Wales. He has also held appointments at the Australian National University and the Centre for Russian and East European Studies, University of Birmingham. His publications include *The Communist Party and Soviet Science* (Macmillan: 1986), and *Science Policy in the Soviet Union* (Routledge: 1990)

Leslie Holmes is Professor of Political Science at the University of Melbourne. As well as many journal articles, he has written *The Policy Process in Communist States* (Sage Publications: 1981), *Politics in the Communist World* (Oxford University Press: 1986), and *Crisis, Collapse and Corruption in the Communist World* (Polity Press: 1991).

Eugene Kamenka is Professor of the History of Ideas, Research School of Social Sciences, The Australian National University. He is the author of *The Ethical Foundations of Marxism* (Routledge & Kegan Paul: 1962, 1972), *Marxism and Ethics* (Macmillan: 1969), *The Philosophy of Ludwig Feuerbach* (Routledge & Kegan Paul: 1970), and *Bureaucracy* (Basil Blackwell: 1989).

Leszek Kolakowski is Senior Research Fellow at All Souls College, Oxford, having previously served as Professor of the History of Philosophy at the University of Warsaw. His publications include *Marxism and Beyond* (Pall Mall: 1969), *Husserl and the Search for Certitude* (Yale University Press: 1975), *Main Currents of Marxism* (Oxford University Press: 1978), *Religion* (Fontana: 1982), and *Modernity on Endless Trial* (University of Chicago Press: 1990)

Chandran Kukathas is Lecturer in Politics, University College, The University of New South Wales. He has held appointments at Lincoln College, Oxford, George Mason University, and The Australian National University, and his publications include *Hayek and Modern Liberalism* (Oxford University Press: 1989), *Rawls: A*

220 THE TRANSITION FROM SOCIALISM

Theory of Justice and its critics (Stanford University Press: 1990) (with Philip Pettit), and *The Theory of Politics: An Australian Perspective* (Longman Cheshire: 1990) (with David W. Lovell and William Maley).

David W. Lovell is Lecturer in Politics, University College, The University of New South Wales. He is author of *From Marx to Lenin: An evaluation of Marx's responsibility for Soviet authoritarianism* (Cambridge University Press: 1984), *Trotsky's Analysis of Soviet Bureaucratization: A critical essay* (Croom Helm: 1985), *Marx's Proletariat: The making of a myth* (Routledge: 1988), and *The Theory of Politics: An Australian Perspective* (Longman Cheshire: 1990) (with Chandran Kukathas and William Maley).

William Maley is Tutor in Politics, University College, The University of New South Wales. His publications include *The Soviet Withdrawal from Afghanistan* (Cambridge University Press: 1989) (coedited with Amin Saikal), and *The Theory of Politics: An Australian Perspective* (Longman Cheshire: 1990) (with Chandran Kukathas and David W. Lovell).

T.H. Rigby is Professor of Political Science, Research School of Social Sciences, The Australian National University. He is author of *Communist Party Membership in the USSR 1917–1967* (Princeton University Press: 1968), *Lenin's Government* (Cambridge University Press: 1979), *Political Elites in the USSR: Central leaders and local cadres from Lenin to Gorbachev* (Edward Elgar: 1990), and *The Changing Soviet System: Mono-organisational Socialism from its Origins to Gorbachev's Restructuring* (Edward Elgar: 1990).

Vladimir Shlapentokh is Professor of Sociology at Michigan State University. His publications in English include *Love, Marriage, and Friendship in the Soviet Union* (Praeger: 1984), *Soviet Public Opinion and Ideology* (Praeger: 1986), *Soviet Ideologies in the Period of Glasnost* (Praeger: 1988), and *Public and Private Life of the Soviet People* (Oxford University Press: 1989).

Alice Erh-Soon Tay is Professor of Jurispridence at the University of Sydney, President of the International Association for Philosophy of Law and Social Philosophy, and Editor of the *Bulletin of the Australian Society of Legal Philosophy*.

Carlyle A. Thayer is Associate Professor of Politics, University College, The University of New South Wales. He is author of *War By Other Means* (Allen & Unwin: 1989), and he coedited *The Soviet Union as an Asian Pacific Power* (Westview Press: 1987).

INDEX